Breakthrough
DEPRESSION SOLUTION

Breakthrough DEPRESSION SOLUTION

A Personalized Model for Relief from Depression

Mastering Your Mood with Nutrition, Diet and Supplementation

SECOND EDITION

JAMES M. GREENBLATT, MD
with Winnie To, BS

Sunrise River Press

SUNRISE
River Press

Sunrise River Press
838 Lake Street South
Forest Lake, MN 55025
Phone: 651-277-1400 or 800-895-4585
Fax: 651-277-1203
www.sunriseriverpress.com

Edit by Mary Van Beusekom
Layout by Connie DeFlorin

ISBN 978-1-934716-61-8
Item No. SRP615

Library of Congress Cataloging-in-Publication Data

Greenblatt, James.
The breakthrough depression solution / James Mark Greenblatt, MD. -- [Updated edition.]
pages cm
Includes bibliographical references and index.
ISBN 978-1-934716-61-8
1. Depression, Mental--Diet therapy--Popular works. 2. Depression, Mental--Nutritional aspects--Popular works. I. Title.
RC537.G724 2016
616.85'270654--dc23
2015035685

Printed in USA

10 9 8 7 6 5 4 3 2 1

Contents

Acknowledgments

I would like to thank my family for their patience and understanding during my many morning and weekend disappearances to work on this project. I also want to thank my parents, who have provided a lifetime of unwavering support and encouragement. Finally, this book could never have been written without the research, writing, and editing assistance of my coauthor, Winnie To.

Most important, I would like to thank the thousands of patients who have led me to think about what truly helps rather than what is supposed to help.

Introduction

I am grateful to have the opportunity to write an updated edition of *The Breakthrough Depression Solution.* The core concepts have been verified by thousands of research papers by scholars around the world, and many of these new references have been described in this edition.

The growing body of scientific literature clearly dispels the myths and demolishes the concept of alternative medicine. What used to be described as "alternative" medicine is now commonly recognized as integrative medicine. Integrative medicine represents the combination of conventional and alternative methodologies derived from evidence-based medicine. The field of psychiatry has lagged far behind in understanding the value of integrative medicine in the treatment of mental illness, particularly depression.

Depression cannot be seen, heard, or felt during a physical exam. Yet depression is a life-threatening, life-robbing, and disabling disorder. According to the World Health Organization, it is the leading cause of disability worldwide. The notion that we have such vague, unfounded ideas about how to effectively treat this disorder should be unacceptable to medical professionals.

Depression presents complex challenges to those who suffer from it and to those who treat it. Unlike diseases due to a single cause, such as a poison or infection, depression springs from many sources. Depression is capable of destroying every aspect of one's life and often is chronic and relapsing. The devastating effects of depression are seen by all, yet the understanding of what causes depression and, more important, how to treat depression, remains elusive to my medical colleagues and to practicing psychiatrists around the world.

Many of my colleagues in psychiatry have embraced a pure drug model. They provide no therapy, practicing medicine by seeing patients for ten to fifteen minutes at a time to do "med checks," in which they adjust doses or change medications. Med checks are encouraged by insurance companies, which have created special billing codes for these visits.

Because many patients do not respond well to the first medication prescribed, the med check concept actually encourages the addition of a second or even third medication. It's not unusual for patients to be given three to five medications to treat a single diagnosis. As side effects worsen, patients often become increasingly frustrated with the medication approach, decide that all medications are evil, and refuse them.

Consumer groups are organized and relentless when spreading information on the dangers of antidepressant medications. This leaves many patients feeling stuck in the middle, wondering, "Who do I listen to?"

The medical treatment of depression is currently not good enough. New treatments are being researched, but too many patients are still suffering. Psychiatry continues to blame you for our failures. You can see this in the terms we use: you have "failed treatment" or are "treatment resistant." But if you are taking a medication prescribed by your doctor and are unable to recover, who has failed? I believe it's time we stop failing millions of people like yourself who come to mental health professionals seeking relief from depression.

We can do better, much better, if we consider decades' worth of largely ignored research that shows that depression is not "all in your head." The mind and body are one; what happens in the body affects the mind and vice versa.

It's time for an approach to depression that combines traditional medical science with nutritional and metabolic therapies. To be truly successful, this approach must also be scientific, basing each and every prescription or recommendation on objectively measured problems in the body instead of subjectively compiled lists of symptoms matched to a manual. An approach to depression based on each person's different biochemical makeup does not ignore medications but focuses on the nutritional and/or metabolic abnormalities that may be contributing to the problem. This approach is able to successfully treat many individuals suffering from depression.

It was truly amazing to recently read about the U.S. spaceship that was sent on a decade-long journey to travel billions of miles to take photos of the dwarf planet Pluto. This amazing feat of human engineering and science seems to overwhelm the limited knowledge that science has provided in understanding how to treat depression.

This book offers hope and treatment models that are simple, safe, and effective. I have been using these therapies for more than twenty-five years and have seen thousands of patients improve and recover from depression. As you read on, you will begin to appreciate the complexities of depression and realize that it cannot be cured by a magic-bullet approach. A personalized model of integrative medicine for mental health can result in relief from depression and a renewed sense of emotional health.

Hope is fundamental to recovery. Hope is your fuel—the energy to support your efforts in full recovery and peace of mind. Hope and healing are possible as you explore the vast landscape of integrative medicine.

Chapter 1

Personalized Medicine

Another book about depression? You've probably gotten excited before about the promise of a new therapy or the advertised benefits of the latest drug. You have good reason to be frustrated and cynical, especially if you are still depressed.

I understand. I have been treating patients with depression for more than twenty-five years. In that time, I have talked to young children who claimed that they would rather die than live with their "sadness." I have treated teens who cut themselves to relieve the emotional pain of depression. And I have helped adults who can no longer function at work and whose relationships have been destroyed by the ravages of depression.

But I urge you to restore hope once again and to read on. In this book, I am not promoting a particular therapy or a new drug. In fact, I am not hyping any one treatment for the complex illness of depression, a disease so common that it threatens to become the major cause of disability worldwide by the year 2020.

Depression has many causes. Unless treatment targets the particular causes of an individual's case of depression, it is doomed to fail.

In this book, I offer a method designed to ensure personalized treatment of depression.

Personalized Medicine

We recognize early in life that the people we know have many differences in appearance and personality. It shouldn't be hard to realize, then, that we are also biochemically unique, meaning that our bodies each function differently. For example, your body requires different amounts of vitamins and minerals for optimal function than your mother's or father's or a complete stranger's body. These biochemical differences affect our brains, our moods, and our recovery from depression.

My approach to treating depression is grounded in personalized medicine. The belief underlying this approach is that, just as your personality and appearance are unique, so are the factors that contribute to your depression. By identifying and treating these factors—many of which have long been ignored in traditional psychiatric treatment—you can get well.

Traditional treatment methods are based on the results of research studies. These studies collect data from large populations. But we can't be sure that a particular treatment will work for you based on that data.

Personalized medicine, on the other hand, seeks to identify all the factors that may be causing your depression. This approach includes nutrition, genetics, stress, and, when needed, technology to ensure that medications are targeted toward your individual makeup. The goal of personalized medicine is a treatment approach designed especially for you.

As a way to help you remember each part of this method of personalized medicine, I've devised a mnemonic: THE ZEEBRA. In chapter 7, I explain what each letter stands for, but now just a word about the animal that inspired the acronym.

Since childhood, I have been fascinated by zebras. I learned that zebras are sensitive and alert. They move in a zigzag pattern to avoid their predators, and because of their stamina, they can usually outlast them. Zebras have excellent eyesight, hearing, sense of smell, and taste. But the most interesting thing about zebras to me—both then and now—is that each zebra has a unique stripe pattern. Zebras may all look alike to the untrained eye, but a closer look reveals that some zebra stripes are brown and others are black. There are even some black zebras with white stripes. Each zebra's stripe pattern is unique.

The uniqueness of each zebra's stripe pattern symbolizes this book's message about depression. While the illness of depression has enough common features to be considered a diagnostic category, each person's version of depression is unique. Therefore, to be effective, treatment for depression must consider the particular mix of factors that contribute to each person's disease. We cannot assume that people, any more than zebras, are of the same stripe.

I am not interested in pinpointing the blame for depression on your past, your parents, or (least of all) you. I want you to recognize that what happens in the brain is not separate from the body. The health of the brain, or what we might call the mind, depends directly on the health of the body. A complex mix of factors—nutrients, hormones, genetics, and stress—operates together to affect how the mind works and how the individual responds to life events. The slings and arrows that beset us in the world, in other words, are only one set of factors that determine whether we will be mentally healthy or have depression.

Let me mention just a few of the major factors I address in this book.

Nutrition

After twenty-five years of practicing psychiatry and seeing thousands of patients, I have come to believe that feeding the brain well is fundamental to the effective treatment of depression. Yet this simple truth is often overlooked. Physicians tend not to think in terms of nutrition, partly because they do not learn about it in medical school. Graduates of U.S. medical schools receive inadequate training in nutrition, according to a study conducted by the National Academy of Sciences. A follow-up survey in 2006 drew the same conclusion. Physicians lack the training they need to understand the importance of nutrition and to counsel their patients. Fast Forward to 2015, and very little has changed.

If nutrition is critically important in treating depression as well as other diseases, why has the medical community been slow to accept simple, inexpensive nutritional interventions? Partly because they are simple and inexpensive! Companies fund research studies to test drugs that will generate profit. The glossy advertisements for antidepressants that come across your doctor's desk or the TV commercials our children watch promote drugs that will profit the drug companies. Physicians choose treatment options that are familiar to them, like the ones they read about in medical journals. These medications are considered standard practice because research articles (usually funded by the companies making the drugs) support their use.

The medical profession has been slow to accept nutritional therapies in general. In a study on spreading the word about health innovations, Dr. Donald Berwick tells the story of Captain James Lancaster, a British sea captain who discovered in 1601 that lemon juice can prevent scurvy, a disease that occurs in people who don't get enough vitamin C. The British government did not adopt this simple and inexpensive intervention right away—but 264 years after, it was proven to work. Just because physicians largely ignore the benefits of nutritional therapies does not mean that these interventions don't work. What is even more fascinating about the history of scurvy is that a deficiency in a single nutrient is able to create a diverse range of symptoms, highlighting the core concept in this book that each person's depression is unique.

A phenomenon called the Tomato Effect helps explain why the medical community is slow to recognize the benefits of nutritional therapies. The Tomato Effect was defined by Dr. James Goodwin in 1984 in the *Journal of the American Medical Association.* He wrote, "The Tomato Effect in medicine occurs when an efficacious treatment for a certain disease is ignored or rejected because it does not 'make sense' in light of accepted theories of disease mechanism and drug action." In other words, doctors ignore treatments that don't fit with what they know about diseases or the way drugs work.

The rejection of a potentially useful treatment because "everyone knows it won't work" is named for Americans' mistaken yet stubborn belief—from the sixteenth to the nineteenth century—that tomatoes were poisonous.

Understanding why people tend to reject a treatment outside of their frame of reference—even when it has been proven to work—helps explain why doctors still resist using nutritional therapies to treat depression. Still, we can no longer accept this slow progress in identifying treatments for depression. The costs of depression—in terms of joy, energy, opportunity, relationships, even life itself—are high. Physicians owe it to patients and their families to break free from long-held but mistaken beliefs.

Medication

Instead of looking first at a patient's nutritional status, psychiatrists today are much more likely to prescribe a medication. Individual psychiatrists tend to favor particular drugs; one may tend to order Prozac first, another Lexapro. Sometimes, the first prescription helps; more often, however, the patient's depression lingers. Usually, another drug is prescribed, and sometimes, a third, often to medicate the side effects of the first or second. Doctors continually prescribe more medications partly because they don't fully understand how antidepressants work, although it appears that they affect chemicals in the brain called neurotransmitters. If these drugs were completely without risk, the patient would waste only money and time during this trial-and-error method. But living with depression itself brings risk, and the longer one suffers, the more difficult it is to recover. Plus, we probably do not yet fully appreciate the potential risks of prescription medication, especially to children and elderly persons.

Recognizing that psychiatrists rely too much on prescription drugs, Dr. James Watson, winner of the Nobel Prize in Physiology and Medicine for determining the structure of DNA, has urged doctors to focus research and funding on a better understanding of mental illness. In 2010, he said that we need breakthroughs to find out what causes mental illness and to develop treatments based on their results.

By using nutritional and other types of testing and measuring how well prescription drugs work, we can understand the nature of depression in each person. Only then can treatment be tailored to the patient. Until you know the stripes, you can't know the zebra.

Overcoming Stigma

Even today, despite advances in educating the public, mental illness carries a stigma, or negative mark. In addition to suffering from depression, people with depression tend to live in the shadows of guilt and self-blame. I believe the stigma is due in part to our culture's tendency to explain depression in vague psychological terms, with phrases like it is just "in your head" and beliefs that you can simply "fix it."

Of course, our life experiences influence our moods. Our genes, the gift or curse we inherit from our parents and grandparents, affect how likely we are to be healthy or ill. Yet we are made up of more than our life experience and genes. Our culture's lack of attention to other biological factors that may influence depression makes it easy to blame oneself. People are not likely to feel guilty if they have celiac disease, a shortage of zinc in their blood, or a low thyroid level.

This book is a guide to the many things that could be making and keeping you depressed. Because everyone is unique, this book cannot give you the one treatment that will end your depression; instead, this book gives you the tools to ask the right questions.

As you begin to address the biological causes of depression, you will find hope, motivation, and strength for recovery. A patient of mine said that being depressed was like being in a dark hole. He was at the bottom, and although there was a ladder that led to the light, it had no rungs, and he was powerless to climb out.

The tools in this book will be your rungs, and you will understand how psychological and biological factors work together. THE ZEEBRA approach emphasizes recovery and remission from depression and will help you find the light.

Chapter 2

What Is Depression?

Now and again, almost everybody experiences depression: feelings of sadness, a lack of energy, fatigue, and sometimes even hopelessness. Depression, whose name comes from the Latin word *deprimere*, meaning "pressing down," certainly can feel as if a heavy weight were pressing on your head, shoulders, or heart.

In difficult or frustrating situations, such as the death of a loved one, loss of a job, or divorce, these sad or "down" feelings are perfectly normal. But when the sad feelings are stronger, they stay for no apparent reason, or they go on longer than seems normal, they can indicate depression.

Symptoms of Depression

You know it if you feel down. But how do you know if you truly have depression? No test can firmly tell you you're depressed, because it isn't a disease such as diabetes or rheumatoid arthritis with the same cause or path. Depression is different things to different people. It can show up as any mix of symptoms, from the emotional to the behavioral to the physical. In some people, these symptoms are obvious, but in others, they are quite vague, making depression difficult to correctly diagnose.

Still, certain symptoms point to depression. The *Diagnostic and Statistical Manual of Mental Disorders (DSM)* is the guidebook that psychiatrists use to organize psychiatric diagnoses. The current version, *DSM-V*, is the fifth edition of the manual, published in 2013. According to the *DSM-V*, people with major depression have at least five of the following symptoms during the same two-week period, including at least one of the first two symptoms on the list:

- Persistent sadness, anxiety, or a feeling of emptiness most of the day, nearly every day
- Marked decrease in interest or pleasure in almost all activities nearly every day

- Binge eating/weight gain or anorexia/weight loss
- Sleeping too much or not being able to sleep
- Fatigue or lack of energy
- Feeling restless or "slowed down"
- Feelings of worthlessness or guilt
- Trouble concentrating and remembering
- Feeling suicidal

So does it mean that you *aren't* depressed if you don't have any of these symptoms? Not necessarily. Many less obvious symptoms may also point to depression, but they aren't on the list. These include physical symptoms such as a persistent stomachache, emotional symptoms like irritability, and behavioral symptoms like working too much. (Then again, these symptoms might indicate something entirely apart from depression.)

Here are some of the wide-ranging symptoms that may point to depression:

- Aches and pains, stomach problems, or other physical complaints for which treatment doesn't work
- Alcohol or drug abuse
- Chain smoking
- Constant exhaustion or tiredness
- Crying a lot
- Decreased physical activity just about every day
- Behaving recklessly or doing risky things
- Great difficulty getting up in the morning
- Irritability or frustration
- Lack of energy or motivation
- Reduced sex drive
- Working unnecessarily long hours
- Long-term difficulty sleeping

Depression can negatively affect a person's life in many ways. It makes it hard to function at work, which can result in job loss and decreased income. It can cause a withdrawal from life that leads to the loss of relationships with family and friends. It can negatively affect physical health by contributing to or worsening other illnesses, or because the depressed person simply doesn't have the energy or will to take care of himself or herself. It can also increase the risk of disease and death. According to the National Institute of Mental Health, people with depression are four times more likely to have a heart attack than those with no history of depression. And after someone suffers a heart attack, his or her chances of having another one are much higher. Depressed people are also more likely to abuse alcohol or drugs.

When depressed people first go to their doctors for help, they usually complain of fatigue, sleep problems, or unexplained pain rather than feeling sad or "low." Most people first mention these problems to their regular health care professional rather than to a psychiatrist. These doctors often try to treat the problem before sending patients to psychiatrists, which means that prescriptions for most drugs to treat depression (antidepressants) and anxiety (antianxiety drugs) are written by nonpsychiatrists. Indeed, research has shown that general practitioners (doctors, physician assistants, and nurse practitioners) write 62 percent of prescriptions for antidepressants and 65 percent of prescriptions for antianxiety medications, with psychiatrists and addiction specialists writing only 21 percent of antidepressant and 13 percent of antianxiety prescriptions.

The fact that people generally notice a physical problem first means that diagnosing depression can be tricky, especially if you're trying to diagnose yourself. That's why it's important to see a mental health professional if you think you may be depressed. Depression can be treated. If left untreated, it can affect your mental, emotional, and physical health.

Kinds of Depression

The *DSM-V* lists many kinds of depression, the most common types being major depressive disorder and persistent depressive disorder. Several "new" depressive disorders, including disruptive mood dysregulation disorder and premenstrual dysphoric disorder, are listed in the *DSM-V*. Other kinds of depressive disorders include bipolar disorder, substance/medication-induced depressive disorder, depressive disorder due to another medical condition, peripartum onset, psychotic depression, depression with seasonal pattern, atypical depression, anxious distress, double depression, secondary depression, masked depression, and chronic treatment-resistant depression. I discuss the confusing concept of the *DSM-V* further in chapter 3. It does appear at first glance a little odd for the medical community to change the names and add diagnoses each year.

Major depressive disorder

Major depressive disorder can lead to a variety of emotional and physical problems and can decrease the ability to function at work and at home. The essential characteristic of a major depressive episode is either depressed mood or the loss of interest in nearly all activities. The diagnostic criteria for major depressive disorder include the following symptoms:

- Feeling sad, empty, hopeless, irritable, or discouraged
- Noticeably reduced interest in or pleasure taken from almost all activities once enjoyed
- Significant unintended weight change
- Difficulty sleeping or sleeping excessively
- Agitation and restlessness or slowed movements and speech
- Fatigue or loss of energy
- Feeling worthless or excessively guilty
- Difficulty thinking, concentrating, or making decisions
- Frequent thoughts of death

Symptoms must be present for most of the day, nearly every day, for at least two consecutive weeks. At least one of the first two symptoms on the list and at least five other symptoms must be present. A diagnosis based on a single episode is possible, although most people have several episodes. In a given year in the United States, about 7 percent of people suffer from major depression.

Depression is different from sadness or grief. It is normal to feel sad and grieve in a difficult situation, such as the death of a loved one, the loss of a job, or the ending of a relationship. In grief, painful feelings come in waves, often mixed with positive memories. In major depression, mood, interest, and pleasure are decreased for most of two weeks. In grief, self-esteem is usually maintained. In major depression, feelings of worthlessness and self-loathing are common. For some people, the death of a loved one, the loss of a job, or being a victim of a physical assault or a major disaster can lead to depression.

Persistent depressive disorder (dysthymia)

The main characteristic of persistent depressive disorder (dysthymia) is depressed mood for most of the day, for more days than not, for at least two years. In children and adolescents, mood can be irritable, and duration must be at least one year. Major depression may come before persistent depressive disorder, and major depressive episodes may occur during persistent depressive disorder. Persistent depressive disorder often has an early and subtle onset and a chronic course. Early onset (before age twenty-one) is associated with a higher likelihood of co-occurring personality disorders and substance use disorders. About 2 percent of people in the United States have persistent depressive disorder.

Disruptive mood dysregulation disorder

Symptoms of disruptive mood dysregulation disorder go beyond those that describe temperamental children. They describe those with a severe impairment that requires medical attention. The primary feature of disruptive mood dysregulation disorder is chronic, severe, persistent irritability. This severe irritability has two important clinical signs.

The first sign is severe, frequent (on average, three or more times per week) temper outbursts expressed verbally (verbal rages) and/or behaviorally (physical aggression toward people or property). The outbursts are completely out of proportion in intensity or duration to the situation. They must occur over at least one year in at least two settings, such as the home and school, and they must be developmentally inappropriate. When the child is not having an outburst, the second sign of severe irritability—a chronic, persistent irritable or angry mood—can be seen. This irritable or angry mood must be characteristic of the child, be present most of the day, nearly every day, and be noticeable by others in the child's environment. It is important to note that this diagnosis can be made for the first time only for those aged six to eighteen. The onset of disruptive mood dysregulation disorder must be before age ten.

This disorder is associated with significant disruption in a child's family and peer relationships, as well as in school performance. Children with this disorder have extremely low frustration tolerance and therefore may have difficulty succeeding in school and are often unable to participate in the activities typically enjoyed by healthy children. Family life is severely disrupted by their outbursts and irritability, and they may have trouble initiating or sustaining friendships. The estimated occurrence among children and adolescents is 2 to 5 percent. However, rates are higher in males and school-aged children than in females and adolescents.

Premenstrual dysphoric disorder

Many women experience emotional and physical changes around the time of their period. However, for some women, these changes can be disabling and can disrupt their lives. Premenstrual dysphoric disorder is a severe form of premenstrual syndrome (PMS). In most menstrual cycles, symptoms must be present in the final week before the period, start to improve a few days after the period begins, and become minimal or absent in the week after. One or more of the following symptoms must be present:

- Emotional changes (mood swings, feeling suddenly sad or tearful, or increased sensitivity to rejection)
- Irritability, anger, or increased conflicts with others
- Depressed mood, feelings of hopelessness, or self-deprecating thoughts
- Anxiety, tension, or feeling on edge

One or more of the following symptoms must also be present, to reach a total of five symptoms when combined with symptoms listed previously:

- Decreased interest in usual activities
- Difficulty concentrating
- Lack of energy
- Change in appetite, overeating, or specific food cravings
- Difficulty sleeping or sleeping too much
- Feeling overwhelmed or out of control
- Physical symptoms such as breast tenderness or swelling, joint or muscle pain, bloating, or weight gain

These symptoms are linked to significant distress or interference with work, school, usual social activities, or relationships with others. Many women report that symptoms worsen as they approach menopause. About 2 to 6 percent of menstruating women in the United States have premenstrual dysphoric disorder.

Substance/medication-induced depressive disorder

In substance/medication-induced depressive disorder, the symptoms of a depressive disorder are present, but here the depressive symptoms are associated with the ingestion, injection, or inhalation of a substance (drug, alcohol, toxin, or medication). Most often, the depressive disorder begins within the first few weeks or first month of the substance use. Once the substance use is stopped, the depressive symptoms usually decrease within days to several weeks, depending on the substance/medication and the presence of withdrawal symptoms.

Depressive disorder due to another medical condition

Depression is clearly linked, through nervous system anatomy, with stroke, Huntington's disease, Parkinson's disease, and traumatic brain injury. In fact, depression is considered the first psychiatric symptom of Huntington's disease. Cushing's disease and hypothyroidism (low thyroid hormone) are the two nervous system/endocrine system conditions most closely linked to depression. The risk of suicide of major depressive episodes connected to medical conditions might be greater than that for other forms of depression; there is a clear link between serious medical illnesses and suicide, particularly shortly after diagnosis of the illness.

Depression with anxious distress

High levels of anxiety have been linked to higher suicide risk, longer length of illness, and a greater likelihood of not responding to treatment. Anxious distress is defined as the presence of at least two of the following symptoms during most days of a depressive episode:

- Feeling anxious or tense
- Feeling unusually restless
- Difficulty concentrating because of constant worrying
- Fear that something awful may happen
- Feeling that one might lose control

Depression with atypical features

Despite its name, atypical depression does not imply that the individual has an uncommon or unusual disorder. Those with atypical depression have mood reactivity, which is the ability to be cheered up when presented with positive events. The mood may even become euthymic (not sad) for long periods if the environment is positive. Other symptoms of atypical depression are significant weight gain or an increase in appetite, sleeping at least ten hours a day, leaden paralysis (feeling weighted down, usually in the arms or legs), and rejection sensitivity.

Depressive disorder with peripartum onset (postpartum depression)

For some women, having a baby can be more stressful and challenging than blissful. Up to 70 percent of all new mothers experience the "baby blues." But postpartum depression is different from the baby blues, which is a short-term condition (lasting days to two weeks), with feelings of worry, unhappiness, and fatigue. A woman experiencing postpartum depression may first appear to have the baby blues. But with postpartum depression, the symptoms usually become worse and last longer. Women who become depressed around the time of giving birth may have the following symptoms during pregnancy or in the four weeks following delivery:

- Sluggishness or fatigue
- Feeling sad, hopeless, helpless, or worthless
- Difficulty sleeping or sleeping too much
- Changes in appetite
- Difficulty concentrating or confusion
- Crying for no reason
- Lack of interest in the baby or family and friends
- Fear of harming the baby or oneself
- Difficulty bonding with the baby

An estimated 9 to 16 percent of new mothers experience postpartum depression. These women often have severe anxiety and even panic attacks. Rapid changes in hormones and thyroid levels after delivery have a strong effect on mood and may contribute to postpartum depression. A lack of sleep, stress, a family history of depression, or a lack of a support system may also play a role.

Depression with seasonal pattern (seasonal affective disorder)

Seasonal affective disorder (SAD) is present when there is a relationship between the start of depressive episodes and a particular time of year. Symptoms of major depressive episodes that occur in a seasonal pattern include loss of energy, sleeping too much, overeating, weight gain, and a craving for carbohydrates. SAD has been linked to a biochemical imbalance in the brain caused by shorter daylight hours and less sunlight in winter. SAD is most common in people living far from the equator, with reduced hours of sunshine in the winter. Less commonly, SAD occurs in the summer, possibly in response to high heat and humidity. During this period, the depression is more likely to cause symptoms of insomnia, decreased appetite, weight loss, and agitation or anxiety. Young adults and women are at a higher risk than others. SAD may begin at any age, but the average age of onset is eighteen to thirty years.

Who's Most at Risk for Depression?

Depression is surprisingly common, affecting about 120 million people worldwide. The National Institute of Mental Health estimates that depression affects nearly 15 million American adults each year, or almost 7 percent of the population older than eighteen. Depression can surface at any age; however, the average age is thirty-two.

Both men and women can be affected by depression, although women are at least twice as likely as men to have it, no matter their race or how much money they make. But not just adults suffer. As many as one in eight teenagers of both sexes and one in thirty-three children have clinical depression (depression serious enough to require treatment). Yet less than one-third of those with depression actively seek or receive treatment.

Depression tends to run in families, and those with a family history of depressive disorders are as many as three times more likely to have the illness than those in the general population. Another risk factor is depression itself. Those who have had an episode of major depression not connected to a general medical condition are at least 50 percent more likely to have another one. And the risk rises to 90 percent after several such episodes.

The cost of depression is high. Over the next twenty years, depression is projected to become the No. 1 cause of disability in high-income countries such as the United States and the No. 2 cause worldwide. In the United States alone, the yearly cost of depressive illness is about $30 to $44 billion. But the personal cost of depression is impossible to estimate, as the amount of pain, suffering, lost wages, and destruction of relationships simply cannot be measured. And some people with depression pay the highest price of all—the loss of life. More than 90 percent of those who commit suicide had a mental disorder, usually involving depression or substance abuse.

Depression and Suicide: Stats and Facts

Suicide is the eighth leading cause of death in the United States, accounting for thirty-two thousand deaths each year. More than two-thirds of reported suicides are caused by depression.

- Although depression is diagnosed two or three times more often in women than in men, men are more than four times more likely to die by suicide. Women, however, are up to three times more likely than men to attempt suicide.
- The risk of suicide increases around the time of an important anniversary, during periods of high anxiety, in conjunction with drug or alcohol abuse, and when depression is either untreated or not treated enough.
- Suicide risk also increases in those who tend to be impulsive or have a family history of mental illness, substance abuse, suicide, separation, divorce, or family violence of any kind.
- Treatment of those at high risk for suicide is surprisingly lacking. In a large study in Canada, nearly half of the patients who had thought about suicide and one-fourth of those who had attempted it said that they had not received care or even thought they needed it.
- About 15 percent of depressed people whose depression is untreated commit suicide.

Causes of Depression

Doctors used to believe that depression was the result of certain thoughts or triggers. But research shows that it's far more complicated than that. Depression is rarely due to a single cause; it's more likely the result of a combination of biochemical, physical, genetic, and/or psychological factors.

Biochemical factors

Brain scans have shown that the brains of depressed people function differently from those of "normal" people in the areas regulating mood, behavior, appetite, sleep, and thinking. This may be due to the fact that those with depression typically have imbalances in levels of brain chemicals called neurotransmitters—specifically serotonin and norepinephrine, and possibly, dopamine. Imbalanced levels of serotonin are linked to sleep problems, binge eating, and irritability, while imbalances norepinephrine can cause low mood and fatigue. In the case of dopamine, the problem may be due to either too much or not enough of the neurotransmitter for long periods.

Why do neurotransmitter levels change? It may be because the body is having problems making them. Deficiencies in amino acids or vitamin and mineral cofactors may result in decreased production of critical chemicals affecting mood. Or it may be that the body is breaking down the neurotransmitters too quickly. Many things can account for neurotransmitter imbalances.

Physical factors

A large percentage of people with certain medical conditions or illnesses suffer from depression.

Condition	***Percent of sufferers***
Cancer	15 to 25
Eating disorders	94
Heart attack survivors	20 to 40
HIV	10 to 20
Huntington's disease	50
Chronic (long-term) pain	30
Parkinson's disease	50
Stroke survivors	25 to 50
Disabling tinnitus	60
Drug or alcohol abuse	27
Alzheimer's disease	30 to 35

In addition, depression is often seen with anxiety disorders and nicotine (tobacco) addiction. Depression may be caused by some of these conditions, and it can also contribute to others, including eating disorders and substance abuse. Researchers have also found that depressed people are more likely to have type 2 diabetes and heart disease. And with certain conditions, such as Alzheimer's disease and substance abuse, depression may be both a cause and an effect.

Certain medications, whether prescription, over the counter, or recreational, may also contribute to depression. These include antipsychotic drugs, antihistamines, beta blockers, birth control pills, high blood pressure medications, anti-inflammatory medications, adrenal hormone agents, and corticosteroids.

Medications That Can Cause Depression

Medications or street drugs that can bring about depression as a side effect include the following:

- Alcohol
- Amphotericin B (Fungizone)
- Antipsychotic drugs
- Beta blockers (betaxolol, nadolol, propranolol, timolol)
- Bismuth nitrate
- Carbamazepine
- Cis-retinoic acid
- Birth control pills
- Corticosteroids
- Cycloserine (Seromycin)
- Cyclosporine
- Digitalis
- Estrogen therapy
- Flunarizine
- H_2 blockers (cimetidine, ranitidine)
- Interferon
- Levodopa
- Mercury
- Methyldopa
- Methylxanthines (caffeine, theophylline)
- Metoclopramide (Reglan)
- Metronidazole
- Nifedipine
- Organic nitrates
- Phenytoin
- Psychostimulants (fenfluramine, methylphenidate, pemoline, phenylpropanolamine)
- Reserpine
- Sedative-hypnotics (barbiturates, benzodiazepines, methaqualone)
- Thallium
- Thiazide diuretics
- Vinblastine
- Vincristine

An overactive immune system

"Sickness behavior" is a normal reaction to infection that causes fatigue, sleepiness, poor concentration, and a lack of desire to do anything productive. Interestingly, sickness behavior and depression have many symptoms in common. It shouldn't be surprising, then, that there is a link between depression and an overactive immune system (the system that fights off infection) due to an infection or injury.

During long-lasting infection or injury, chemicals called proinflammatory cytokines can contribute to depression by causing changes in the levels of neurotransmitters. Cytokines can also lead to a lack of certain neurotransmitters by continually stimulating their release.

Recent studies have found changes in the cytokine levels of patients with major depression. Several studies have shown that high levels of proinflammatory cytokines and low levels of anti-inflammatory cytokines appear in people with depression. One study involving twenty-three subjects with depression and twenty-five healthy controls measured the cytokine levels of the patients at admission into the study and after eight weeks of antidepressant treatment with sertraline (Zoloft). At admission, proinflammatory cytokines were much higher in patients with depression. The anti-inflammatory cytokines IL-4 and TGF-beta1 in subjects with depression were much lower. After treatment with sertraline, there was a noticeable decrease in proinflammatory cytokines and an increase in anti-inflammatory cytokines. This and several other studies support the idea that depression may, in some cases, be due to an overactive immune system.

Depressed patients with increased inflammatory biomarkers, measurable substances in the body that help indicate a disease, have been found to be less likely to respond to conventional antidepressant treatments. Patients with a history of nonresponse to antidepressants have been found to have increased concentrations of chemicals in the blood that accompany inflammation compared with treatment-responsive patients. Genetic variations in our inflammatory responses may increase the risk of depression and may be associated with reduced responsiveness to antidepressant therapy.

Inflammatory brain illnesses are linked to high rates of major depressive episodes. The most compelling evidence to date of brain inflammation and major depressive disorder comes from a 2015 Canadian study.

Inflammation in areas of the brain dealing with mood regulation was 30 percent higher in clinically depressed patients. More inflammation was associated with a more severe depressive episode, supporting the idea that inflammation may contribute to sickness behaviors that overlap with the symptoms of major depressive episodes. While many studies have looked at blood biomarkers of inflammation, this study is the first to find conclusive evidence in the brain.

The role of the immune system needs to be considered whenever depressive symptoms occur. Many treatments for depression focus only on balancing neurotransmitters, yet these imbalances may result from increases in immune system activity that trigger an inflammatory response in the brain.

Hormonal factors

Hormones are also linked to depression. Although teenage girls are no more likely than boys of the same age to have depression, in adulthood, women with depression quickly outnumber men with depression.

In women, short episodes of depression can occur seven to ten days before the menstrual period (premenstrual syndrome or, in more serious cases, premenstrual dysphoric disorder) and during the first fourteen days after delivering a child ("baby blues" or, in more serious cases, postpartum depression). Depression can also be a symptom of perimenopause and menopause.

In men, low levels of the male hormone testosterone may be linked to depression. Low or low-normal levels of testosterone have been found in men who were not helped by standard antidepressants, and testosterone replacement has been used with success in men with depression.

When thyroid hormone levels are low, many organs slow down, creating a wide range of symptoms, including depression. The thyroid gland is a small butterfly-shaped organ in the neck below the Adam's apple. Thyroid hormones can affect energy level, mood, body temperature, and even weight. The thyroid is regulated by the pituitary gland, a pea-sized structure in the brain. The pituitary gland continuously monitors levels of hormones in the blood, including thyroid hormone. The thyroid gland and the pituitary gland work together to secrete a steady amount of thyroid hormone into the bloodstream. When blood levels of thyroid hormones fall, the pituitary gland uses a chemical signal called thyroid-stimulating hormone (TSH) to tell the thyroid to increase hormone production. In response, the thyroid produces two hormones, T_3 and T_4. In the condition hypothyroidism, the thyroid gland does not entirely respond to TSH, so blood levels of T_3 and T_4 remain low.

Subclinical hypothyroidism (normal T_4 with raised TSH) occurs in up to 40 percent of patients with mood disorders. In a 2015 study including more than five thousand females, the risk of depressive symptoms was increased in those with the highest TSH level compared with those with the lowest TSH level. A high TSH level occurs in hypothyroidism because the pituitary gland is using much more effort to stimulate the unresponsive thyroid gland. In addition, low thyroid function has been linked to poorer responses to depression treatment and a lower rate of recovery.

Thyroid hormone supplements appear to speed up and increase the response to antidepressant drugs. According to the American Association of Clinical Endocrinologists, "The diagnosis of subclinical or clinical hypothyroidism must be considered in every patient with depression."

Genetic factors

Studies have shown that depression occurs at much higher rates in families in which either a grandparent or parent has had depression. In fact, a family history of depression can increase one's risk of depression by as many as three times, although it's just the tendency to have depression that is inherited, not the disorder itself. In addition, easily inherited personality traits such as anxiety and neuroticism also are strongly linked to depression.

To determine the extent to which genes play a role in an illness, scientists look at patterns of illness in families to estimate heritability (what percentage of the cause is due to genes). Many research studies trying to identify specific genes influencing the risk of depression are done with identical twins because they share the same genetic makeup. Researchers have found that, when one twin becomes depressed, the other one also becomes depressed about 76 percent of the time. Even when the identical twins are raised separately, the likelihood of both twins having depression is about 67 percent, implying that there is a strong genetic influence. Because the rate is not closer to 100 percent, we know that a strong genetic factor predisposes the individual to depressive disorders but that environmental factors such as stress, traumatic events, and other illnesses may be the tipping point.

Psychological factors

Stress is among the most important risk factors for depression. Stressful or traumatic situations such as the death of someone close, divorce, disability, lack of social support, chronic illness, an accident, the loss of a job, or loss of personal dreams or goals can trigger or contribute to depression. In addition, people who have suffered many difficult life events, had a very stressful early life, or tend to be negative thinkers may be more likely to have depression.

Aging appears to be another trigger, with about 16 percent of older people suffering from depression, some for the first time in their lives. This is not too surprising, considering that older people are more likely to experience the loss of loved ones, social isolation, the end of an important relationship, chronic illness, a decrease in income, or a loss of independence. They are also more likely to have nutritional problems because they eat less and their bodies can't absorb nutrients as well as when they were younger, which can increase the risk of depression.

Chapter 3

How Do We Evaluate Depression?

Depression is a disabling illness that strangles one's life and spirit and severely reduces both psychological and physical well-being. It is surprisingly common, affecting more than 15 million people in the United States alone. However, standard treatment for depression brings about a complete recovery or nearly complete elimination of symptoms in only 33 percent of patients, and in roughly 70 percent of those, depression happens again.

Most of us do not need numbers to know that depression is a widespread problem that is difficult to resolve. We see the devastation in our lives and in the lives of family members and friends with depression. I have listened to patients suffering from depression for more than twenty years, and it is very clear to me that our current treatments are not enough.

> Susan is twenty years old and has been in therapy for the last eight years. She has tried eight different medications over the years, with no sign of relief from her depression and mood swings.
>
> Harold, a twenty-six-year-old living with his parents, has had depression since high school. He has attempted suicide twice and has been hospitalized for severe depression four times. Although he is very bright, he has been unable to complete college.
>
> Melanie wakes up every morning asking why she should get out of bed. She always feels irritable with her two children and her husband, and she often explodes with anger. "I have been in therapy for years. I have tried every medication they make, and nothing works for me."

What Is a Psychiatric Evaluation?

Numerous scientific articles have looked at the reasons for our difficulties in treating depression, but let's instead consider what happens when the typical patient visits a psychiatrist. In fact, let's imagine that it's you stepping into the office. You've been sent to a psychiatrist by your doctor, who has been prescribing you antidepressants for sleep problems, fatigue, anxiety, and depression.

One of the first things you notice when you enter the psychiatrist's office is that it is not a usual medical office. There are no stethoscopes, blood pressure cuffs, or other instruments that doctors use to take measurements of patients. Instead, there are two chairs and a box of tissues. Clearly, this is not going to be a standard medical exam, despite the fact that psychiatrists are doctors who go to four years of medical school after college, followed by at least four years of specialized training in psychiatry. You start to feel a little anxious.

The doctor sits down, offers you a seat, and encourages you to describe your symptoms: "So, what brings you in today?" You feel even more anxious because you are not sure where to begin. If you're feeling depressed, your symptoms might include loss of interest in activities you used to enjoy, crying spells, increased irritability, fatigue, changes in your sleep patterns, and a feeling of worthlessness. The psychiatrist writes down these symptoms and interviews you to get the information she needs to make a diagnosis.

You start to wonder, *What is a psychiatric diagnosis?* You may continue to wonder how a psychiatrist can make a diagnosis based only on talking with you rather than from test results or a physical exam. So you feel even more anxious and confused than when you walked in the door.

The psychiatrist opens the *DSM-V,* a big, gray book that sits behind her on the bookshelf. She is trying to come up with a list of symptoms from the things you've told her that match one of the lists of symptoms in the book. For example, the *DSM-V* lists the following symptoms under the category of a major depressive episode:

- Depressed mood most of the day, nearly every day
- Markedly reduced interest in activities
- Noticeable weight loss (when not dieting) or weight gain
- Sleeping more than usual or having difficulty sleeping
- Feeling fatigued nearly every day
- Feeling worthless or guilty for no reason
- Having difficulty concentrating or making decisions
- Thinking about death or attempting suicide

About Those *DSM* Lists

As psychiatry became a field of medicine, it became necessary to have clear diagnostic categories so that professionals could discuss and research the difficulties of patients with mental illness. The goal was to create precise categories, but how precise was the science behind their development?

The first edition of the *DSM*, published in 1952 by the American Psychiatric Association, described 107 mental illnesses. Members of the association voted on the list of disorders to be included; about 10 percent of the membership was asked to approve a draft of the initial *DSM*. Somewhat less than half of those (or less than 5 percent of the total membership) voted to adopt the *DSM*. That means that 95 percent of members had no say in a document that would be accepted as the standard for mental health diagnosis.

Exactly what should be labeled as mental illness? How do we decide if someone is mentally ill? The different symptom lists in the *DSM* are simply the opinions of experts. They can't be any more than that, for there is no germ, blood test, or other test that can diagnose mental illness. The best that psychiatrists can say is, "We know it when we see it." And, apparently, we see a lot of it, for the *DSM-IV*, which was published in 2003, lists 297 disorders, nearly three times more than the original *DSM*. Are there really that many more mental illnesses these days? Or have we labeled every little problem a disorder? That's a matter of opinion—and opinions change. For example, early versions of the *DSM* listed homosexuality as a mental illness; modern editions do not.

The new and revised *DSM-V* was released in 2013, after a decade of editing work on the last edition, *DSM-IV*. The *DSM-V* strives to include elements and diagnostic criteria that were lacking in the *DSM-IV*.

Several structural changes were made in the *DSM-V*. First, chapters in the *DSM-V* are grouped around symptoms and vulnerabilities rather than around scientific or clinical advances. This arrangement allows health professionals to better diagnose and treat patients based on similar symptoms and causes of disease across all groups. Also, the *DSM-V* is aligned with the *International Classification of Diseases*, eleventh edition, published by the World Health Organization (WHO). The WHO publication helps mental health professionals consistently and efficiently communicate with people about all spectrums of disorders.

With the *DSM-IV*, a patient either had or did not have a specific symptom and had to reach a certain number of symptoms to receive a diagnosis. The *DSM-V* evaluates not only the patient's symptoms but also the severity of the diagnosis: very severe, severe, moderate, or mild. The *DSM-V* also attempts to overlap and link related diagnoses. All these changes might improve the diagnostic criteria for patients with depression. Is the *DSM-V* really better than the *DSM-IV*? The real question is: Did these changes result in improved treatment for patients suffering with depression? The answer is simply no.

What's Missing From Your Psychiatric Evaluation?

It's also important to consider what was *not* included in the hypothetical initial psychiatric evaluation mentioned above. Psychiatrists do not always ask you about medical illnesses and physical symptoms that you, your siblings, your parents, and your grandparents have or have had. Rarely would a psychiatrist listen to your heart, monitor your pulse, examine your eyes, look at your skin, or otherwise try to determine if any of your physical symptoms might be related to your depressed mood, lack of energy, or insomnia. Your hypothetical evaluation did not include a discussion of what you typically eat or which chemicals you have been exposed to. Neither was there any order for laboratory work to check your nutritional status and hormone levels or to measure the environmental toxins that may have built up in your body. In addition, no attempt was made to discover whether allergies you may or may not be aware of could be affecting your mood.

These omissions clearly show that psychiatry does not operate on the principle that what occurs in the body affects what occurs in the mind. To those in the psychiatric profession, the brain is the brain, and the body is the body; they are two separate and very different things. This separation of brain and body often prevents physicians and mental health professionals from finding the real cause of depression.

A Shot in the Dark

Back to your hypothetical psychiatric evaluation. Now it's time to decide on the treatment strategy, which is much more difficult than making the diagnosis. Why? Because psychiatrists prescribe medications without understanding the causes of the disorders they seek to treat. They are, in essence, guessing.

Internists, cardiologists, gastroenterologists, and other medical specialists offer patients specific medical treatments designed to treat an underlying biological problem. In the case of a bacterial infection, for example, a physician prescribes antibiotics; for high cholesterol, he may recommend a statin drug or exercises and dietary changes to reduce it. An internist or infectious diseases specialist studies a sample of blood to determine exactly which bacterium is triggering the symptoms and then prescribes the antibiotic best suited to getting rid of it.

Psychiatrists, on the other hand, have no way of knowing what may be causing the depression because there are no "depression germs" or other brain problems that obviously cause mental disorder. Yes, certain genes are linked to some mental disorders, but these genes increase the tendency toward a disorder rather than predict it. Certain imbalances in brain chemistry also appear to influence depression, but no one has ever shown that they actually *cause* depression.

Thus psychiatrists make treatment decisions based on educated guesses, prescribing one medicine after another, hoping that one, or some combination, will work. Most psychiatrists rely on their personal favorites. Some favor older medications for depression, such as Zoloft and Prozac, while others lean toward newer ones, such as Cymbalta and Remeron. Either way, patients usually take multiple kinds of psychiatric medications over time and are typically prescribed two or more antidepressants to take at the same time, in addition to medication for sleep and, perhaps, anxiety. A study published in the *Archives of General Psychiatry* confirmed this trend, finding that 59.8 percent of visits to office-based psychiatrists resulted in two or more psychiatric medication prescriptions. About one-third of the office visits resulted in three or more prescriptions. And if the first prescription didn't solve the problem, new ones were offered.

This means that your psychiatrist will try one medicine after another to see what works. Most likely, the first medicine won't provide enough relief, so you'll be given a second, third, fourth, and even fifth kind of medication. Some doctors keep adding medications without stopping ones that don't work. This rapidly growing trend, called polypharmacy, is the sad reality of treating depression.

> Jason, a forty-four-year-old lawyer, was placed on disability because of his chronic depression. Fifteen different medications and electroconvulsive therapy (ECT, formerly called shock therapy) did not help Jason feel better. By the time I met him, he was unable to work, and all he was doing was visiting therapists, specialists, and doctors. His promising career was destroyed by depression that kept coming back. However, after a thorough evaluation, including different kinds of testing, Jason is now on his way toward recovery. With two medications and a strict gluten-free diet after a diagnosis of celiac disease, Jason is back at work.

Missing the Target

Medications are great blessings in modern life. They help hundreds of millions of people every year. During many years in practice, I have seen psychiatric medications give health and function back to many people. But our ability to treat depression with medications is not as good as we once thought. Two-thirds of patients with depression who have been "effectively" treated with antidepressants continue to have symptoms that impair their day-to-day functioning, with 28 percent having mild impairment, 23 percent moderate impairment, 12 percent severe impairment, and 4 percent very severe impairment. This means that a large percentage of those "cured" by standard medications continue to have symptoms of depression that impair important aspects of their lives.

There is not all that much evidence showing that antidepressants work. The medical literature (based on studies from 1987 to 2004) suggests that 94 percent of antidepressant studies show that antidepressants work, but the actual number is closer to 51 percent, because about one-third of the studies showing that they didn't work submitted to the U.S. Food and Drug Administration (FDA) were never published. That means that about half of the studies failed to show any benefit beyond that of a placebo, a pill that contains no medication at all.

Sadly, I've seen psychiatric treatment for depression not work many times in patients of all ages. The struggles with depressed mood, irritability, and fatigue stay despite the patients trying many different medications.

Much of what we know about antidepressant medications and their efficacy is still unclear. In 2001, the pharmaceutical company that created the SSRI Paxil supported a research study that claimed that Paxil was safe and effective for teenagers. Fourteen years later, in 2015, a group of researchers published a report in the *British Medical Journal* that analyzed the same data presented in the original study; only they came up with the opposite conclusion.

The analysis found that the original study mislabeled several side effects brought on by Paxil, including suicidal thoughts and behavior. For example, one of the teenagers enrolled in the research study was hospitalized after overdosing on Tylenol tablets, while another was admitted to a psychiatric hospital for severe suicidal and homicidal ideation toward his parents. This was misrepresented as "emotional lability."

I talk more about the controversy regarding psychiatric medications in chapter 4. For now, it's enough to note that much of the "science" behind antidepressant effectiveness may, in fact, be myths created by drug companies.

Chapter 4

Current Treatments Are Less Effective Than We Think

Earlier, I pointed out that medications are effective in only 33 percent of patients who seek help for depression and that, in 70 percent of those who seem to recover, symptoms return.

The usual treatment for depression isn't good or even good enough. I think the numbers, and the fact that so many people have symptoms return or simply stop treatment in despair, prove that we are failing to help many who suffer from depression. For too many patients, the usual treatment is not successful.

Most psychiatrists and psychiatric researchers support our current practices. And they justify their support by pointing to thousands of studies that show the effectiveness of antidepressants and other medications used to treat depression.

And their support is based on evidence. Stacks of studies conducted by well-known researchers from Harvard, Yale, Stanford, Mayo Clinic, and other important universities, research centers, and hospitals around the world show that antidepressants and other medications are effective in treating depression. Can all of these studies be wrong? They are not filled with errors; however, some are not trustworthy because the researchers received money from the same drug companies that may earn millions (perhaps billions) of dollars if the studies come out "right." Let's take a look at these problems with psychiatric research.

Pharmaceutical Support Undermines Credibility

In the United States, hundreds of millions of dollars are spent every year on studies testing the effectiveness of psychiatric medications. This research is supported by the government, universities, and, most of all, the same drug companies that make these medications. Estimates vary,

Direct-to-Consumer Advertising

Billions of dollars are spent every year on direct-to-consumer advertising (DTCA), with an estimated $3.2 billion spent in 2003. Direct-to-consumer ads target consumers via TV, billboards, radio, and other media. But how do these ads influence patients and their doctors?

First and foremost, DTCA is an issue only in the United States and New Zealand, because it is illegal in the rest of the world. People for DTCA argue that those who may go untreated can receive valuable information that may improve their health. On the other hand, people against DTCA argue that DTCA may lead many healthy people to take medications they don't need, perhaps harming them and increasing their medical costs.

These arguments aside, what we do know is that DTCA increases the use of medication. Although DTCA has no effect on specific antidepressant choices, evidence suggests that when DTCA spending is increased by 10 percent for a certain kind of medication, use of that drug class increases by 1 percent. In the case of antidepressants, Adam Block, economist for the Joint Committee on Taxation in the U.S. Congress, showed that people who were not depressed accounted for 94 percent of new antidepressant use due to DTCA. DTCA may lead to as many as fifteen nondepressed people receiving antidepressant treatment for each depressed person who does so.

This general trend toward prescribing too much medication or prescribing it for the wrong people is reflected in an FDA survey in which 73 percent of primary care doctors and 63 percent of specialists said that they felt pressured to prescribe because their patients had seen or heard DTCA. This patient demand has led to changes in the way doctors prescribe medications. In a separate study, 23.5 percent of physicians reported that DTCA changed the way they prescribe medications.

but it's safe to say that drug companies fund the largest percentage of this research.

At first glance, this seems reasonable. Why wouldn't the companies that make and sell the medications want to do research proving that their products are safe and effective? Indeed, shouldn't we consumers demand that they do? The problem is that drug companies doing or sponsoring their own research have a major conflict of interest. On one hand, they want to make the best possible medications, but on the other hand, they want to sell as many drugs as possible. Because the companies are for-profit businesses, their desire to increase sales often wins.

Drug studies can be very expensive. It can cost millions of dollars to create the study plan, pay for the researchers and laboratory equipment, recruit and possibly pay volunteers, hire statisticians to crunch the numbers, and so on. The government and universities usually don't want to spend that kind of money on researching an unproven medication, so the cost must be paid by the drug company. But the company doesn't really mind, because writing the check means it gets to control what happens during and after the study.

An Industry-wide Problem

By publishing only positive antidepressant studies, drug companies are misleading the medical community and the public into believing that antidepressants are more effective than they are.

In the United States, the FDA is trying to stop this practice by creating a registry and database. In 1997, Congress passed legislation allowing public access to information about ongoing clinical studies. Under this law, drug companies must register all clinical studies they intend to use in support of their drugs during the FDA approval process. The Internet-based registry www.clinicaltrials.gov was created in 2000 to provide the public database. Due to problems with the database—including incomplete information—in 2007, the FDA's Amendments Act was passed. According to the act, the registry must be updated, with information on the participants and study results, within twelve months of study completion (twenty-four months if the drug is currently under FDA review).

These changes may help solve some of the selective publication problems, but they don't address the issue of financial conflicts in drug research. As a group of researchers from Harvard Medical School's Massachusetts General Hospital pointed out, "Financial conflicts of interest are exceedingly common in biomedical research. Investigators with conflicts of interest are more likely to arrive at positive conclusions, perhaps as a result of biased study design, industry suppression of negative results, preferential funding by industry of projects that are likely to succeed or biased interpretation of results."

Three Yale University School of Medicine researchers came to similar conclusions about conflicts of interest that arise when scientific researchers and universities hired to conduct research are financially tied to drug companies. They found, among other issues, that the universities hired to perform drug research were often part owners of the very companies that hired them. This means that the universities are often part owners of the medications they are testing, meaning that they could make a lot of money if the results come out "right."

Does this really make a difference? Aren't medical researchers really interested in finding the best treatments? Of course they are. But when money enters the picture, vision can begin to cloud a bit. That may be why studies are much more likely to "prove" that a drug is better than a placebo when they are funded by the drug industry or when the researchers have a financial interest in the study outcome. Indeed, as researchers from Harvard Medical School pointed out in the *American Journal of Psychiatry*, studies supported by a drug company and studies in which at least one of the researchers has a financial conflict of interest are 4.9 times more likely to report that the medication being studied "works" when compared against studies that are not financially tied to drug companies.

Do Our Pills Really Work?

Even if psychiatric medications, like all medications, are oversold by drug companies, and even if these companies are much too cozy with psychiatrists and doctors, we still need the answer to a key question: Do the medications work?

If you looked at the thousands of published studies on the effectiveness of psychiatric medications, you would have to conclude that the answer is yes, to some degree and for many people. But, as I said earlier, many studies that produce negative results are never published, so it's difficult to get an accurate picture of the true effects of a given medication. You can be sure of one thing: those "buried studies" most likely indicate that the medications being studied don't work well—if at all.

A small number of researchers and practicing psychiatrists have been asking if psychiatric medications work for quite some time. British psychiatrist Joanna Moncrieff published a paper in which she boldly stated, "There are no signs that the rapidly escalating use of antidepressants is reducing the burden of depressive disorders." In other words, although more and more people were being diagnosed with depression and treated accordingly, the situation was not improving.

A decade and many millions of antidepressant prescriptions later, her words continue to ring true. Indeed, a study published in the *Journal of the American Medical Association* in 2010 found that standard antidepressants are no more effective than placebo for people with the less severe forms of depression, despite the fact that antidepressant medications are considered "the best established treatment for major depressive disorder." Specifically, the researchers found that Paxil (an SSRI related to Prozac) and imipramine (an older antidepressant) did not reduce symptoms effectively in people with mild, moderate, or severe depression. That is, these drugs may have slightly lowered the numbers on the Hamilton Depression Rating Scale (HDRS), a test used to measure the severity of a patient's depression, but the reduction was so slight that it didn't make any difference in patients' day-to-day functioning. The antidepressants made a difference only for those in the "very severely depressed" category—that is, those with a Hamilton score of 25 or higher. For everyone else, the benefits of taking antidepressants compared with placebo "may be minimal or nonexistent."

The results of this study are shocking, especially when you consider that about 70 percent of patients begin with Hamilton scores below 22, meaning that for them, *no* antidepressant will be much more effective than a placebo. Yet almost all patients diagnosed with depression are given prescriptions for antidepressant medications.

Depression Is Growing Worse, Despite a Flood of "Miracle" Medicines

In *Anatomy of an Epidemic,* Robert Whitaker carefully looks at fifty years of psychiatric literature and reveals a rather embarrassing secret: Over time, many patients who are *not* medicated do better than those who are. Throughout the 1970s, before the advent of "second-generation" psychiatric medicines such as Prozac, relatively few people suffering from depression were given antidepressants. Those with mild or moderate symptoms were especially unlikely to take them. A large number of mildly or moderately depressed patients recovered over the course of several months, and most were well for years before another bout of depression hit—if it struck at all. Today, however, doctors often prescribe psychiatric medicines right away, which Whitaker argues can set the stage for chronic, recurring depression and lifelong medication use.

Whitaker notes that, in 1987, 1.25 million Americans were on disability because of mental disorders. In 2013, that number more than tripled to 4 million. If psychiatric treatment is as good as the psychiatrists say it is, why has the number of these patients more than tripled over the past thirty years? During this same time, many new medications were introduced; some were described as the next "wonder drug." And why has the number of children on disability due to mental illness skyrocketed from about sixteen thousand to six hundred thousand?

As Whitaker points out, a careful analysis of published studies shows that only about 15 percent of depressed people treated with medication remain healthy over time; the other 85 percent have chronic depression. Over the past several decades, then, most patients have shifted from having isolated episodes of depression, often spaced years apart, to suffering long-term emotional disability.

The problem has occurred because we rely almost totally on short-term studies, typically lasting only six weeks, that claim to prove that antidepressant medications work. Yes, medication may help many people, but these studies almost always fail to track patients during the years and decades that follow. Thus we don't know what happens after a study has ended. They also usually don't compare people who are medicated with those who are not. There is a major gap in our knowledge, for the few studies that *have* tracked long-term results and compared the medicated to the nonmedicated suggest that many people would be better off taking no medication at all.

What about the Side Effects?

The list of side effects that may be caused by antidepressants is long:

- Agitation or restlessness
- Blurred vision
- Constipation
- Decreased sex drive
- Dizziness
- Dry mouth
- Erectile dysfunction
- Fatigue
- Insomnia
- Osteoporosis ("soft" bones)
- Nausea
- Weight gain

Some of these side effects may be easy to avoid or stop. For example, taking the medication with food or eating smaller meals often gets rid of nausea for many people. But other side effects, including weight gain, decreased sex drive, and severe constipation, may be more difficult to deal with and require more medications or significant adjustments in lifestyle. Psychiatrists often add new medications to the ones patients are already taking to try to reduce side effects, but that means that patients risk having new side effects, which may require even more medication.

> Heather, a twenty-three-year-old female, started our first meeting together by saying, "I am not taking any medications that cause weight gain! I gained thirty pounds on the last antidepressant, and I can never do that again."
>
> Jim, a forty-eight-year-old who has had depression for more than a decade, sighed as he said, "Sometimes I don't know what's worse, the depression or the side effects. I've completely lost my sex drive, and things are stressful enough between my wife and me."

Certainly, the most worrisome side effect of antidepressant use is the increased risk of suicide. In March 2004, the FDA told the makers of a number of antidepressants to add a warning to their labels making doctors and patients aware that these medications had been linked to a worsening of depression and/or to an increased risk of suicide.

The FDA warning noted, "Anxiety, agitation, panic attacks, insomnia, irritability, hostility, impulsivity, akathisia ([severe] restlessness), hypomania and mania have been reported in adult and pediatric patients being treated with antidepressants for major depressive disorder as well as for other indications, both psychiatric and nonpsychiatric."

In May 2007, the FDA issued a new warning about the increased risk of suicide among young adults taking antidepressants. Nearly all antidepressant medications today have a "black box" label warning that antidepressants may increase the risk of suicidal thinking and behavior.

Possible Side Effects of SSRI Medications

The most commonly prescribed medications in the treatment of depression and mood disorders are selective serotonin reuptake inhibitors (SSRIs). These medications counteract symptoms of depression by blocking the reuptake of the neurotransmitter serotonin in the brain, resulting in improved mood. Some of the most commonly prescribed SSRI medications include sertraline (Zoloft), fluoxetine (Prozac), citalopram (Celexa), escitalopram (Lexapro), paroxetine (Paxil), and fluoxamine (Luvox).

While many of these medications are considered safe and effective, side effects may occur with their use. According to a report in the journal *Psychiatry*, about 40 percent of people taking an antidepressant reported side effects, and about 25 percent of them regarded those side effects as negatively affecting their quality of life. Some of the most common side effects reported included:

- **Sexual side effects.** About 60 percent of people on SSRIs experience impaired sexual function and decreased libido, although only 14 percent of patients report symptoms of sexual dysfunction, due to patients' and physicians' hesitation to address it. Usually, sexual problems include impotence, decreased sex drive, male ejaculatory disorder, and female orgasm disorder. Sexual side effects often cause patients to stop treatment. Patients may lower the dosage of antidepressants to avoid these side effects and not receive the dose of medication they need, resulting in continued depression. Sexual dysfunction is a common side effect in medications such as Celexa, Cymbalta, Lexapro, Paxil, Prozac, and Zoloft.

- **Weight gain.** Weight gain is often a side effect brought on by long-term use of antidepressant medications, and many patients discontinue antidepressant therapy because of it. About 25 percent of patients on antidepressants gain weight after six months of antidepressant use. Although there is no clear reason why antidepressants cause weight gain, it may be due to changes in both appetite and metabolism.
- **Physical symptoms, including headache, nausea, and stomach problems.** Nausea and stomach problems occur in 17 to 26 percent of patients on antidepressant medications. These symptoms are more prevalent during the first two weeks of use, and they typically disappear over time. However, your doctor might recommend dividing up doses or taking medications with meals to minimize nausea. Some patients also consume foods or drinks containing ginger to calm an upset stomach.

If you are having side effects that interfere with your quality of life, it is important to speak to your doctor and have the medications adjusted. You should not stop taking medications on your own. Antidepressant medication withdrawal is a big concern for many of my patients who want to stop medication use. It is not uncommon for a patient to quickly dismiss the use of medications due to side effects after being on a medication for no more than two weeks. It is critical to understand that stopping medications abruptly can result in a host of withdrawal symptoms.

Recognizing Medication Withdrawal

We often associate withdrawal symptoms with disorders of addiction, but patients who stop taking their medications may experience a phenomenon known as medication discontinuation syndrome (MDS). Long-term use of SSRIs is thought to increase levels of serotonin in the brain by blocking its reuptake, allowing the serotonin molecules to stay around longer, which helps regulate mood.

Because antidepressants essentially alter the function and production of mood-regulating substances in the brain, abruptly stopping medications does not allow the brain to adjust to rapid changes, leading to uncomfortable and sometimes dangerous side effects.

Research demonstrates that about 20 percent of patients stopping antidepressant use experience symptoms of MDS. However, in my clinical experience, that percentage is much higher. It is difficult to predict who will have withdrawal symptoms, but from my experience, those who feel slight withdrawal symptoms whenever they miss a dose may be vulnerable to MDS.

Symptoms of Medication Withdrawal

Emotional or Psychological Symptoms	*Physical Symptoms*
Increased irritability or agitation	Profuse sweating
Restlessness and insomnia	Racing heart or palpitations
Migraines and headaches	Nausea, vomiting, or diarrhea
Inability to focus	Difficulty breathing
Increased feelings of depression	Sensory disturbances

Symptoms of MDS resemble flulike symptoms and last for one or two weeks for most patients, but for some people, MDS may cause disabling symptoms for many months. Symptoms can range from mild to severe and can be alleviated by starting the medication again. Failure to recognize these symptoms may result in costly, unnecessary, and potentially risky medical visits.

While some medications are metabolized quickly, others take a long time before they are completely eliminated from your body. The medications that are metabolized more quickly are known to have shorter half-lives. A half-life is the length of time needed to clear half the medication from the body. Research indicates that individuals on medications with short half-lives are more likely to experience symptoms after stopping the medication. One study compared Paxil, a medication with a short half-life, to Prozac, a medication with a longer half-life. Patients who were on Paxil experienced more withdrawal symptoms than those on Prozac.

A number of class-action and individual lawsuits have been filed against drug companies such as GlaxoSmithKline, the maker of Paxil, for not properly warning patients of potential side effects regarding the use and stopping of the medication. Early research from the 1980s found that about 50 percent of healthy volunteers experienced symptoms from Paxil withdrawal, and in 2001 the FDA ordered stronger warnings about the drug's side effects on the label.

One of the most important tools we can use to minimize medication withdrawal symptoms is to taper medications slowly. The longer someone has been on an antidepressant, the more slowly the taper should be. I commonly use extremely low compounded doses of medications for this kind of slow taper. My recommendation for antidepressant tapering is typically three months, along with the nutritional support described in THE ZEEBRA approach. The most important goal is to withdraw someone safely from antidepressant medication. Speed is not of the essence.

Much of the scientific literature on managing medication withdrawal symptoms is grounded in patient education. Educating the patient about potential side effects before prescribing a medication is standard practice. However, such education does not change the fact that the patient may still feel miserable. I do not believe that simply warning a patient to expect to feel terrible and asking him or her to cope with it is an adequate solution. I discuss several strategies to safely minimize withdrawal side effects in THE ZEEBRA approach.

A New Way

I am not against medication. The problem is not the medications themselves; it's in the way they are researched, advertised, and used. Antidepressants can help restore health when used as part of an approach that combines personalized medicine and nutritional biochemistry. This approach requires that we find just the right medicine in the right dosage for each patient. It requires a better understanding of the research and conflicts of interest between medicine and the drug industry. As you will see, personalized medicine for the treatment of depression has finally become a reality.

Chapter 5

Depression and Biochemical Individuality

Measurement is the basis of scientific medicine. When you visit your doctor for a routine examination, the measurements begin as soon as you step into the exam room—or perhaps while you're still in the hallway and the nurse asks you to step on the scale to check your weight. The doctor's physical exam includes semiobjective measurements, such as asking how much it hurts when a certain area is pressed or noting whether your throat looks red, plus a series of objective measurements of, for instance, your heart rate, cholesterol levels, and liver and thyroid function. All these measurements help the doctor construct a profile of your body and determine the presence of any disease or damage.

While psychiatry is a branch of medicine, it is "the measureless medicine," the only specialty that does not use objective measurements to diagnose and treat disease and then see how well the treatment is working. We *cannot* measure the problems psychiatrists see objectively, because we truly have no idea what we're looking for. Exactly what *is* psychiatric disorder? What triggers it? How does it damage the brain, if at all? We don't know the answers.

We can see the results of mental illness in the form of symptoms, but we have no idea what causes it. We cannot, for example, find and treat the "depression tumor," kill the "depression germ," or fight the effects of the "depression gene." We cannot even find a marker of psychiatric distress, something that serves as a red flag, such as the low iron levels in anemia or high blood sugar in diabetes. In short, objectively speaking, we don't always know what we're trying to treat or how to find it, we don't know what our treatments should do, and we can't tell if they work.

Treating the Crowd, Not the Individual

I've already talked about some of the problems caused by the inability to measure, count, quantify, and objectify the causes and cures of mental illness. Yet another problem is the inability to personalize both diagnosis and treatment. This is a severe handicap.

Most physicians try to tailor a treatment to the individual's needs. An internist, for example, can send a blood sample to the lab to find out exactly which bacterium is causing a disease and can then select the best antibiotic to fight it. An oncologist can measure and stage a cancerous tumor to determine how advanced and aggressive it is and can then narrow the list of potential treatments. A cardiologist can create a heart-healthy diet tailored to a patient's food likes and dislikes. And a dermatologist can look at a rash and have a pretty good idea of which medication will make it go away.

Treatment of the physical body can also be evaluated fairly accurately. The internist can retest the blood to see if the bacteria have disappeared; the oncologist can measure the tumor to see if it is smaller; the cardiologist can recheck levels of cholesterol; and the dermatologist can see if the rash is gone. If the treatment hasn't worked well, another can be tried. But when it comes to the mind, all the psychiatrist can do to measure treatment is ask the patient about any changes in symptoms or perhaps give the patient a subjective paper-and-pen survey that asks questions about how the patient feels.

Unable to measure the thing that is causing a patient's distress or to determine how that distress is different from that of others, the psychiatrist cannot find the approach that has the greatest chance of success for that individual. It's like trying to treat anemia without knowing if it's caused by low levels of iron, lead poisoning, a copper shortage, or a genetic disorder. So the psychiatrist must take a shot-in-the-dark approach, starting at the top of the list of medications recommended for that condition and working his way down, hoping to hit the mark. Yet these recommendations are based on studies involving hundreds of people, which means that such medication solutions are, by definition, impersonal.

Not only is this approach impersonal, but it is also prone to error. Nonpersonalized psychiatric medicine is *almost guaranteed* to produce one treatment error after another until the doctor stumbles on the right approach or the patient says, "Enough!" The only way to avoid serial treatment errors is to personalize psychiatric treatment. And the only way to do that is to find a *specific* objective problem, marker, or imbalance that can be used as a guide to diagnosis and treatment.

One Person Is *Not* the Same as Another

The unspoken basis of psychiatry is sameness. From a *DSM* point of view, all patients with a particular type of depression (for example, major depression, dysthymia, or bipolar disorder) have more or less the same condition. For example, a forty-two-year-old mother of three who works as a corporate attorney and has insomnia, fatigue, and binge eating disorder is considered pretty much the same as a seventy-eight-year-old retired repairman dealing with inappropriate guilt and suicidal ideation. As far as the *DSM* is concerned, they both fall into the category of major depression and should, therefore, respond to similar medications.

Likewise, a female college freshman who no longer enjoys the activities she used to enjoy is considered the same as a thirty-five-year-old father of two with anxiety, restlessness, and feelings of emptiness. They both have dysthymia and therefore (according to the *DSM)* should get better after taking the same types of medications. It's all very neat and tidy, complete with distinct *DSM* code numbers for the various types of depression. But effective treatment within these codes is not one size fits all.

According to modern psychiatric principles, the psychiatrist's job is to learn the patient's symptoms, use those symptoms to categorize the illness, and then treat him or her according to recommendations for that category. It's kind of like herding cattle into different corrals according to the colors of their hides. If most patients with major depression treated with one or more of the recommended medications recovered, all would be well. We could say that, even though we don't understand the basis of the disorder, let alone why the medications work, at least our patients are getting better.

But that's not the case. Many people suffering from depression are not helped, even after trying multiple medications. And among those who find relief, the likelihood of the depression returning is high.

Clearly, our current approach is limited. In addition, a great deal of research suggests that the underlying basis of psychiatry is incorrect. Patients with the same disorder are *not* the same and cannot be grouped only according to symptom-based disorder categories. As a matter of fact, symptoms can be misleading indicators of what's gone wrong with the brain or body. That's because each of us is a different person with a unique biochemical and physical profile, which means that diseases affect us differently.

Are the Mind and Brain Separate?

Psychiatry has mostly ignored the physical reasons for depression and most other mental illnesses. Depressed moods may linger over the years, as in long-term emotional abuse that lasts throughout childhood, or they may show up all at once, as in a frontline soldier with post-traumatic stress disorder.

Oddly enough, despite saying that mental illnesses have little to do with the physical brain, psychiatrists treat their patients with medications designed to increase levels of the brain chemicals serotonin or dopamine or otherwise influence the physical brain.

The physiology of the human body includes the brain. If physiological problems exist in the body, it's logical to assume that they affect the brain. The brain, weighing roughly three pounds, needs about 20 percent of the

Can One Disease Have Different Causes and Cures?

Is it really possible that a mental illness such as depression can be made up of different things, each with separate causes and treatments?

We don't know enough about the biochemistry of depression to answer that question. But we can say with certainty that sometimes what we think of as a single disorder is actually a mixture of many.

Cancer, for example, is the uncontrolled and dangerous reproduction of cells in the body, whether it arises in the brain, breast, basal ganglia, or elsewhere. However, breast cancer behaves very differently from leukemia (cancer of the white blood cells), which destroys the immune system, or melanoma (skin cancer), which begins on the surface of the skin and works its way into the body. Sometimes even a single form of cancer can take different shapes. Prostate cancer, for example, may be fast moving and aggressive or slow growing and relatively "safe."

Yet psychiatry is based on the assumption that each kind of psychiatric disorder is the same thing or that at least all those with specific forms of a psychiatric disorder have the same illness.

energy produced by the body. If nutritional or other physiological problems decrease the body's energy production, the brain's incredibly high need for nutrients and energy is not met, and the brain no longer functions its best, which could lead to psychiatric problems. To make matters more complex, each of us has a "biochemical signature" as unique as our fingerprints. This means that every part of the brain and body must be investigated when searching for the cause of psychiatric distress and the most effective treatment.

Is it wise to insist that a given psychiatric disorder is the same thing in all those who have it when we admit that we have no idea what causes or cures it? Asking this question and doing research to find the answer could have taken psychiatry down an entirely new path, one focused on the *differences* among those with depression, for example, rather than on the same symptoms. Instead, psychiatry decided to categorize patients only according to their subjective symptoms.

Psychiatric Symptoms and Brain Function

Well into the twentieth century, all psychiatric disorders were believed to be mental illnesses that arose from internal conflicts triggered by childhood emotional trauma, unresolved sexual issues, being female, or family conflicts. While it was understood that stroke, Parkinson's disease, and certain other conditions were caused by physical damage to the brain, problems such as depression, anxiety, and obsessive behavior were categorized purely as mental illness because no one could find any corresponding brain damage or abnormality.

In the latter part of the century, however, high-tech brain-imaging techniques such as magnetic resonance imaging (MRI) allowed researchers to take a closer look at the brain from many different angles. The brain can now be viewed as a whole, and connections between various brain areas can be mapped. This has enabled us to see how a problem in one part can affect the whole, even if that problem, by itself, does not seem very important. Researchers can also find problems in specific areas of the brain that appear to be linked to individual psychiatric disorders. These new glimpses into the brain do not reveal any bacteria or "wounds" that cause illness, but they do suggest that certain changes in the brain are linked to specific disorders.

Scans have shown, for example, that a small structure known as Brodmann area 25 (BA25), located deep within the front portion of the brain, tends to be hyperactive in depressed people. Furthermore, its activity level becomes more normal as the depressive symptoms are relieved, whether by medication or by psychotherapy.

It makes sense that BA25 would be involved in depression, because it is directly linked to the amygdala, which processes feelings such as anxiety and fear, and the hypothalamus, which plays an important role in the stress response. In addition, BA25 contains a generous supply of special transporter molecules that help us find out how easily brain cells in the area are able to access serotonin. Several psychiatric medications, including Prozac, Zoloft, and Paxil, are aimed at improving serotonin levels in the brain.

The genetic coding for these serotonin transporter molecules comes in two variations, long and short, with the long version triggering production of more transporter molecules. Brain scan studies on healthy volunteers have shown that those with the short gene have smaller BA25s than those with the long gene. In addition, BA25 in these people does not act together with the amygdala and other brain areas as it should.

Is the sped-up activity in BA25 the cause of depression or a result? Perhaps both cause and result? We don't yet know.

We don't know what all this means or how to correct the problem brain areas. We can imagine, however, how difficult it is for a person to maintain "normal" moods when a part of the brain is not working properly or out of sync with the other parts. Think of an orchestra in which the flute section plays faster than the other sections or the violin section plays the piece in C major while all the others play in C minor.

One thing is certain: There *is* a connection between the physiology of the body and the chemistry in the brain.

Chapter 6

Genetics, Epigenetics, and Personalized Medicine

In our search to determine the unique causes of depression, we first ask: Is depression genetic (passed down from parents to children)?

Certain studies of identical twins, adoptees, and others seem to say that the answer is yes, to some extent. In the twin studies, researchers looked for depressed people who were part of a set of identical twins and then checked to see if the other twin was also depressed. In the adoption studies, rates of depression in biological families, their children who were put up for adoption, and the adopting families were compared with genetic influences separate from social or environmental influences. Many of these studies found that genes can cause a tendency toward depression, with the genetic influence accounting for as much as 37 percent in certain forms of the disorder.

This may seem like a very large number, but remember that numbers like this represent averages and may not matter in an individual case. For example, if the number were 50 percent, it could mean that, for some people, the odds of having depression are as high as 100 percent; for others, exactly 50 percent; and for still others, as low as 0 percent. These percentages are based on studies involving hundreds or even thousands of people, which means that they may not describe a specific person's situation at all.

I prefer to think of genes as "suggestions" that incline a person toward or away from a certain illness. In some people, the suggestion is strong, and it doesn't take much to trigger a full-blown problem. In others, however, the suggestion is barely whispered, and the problem may never occur at all.

A Quick Review of Genetics

Genes are the "blueprints" inside of cells that decide the form and function of each cell in the body and therefore make you who you are. They are passed on from generation to generation, but in each new birth, they are combined in a totally unique way, with half the genes received from the mother and half from the father.

Each gene is made up of a section of DNA, which is made up of two strands coiled around each other. There are some twenty-five thousand genes in the human genome (the entire collection of human genes). Not all genes are active at any given time. When the body needs access to the information stored in a particular gene, the correct section of DNA uncoils and exposes the gene so that it can be "read" and acted on. Afterward, the gene coils back up, and the genetic information remains hidden and quiet until it is needed again.

Every single cell in the body contains and is controlled by genes, even though any one particular cell has no use for a lot of the information in the genome. A liver cell, for example, doesn't need to "read" the genes that tell the heart how to beat, while a hair cell can safely ignore instructions for making a baby.

According to genetic theory, genes are very stable. Inherited genetic changes (mutations) occur very slowly, over hundreds of thousands or millions of years. These mutations, which are designed to make a being more successful at survival, are passed from generation to generation and spread very slowly throughout the larger population. Changes that occur during a person's life, however, such as becoming obese or having asthma, cannot be passed on to other generations because they do not change a person's DNA. Thus, according to our understanding of genetics, a man might have depression after an emotionally difficult childhood and have cancer in midlife as a result of exposure to industrial chemicals, but neither the depression nor the cancer will be passed on to his children because the diseases did not change his DNA.

Epigenetics: A Collection of "Overrides"

At any given time, a large percentage of the genes in the genome are inactive, wrapped up in the DNA coil, and ignored for minutes, days, weeks, years, and even decades. The body decides which ones it needs to switch on at any given moment, telling the DNA to activate and inactivate genes as necessary.

But sometimes the genes are switched on or off by outside forces that the body does not control or cannot fight, overriding the body's normal instructions. This group of "overrides" is known as the epigenome, a collection of all the ways in which the genes have been turned on or off.

Epigenetic changes occur in a couple of different ways. In one method, a tiny molecule called a methyl group (one carbon atom and three hydrogen atoms) attaches itself to a specific spot on a gene. It then acts like an override switch, forcing the gene to remain either unwrapped and switched on or coiled up and switched off, no matter which signals the body sends. The gene is not changed, altered, or mutilated in any way. It's simply locked in either the on or off position for a time, which could be years, decades, or even a lifetime.

At first, the epigenetic changes to the genome may be minor, with just a few genes held in the on or off position. But as the years pass, more and more of these changes occur, and eventually, the "genetic instruction book" is rewritten, with a "revised edition" that is quite a bit different from the original. This can be seen most clearly by comparing the epigenomes of identical twins. Young twins typically have very similar sets of epigenomic changes, while the changes in older twins can be different—sometimes vastly.

What Starts the Epigenetic Process?

It is difficult to pin down all the epigenetic factors that may affect human beings because it is not right to expose people to something that may be harmful or to keep them from something necessary for good health. Thus, much of the evidence comes from animal experiments. They have shown that a number of factors, including diseases, substances in food, physical and emotional stress, drugs, and different chemicals, have "epigenetic potential."

Emotional stress and epigenetics

Several animal experiments have focused on the effects of stress early in life on epigenetics and behavior later in life. In one such study, emotional stress was created in newborn mice by removing them from their mothers for three hours each day during the first ten days of their lives. Doing so triggered epigenetic changes that lasted at least a year, which is a long time in the life of a typical mouse, and reduced the ability of these mice to deal with stress and remember things.

Another study looked at epigenetic differences in the brains of two groups of newborn mice. In the "good-mothering" group, newborns received more licking and grooming from their mothers during the first seven days of life. Those in the "bad-mothering" group received less affection. As time passed, the baby mice in the good-mothering group were less anxious and better able to recover from stress than those in the bad-mothering group.

Some might say that this is not a surprise. Good mothers who licked their infants a lot were probably better adjusted mice to begin with and passed on their "well-adjusted genes" to their offspring, while bad mothers probably passed on their "unhappy genes." In other words, this issue could be more genetic than epigenetic.

To test this argument, in another study, researchers switched the newborn mice, placing the offspring of the good mothers with the bad mothers and those of the bad mothers with the good mothers. The results were interesting. When the young mice grew up, they showed the stress-handling abilities of their foster mothers, not their biological mothers. In other words, nurture was more important than nature; environment was more important than genetics.

The same thing happened with infant monkeys. When the babies of abusive and nonabusive mothers were switched, the ones raised by the good mothers showed the same good mothering skills when they grew to adulthood—even though they were the biological offspring of bad mothers.

These and other studies have shown that care received during infancy can trigger changes in a number of different genes that regulate mood and behavior.

Nutrigenomics

Researchers are studying links between nutrition and genetics to discover exactly how the thousands of substances in food can influence the epigenome and how we might use that knowledge to personalize dietary recommendations. In other words, these researchers are figuring out how to use nutrition to switch on or switch off specific genes.

Nutrigenomics does not involve developing genetically modified foods. Instead, the focus is on learning how to switch off, for example, the genes that increase the risk of breast cancer (*BRCA1* and *BRCA2*) or

Shining a Light on Epigenetics

Imagine that you have strings of red, blue, green, orange, and white lights around the outside of your house. You control each lightbulb individually via your computer, which you've programmed in a certain way. You want only red, white, and blue lights to shine on the Fourth of July, green and red ones in December, orange ones on Halloween, blue and white ones during the coldest part of winter, and so on.

One Fourth of July, you notice that the orange lights are on, while the red, white, and blue ones are off. The orange ones stay on through the summer but do not come on for Halloween. During the Christmas season, the blue bulbs come on, while the red and green ones stay dark, ruining the seasonal look. Only red ones come on during the coldest part of winter.

You check your computer program and find that everything looks fine; the computer code has not been changed. The lights should be working. Then you check the light strands and find something unusual. Tiny devices on many of the lights are forcing them to remain in the on or off position, no matter what instructions your computer might give.

Year after year, those tiny devices remain there, overriding instructions to turn on certain lights at certain times. When you inspect the light strands each year, you notice that, while many of the tiny devices remain in place, others have disappeared, so you never know what to expect from your lights. This is much like what happens to your genes as a result of epigenetic changes.

how to switch on genes that strengthen the immune system when disease has already struck. In essence, food and substances in food would be used as medications that act on our genes. The science is just beginning, but the promise is large. I believe that within the next decade we'll be able to prescribe foods or substances taken from foods to people with a variety of ailments. This will be truly personalized medicine at its best, because we'll be able to pinpoint and alter an individual's genetic expressions naturally.

How Do Epigenetic Changes Play Out?

Everyone is born with a genome, a unique assemblage of genes derived from both parents, as well as an epigenome, a set of "switches" that have locked some of those genes into the on or off position.

The fact that the epigenome is passed down from parent to child may seem odd, because every high school biology student learns that any changes to the genome during a person's lifetime (whether due to mutations, exposure to radiation, epigenetics, or other factors) are not passed on during reproduction and that infants are born with a clean genetic slate. However, we've learned in the past several years that this is not true. Research has shown that some epigenetic switches are copied when sex cells divide, as well as when sperm and egg combine, ensuring that the newly created genome is already influenced by an epigenome. More epigenetic changes may occur in the womb as the fetus is exposed to differing levels and types of nutrients, chemicals such as BPA, alcohol, stress hormones generated by the mother's body, and many other substances.

There's something else that the epigenome does. It makes each person unique. Even identical twins, who begin life with the same genomes, accumulate different epigenomic changes throughout life, especially if they have different life experiences, diets, and lifestyles.

We can now see how the epigenome is created and how it influences a person's life, as well as the lives of his or her children—sometimes for many generations. Unfortunately, we have not yet been able to find a certain epigenomic change that leads to depression, and we cannot find a medication, diet, or other approach that reverses that change.

What we *can* do is set the stage for a helpful rather than a harmful epigenome by eating a nutritious diet, reducing stress, and otherwise giving the body the tools it needs to build good health.

New technology can help physicians understand how an individual's unique genetic makeup influences his or her response to medications. This technology has provided very significant changes in the current practice of psychiatric prescribing. A genetic test can help your doctor decide which medication is more likely to work effectively, based on your genetic profile. Often done through a simple cheek swab, this test looks for subtle differences in the genes responsible for metabolizing medications. Instead of a trial-and-error approach, physicians are now able to make informed treatment decisions supported by laboratory results. One study found that tested patients were twice as likely to get on the right medication, reducing their prescription costs by more than $1,000.

Unique Person, Unique Disease

This chapter raises more questions than it can answer, but two points are clear: The brain is linked to the body, and everyone is unique, which means that no two cases of mental illness are identical. These facts have become the foundation for a new way of viewing and treating depression. Now that we understand each patient's uniqueness, we can and must provide personalized medical treatment in psychiatry that will help prevent the endless trial-and-error prescribing so common in the treatment of depression.

Our genes provide the blueprints for who we may become; they do not, however, determine who we are. Mood disorders can be understood, and recovery is based on biochemical individuality. Knowing this simple fact provides optimism and hope.

Chapter 7

Personalized Medicine with THE ZEEBRA Approach

The ideas as to what causes depression are not based on strong science, and our treatments are not working nearly as well as they should. Psychiatry is in crisis. The usual treatment mode (typically based solely on a subjective psychiatric examination and construction of a symptom list) often leads to psychiatrists blindly searching for a medication that might work. Body factors such as nutrition, toxins, hormones, allergies, biochemical risks, and medical disorders are typically ignored.

No amount of changing this approach will work, because the basic underlying concepts are wrong. We need an entirely new way of looking at patients. We must stop treating them according to lists of subjective symptoms, and we must stop acting as if one person were the same as the next. Instead, we must start seeing patients as the individuals they are and then diagnose and treat their disorders accordingly.

The Way It Could Be

Earlier in this book, I asked you to imagine being sent to a psychiatrist by your family doctor because you had sleep difficulties, a lack of energy, agitation, "the blues," and other symptoms. As you recall, during the imaginary psychiatric examination, you were asked only about how you felt, and your answers became the sole basis of your diagnosis of depression and the medications you received.

Now imagine that this psychiatrist asks you, in detail, about your diet, the medications and supplements you take, the health of your relatives, and what you do every day, trying to identify any situations or substances that might be causing your depression.

Next this psychiatrist orders lab tests to look for physical problems that might cause or worsen depression, such as the following:

- Vitamin deficiencies
- Toxic metals
- Hormonal imbalances
- Low levels of certain vitamins
- Amino acid and fatty acid imbalances
- Low or high levels of certain minerals
- Celiac disease or other food sensitivities
- Imbalanced levels of digestive enzymes
- Dysbiosis ("bad" bacteria, yeast, or other flora in your intestines)
- Parasites

When all these tests are completed, the psychiatrist does not give you a prescription, because he wants to see the results before making a treatment decision. After all, your depression may be rooted in a food sensitivity, nutrient imbalance, or something else that can be corrected without the use of psychiatric medications.

When the results have come in and the psychiatrist sees you for a second visit, he may recommend a medication and nutritional support. But the medication will be carefully selected and targeted and therefore will be much more likely to work. It won't be a "Try it and see if it works" prescription based on studies of hundreds of people who are nothing like you; it will be individualized, targeted treatment based on specific genetic markers. In other words, it will be just for you.

Integrative Psychiatry

The approach I just described is called integrative psychiatry, a way of looking at each person as a whole person, with unique biochemistry and nutritional needs, which, when balanced, allow for health and vitality. The practice of integrative psychiatry is based on five basic things:

- Focus on each individual's unique personality, environment, and physical makeup
- Care for the whole patient, not just the disease
- Understanding how the human body and mind are connected
- Restoring health instead of simply reducing symptoms
- Increasing the body's nutrients to promote long-term health

By focusing on the individual as a whole, integrative psychiatry often produces improvement and encourages healing where traditional, symptom-based treatments have failed.

Jill, a thirty-three-year-old single mother with depression and bulimia, had requested a consultation with me. After having tried many medications, she was seeking a natural treatment for her depression. Many of the medications she had tried left her with side effects that either decreased her sex drive or impaired her ability to care for her disabled son. She needed relief immediately; her symptoms of depression and bulimia were interfering with every aspect of her life. After my consultation, I recommended different medications for Jill, though Jill's preference would have been to take no medication. These new drugs greatly improved her symptoms.

Mary was forty-two when I first met her. By that time, she had struggled with alcohol abuse and depression for many years. She was not alone in her struggles, as her siblings and father had also dealt with depression and substance abuse. I ordered a complete metabolic and nutritional evaluation. Based on the results, I found that Mary had a B_{12} shortage and high levels of casomorphin (a morphine-like chemical generated because she could not digest casein in dairy products). After Mary eliminated dairy and all casein from her diet and took B_{12} injections, her depression lifted.

Harry was fifty when he considered "a different approach" to treating his depression. In his five years with fatigue and depression, Harry had been treated with antidepressants, antipsychotics, and antianxiety medications without significant relief. After taking a complete history and testing, I found that Harry had low testosterone, a zinc shortage, and sleep apnea. When these problems were corrected, Harry's symptoms improved. Now Harry has no symptoms of depression.

The fact that each of these patients required a different treatment to return to health is not surprising. One person may need nutritional support and medication, another lots of exercise and psychological guidance but no medication, and yet another medication with relatively little change in diet and lifestyle. That's the difficulty and the beauty of integrative psychiatry. It can be more difficult to sort through all the possibilities to develop a treatment plan, but when your psychiatrist does, it is much more likely to be effective.

THE ZEEBRA Approach

To ensure that every aspect of a person—mind, body, and spirit—is investigated and restored to balance, I've devised a simple mnemonic: THE ZEEBRA.

T is for Take care of yourself.

H is for Hormones and Herbs.

E is for Exclude.

Z is for Zinc (and other minerals).

E is for Essential fatty acids and cholesterol.

E is for Exercise and energy.

B is for B (and other) vitamins.

R is for Restore.

A is for Amino acids and proteins.

It may not be obvious how this list of items relates to depression, but each item is very important. Here I explain the approach briefly; I go into each component further in chapters 8 through 15.

T—Take care of yourself

Psychiatrists have assumed, without proof, that depression results from chemical imbalances in the brain. Treatment has primarily consisted of prescribing medications that may restore proper balance. But even if we had medications that could do so consistently, shouldn't we be looking for the causes of the imbalance?

But how about too much sugar in the diet? The brain is fueled almost entirely by glucose, the form of sugar in the blood, so it should be no surprise that low levels of blood sugar can cause irritability, anxiety, and other mood disturbances, including depression. Although it sounds strange, eating too much sugar can cause blood sugar levels to fall very quickly.

Studies have consistently shown a link between poor diet and depression. In 2012, researchers looking at 8,964 Spanish participants found that eating fast food (but not baked goods) increased the risk of depression. Soft drink consumption has also been linked to aggression and suicidal behaviors in American high school students.

A 2015 study of seventy thousand women showed that a diet high in carbohydrates is linked to a higher risk of depression in women who have gone through menopause. The researchers also found that a diet high in fiber, whole grains, vegetables, and fruits was linked to a lower risk of depression. Similarly, a 2013 study of 4,215 participants aged thirty-five to fifty-five showed that women who followed a healthy diet according to the Alternative Healthy Eating Index had 65 percent less likelihood of recurring depressive symptoms than women who ate a less healthy diet.

The next year, researchers studying 43,685 women aged fifty to seventy-seven who were depression-free for twelve years showed that following a diet likely to lead to chronic inflammation was linked to a higher risk of depression. The researchers concluded that chronic inflammation may underlie the link between diet and depression. The pattern also applies to children and adolescents, who show worse displays of mental health when following an unhealthy diet.

> Heather started the day with a sugary coffee drink, had a doughnut in mid-morning, kept candy and cookies in her desk at work, and ended the evening with a big bowl of ice cream. Her mood crashed right about the same time as her blood sugar, about half an hour after she'd eaten something sweet. I suggested she start the day with a protein-rich breakfast and that she snack on whole grains coupled with a small serving of protein (such as cheese or cottage cheese) to keep her blood sugar levels more stable. She also stopped eating her high-sugar bedtime snack. As a result, Heather's depressed moods improved—without medication.

In addition to excess sugar, sleeping problems—particularly obstructive sleep apnea, which causes one to literally stop breathing repeatedly while sleeping—may play a role in depression. Obstructive sleep apnea is not only linked to depression; it may also interfere with the actions of certain antidepressants. To make matters worse, certain medications used for depression make sleep apnea worse, which can heighten depression. How many people with obstructive sleep apnea or other sleep disorders are caught in a vicious cycle of depression that their doctors cannot break because they don't know about it?

Insomnia has also been implicated in depression. Studies have found a significant relationship between the severity of insomnia and depressive symptoms, with greater insomnia linked to greater depressive symptoms and vice versa. Researchers have found that teens with depression report many more sleep problems than their nondepressed peers and that depression and disturbed sleep are closely related. In fact, poor sleep is a predictor of depression and of disability retirement due to depression. But it's not just a lack of sleep that is the problem; short- and long-term sleep deprivation has been linked to an increased risk of depression in adults.

Poor digestion can also be a factor in depression. Most psychiatrists are aware that depression can interfere with appetite, but few fully understand the relationship between good digestion and good mental health. Proper digestion involves the effective breakdown of food and absorption of nutrients. Key to this process are probiotics, otherwise known as the "friendly" bacteria in the intestines. Probiotics have been shown to improve nutritional status, overall mood, and symptoms of anxiety.

Chapter 8 discusses diet, sleep and stress and their link to depression, along with ways to ensure that problems in these areas are detected and resolved.

H—Hormones and Herbs

The idea that hormones are linked to depression in women is firmly grounded in science and popular culture. You can see the effects of hormones at an early age when pubescent girls, who before puberty were no more likely than boys of the same age to have depression, quickly become much more likely to be depressed. In later years, they may have depression linked to premenstrual dysphoric disorder, postpartum depression, or menopause.

Although it's not as well-known, hormones have also been linked to depression in men. Indeed, the male hormone testosterone used to be prescribed for men with depression, but that practice was stopped decades ago with the introduction of modern antidepressants. But hormone treatment for depression may be making a comeback. A small study conducted at Harvard Medical School's McLean Hospital found that about half the men studied who were not helped by standard antidepressants had low or low-normal levels of testosterone. Chapter 9 discusses why it's important for those with depression to have their hormone levels checked and, possibly, corrected. Adjusting hormones can often relieve or get rid of long-standing depression in many individuals.

Chapter 9 introduces exciting new research on phytotherapy, which is the use of plant-based herbs that have been shown to have positive effects on neurochemistry. The herbs discussed in this chapter include

St. John's wort, curcumin, and rhodiola. Curcumin, a traditional spice used in Indian food, has demonstrated antidepressant-like effects in animal studies. Studies involving humans have also reported improvement in symptoms when curcumin was given jointly with standard antidepressants such as fluoxetine, venlafaxine, and bupropion.

E—Exclude

The integrative medical approach involves testing for and excluding digestive problems that can worsen depressed moods. Celiac disease is a case of the body attacking itself. It stems from a damaged immune system launching a full-scale attack on harmless substances in the body. In the process, it damages the small intestines and other parts of the body. A substance called gluten, found in wheat, barley, and rye, sets off that immune response, which leads to constipation, diarrhea, abdominal bloating, lack of appetite, vomiting, bloody stools, and other symptoms. These other symptoms include depression and low nutrient levels that may develop due to intestinal problems and lack of appetite. If certain nutrients are low, the depression may worsen.

Recent studies have also suggested that another syndrome produces symptoms similar to celiac disease without being true celiac disease. Non-celiac gluten sensitivity may simply be a sensitivity to gluten rather than a true disease. Further study is needed to come up with criteria for diagnosis.

Celiac disease, elevated neuropeptides from improper digestion of wheat and dairy foods, food allergies, and other problems with the digestive system, including Crohn's disease and ulcerative colitis, must be ruled out in a physician's exam. Chapter 10 examines these digestive contributors to depression.

Z—Zinc and other trace minerals

In addition to keeping the immune system strong and the memory sharp, zinc plays an important role in the production and use of neurotransmitters—brain chemicals that help stabilize mood. This is why low levels of zinc have been linked to major depression and why zinc in the form of a capsule or tablet has an antidepressant effect in many people.

Zinc also enhances the effects of antidepressant medications in certain people. A study published in the *Journal of Affective Disorders* reported on sixty people aged eighteen to fifty-five with major depression. They were all treated with imipramine, a standard antidepressant. In addition, half were randomly assigned to receive 25 milligrams (mg) of zinc per day, while the other half received a placebo. When the researchers retested study subjects after twelve weeks, they found that zinc supplementation reduced depression scores in people who had not been helped by antidepressants in the past. This study suggests a major role for zinc in treating depression, especially among those who fail to get relief from antidepressants alone. Every depressed patient should be tested for a zinc shortage and treated if he or she has a low level.

Researchers reviewing all the published papers on randomized controlled studies on the effectiveness of zinc for reducing or preventing depressive symptoms found that zinc lowered patients' depressive symptom scores.

Another mineral that is important to mood is magnesium. Of all the minerals needed for human health, magnesium is the one most likely to be lacking. A magnesium shortage can trigger a host of problems with mental and physical health, including depression, insomnia, irritability, nervousness and anxiety, apathy, and migraine headaches.

Case studies have shown that giving patients 125–300 mg of magnesium per meal and at bedtime can lead to rapid recovery from major depression. In my own practice, magnesium has been invaluable in relieving the insomnia and anxiety often linked to depression.

A great deal of research has clearly shown that a lack of zinc, magnesium, and other minerals can cause or worsen depression and that many people with different forms of depression don't have enough of these minerals.

Lithium is a naturally occurring mineral that is essential to human health. The most common uses involve high pharmaceutical doses for bipolar disorder, although nutritional lithium can also provide effective treatment for depression without medications.

Chapter 11 looks at the problem of mineral shortage among depressed people, explains why these nutrients are vital for mental health, and describes how they can be used either to reduce depressive symptoms or to "supercharge" standard therapy.

E—Essential fatty acids and cholesterol

An imbalance in the right kind of fat can also be involved in depression.

The brain is a fatty organ that cannot function without large amounts of essential fatty acids (EFAs), as well as cholesterol and other members of the fat family. Indeed, 60 percent of the brain's dry weight is fat, and at least 25 percent of its white matter consists of phospholipids from EFAs.

EFAs support the actions of neurotransmitters, and a great deal of research has shown that they play a key role in depression. For example,

- In one study, treatment with 6.6 grams (g) per day of the EFA eicosapentaenoic acid (EPA) and docosahexaenoic acid (DHA) for eight weeks led to much improved Hamilton scores.
- A study of children aged six to twelve showed that EPA and DHA supplementation much improved symptoms of major depressive disorder.
- Research revealed that the lower the EPA, the greater the risk of depression. Likewise, the higher the EPA, the lower the risk of depression.
- Other research found that low levels of DHA in the blood and skewed ratios of omega-6 to omega-3 fatty acids predicted suicide risk.

In one study, treatment with omega-3s was shown to be effective in subjects with major depressive disorder and in patients with depressive symptoms but no diagnosis of major depressive disorder.

Cholesterol is also needed for good mental health. Lower levels of cholesterol in the blood are linked to a higher risk of major depressive disorder, hospitalization, and suicide. A study published in the *Journal of Psychiatric Research* found that depressed men with low total cholesterol levels (less than 165 mg per deciliter [dL]) were *seven times more likely to die early* from unnatural causes such as suicide and accidents.

The link between cholesterol and depression involves the neurotransmitter serotonin:

- Low cholesterol decreases the number of serotonin receptors in the brain.
- Decreasing the number of serotonin receptors may lead to decreases in serotonin levels.
- Low serotonin is linked to an increased level of aggressive impulses.

Simply checking the levels of EFAs, cholesterol, and other fats in all depressed patients may help identify many who will benefit greatly from simple dietary changes or supplements.

Chapter 12, which looks at the relationship between depression and EFAs, cholesterol, and other fats, explains why so many Americans lack key fats and shows how to prevent depression by making sure you get enough of these substances.

E—Exercise and energy

When you're depressed, the last thing you want to do is huff and puff your way through a run or bounce up and down in an aerobics class. Even doing your favorite sport with your friends doesn't sound like fun. Yet exercise fights depression on many levels by triggering the release of endorphins and other brain chemicals that help lift mood, improving sleep and slowing the release of certain immune system substances that can deepen depression.

A great deal of research has shown that exercise is an effective antidepressant in mild to moderate depression. Psychiatrists tend to underestimate the benefits of exercise and rarely prescribe it. British doctors, on the other hand, can actually prescribe exercise as a treatment for depression, with the National Health Service paying some or all of the cost. But patients find it difficult to overcome their feelings of hopelessness and lack of energy to begin moving again.

Chapter 13 explores the relationship between exercise, energy, and depression and offers a "prescription" for getting more energy and starting an exercise program.

B—B (and other) vitamins

Many of the B vitamins are very important for both mood and energy:

- B_1 (thiamine)
- B_3 (niacin)
- B_6 (pyridoxine)
- B_9 (folate)
- B_{12} (cobalamin)
- Inositol

Of these B vitamins, research has strongly linked folic acid and vitamin B_{12} to depression. For example, low levels of folate in the blood have been linked to poor treatment outcomes in patients with major depressive disorder who are taking Prozac, while higher levels of B_{12} are linked to recovery.

Many Americans do not get enough B vitamins in their diet. Even if they do, they unknowingly reduce their supplies by eating refined sugar and carbohydrates, which deplete the body of these precious vitamins.

Ample supplies of other vitamins, including vitamin C and vitamin D, are also needed for good mental health. An increasing amount of research is looking at the link between depression and vitamin D, which influences the growth and regulation of every cell in the body. A study of one thousand senior citizens found that those with major depression or dysthymia were more likely to have much lower levels of vitamin D than other senior citizens in the study. An interesting study with healthy volunteers found that giving people vitamin D in the winter, when levels tend to be lower because of a lack of sunlight, increased their "happy feelings" and decreased their "sad feelings." About 41 to 57 percent of the U.S. population lacks vitamin D, with dark-skinned people particularly at risk because their skin requires more sunlight to make the vitamin.

Chapter 14 is devoted to the B vitamins and other vitamins that play a role in depression. I discuss how they influence mood, what happens when they are in short supply, ways to measure vitamin levels in the body, and how to increase these levels, if necessary.

R—Restore

For centuries, bacteria and germs were perceived as villains that caused illnesses and disease. Now there is a scientific revolution occurring. The bacteria in our gastrointestinal tract can also affect the way we feel and think. Nourishing a healthy gut flora by containing enough beneficial bacteria, is critical for mental health and well-being.

Microbes are one of the target areas for new therapies in depression. Microbes—bacteria, viruses, and fungi—commonly known as germs, are everywhere. In fact, there are ten times more microbes living in and on us than actual human cells. Nearly 100 trillion bacteria that play a role in health live in the human intestine. Together, the microbes in your entire body make up your microbiome.

Each person's microbiome is unique and varied; no two individuals share the same microbiome. Microbial genes outnumber human genes 150 to 1, and it appears that we are more bacteria than we are human.

The microbiome is often called our second brain because the gastrointestinal tract contains the same kind of neurotransmitters that are found in the brain. About 95 percent of the "feel good" neurotransmitter serotonin can be found in our intestines, which may explain why you get a bad feeling in your stomach when you are anxious or afraid. Changes in the microbiome can influence your feelings and behavior.

Several studies show that probiotics, or "good" bacteria, can be useful in the treatment of certain kinds of depression. Chapter 15 reviews all the emerging evidence on how certain strains of bacteria are able to restore bacterial balance in the stomach, which can help improve depressive symptoms.

A—Amino acids and proteins

A lack of protein is not usually thought to cause depression, but a lack of the amino acids that make up protein can contribute to emotional distress. Different amino acids are needed to make all major neurotransmitters, which in turn affect every part of one's emotional health, including thoughts, feelings, and behaviors.

We tend to think that, because we eat plenty of protein, we should have all the amino acids we need. However, eating a lot of carbohydrates has led to a steady decline in the percentage of protein in the diet. In addition, the increasing use of antacids interferes with the body's production of the hydrochloric acid (HCl) and pepsin needed to digest protein. We tend to worry these days that we eat too much protein, but for some people, the real issue is that they are not eating or absorbing the amino acids needed for good physical and mental health.

Chapter 16 looks at the protein–depression link and explains how to tell if protein intake is lacking, what happens as a result, and what to do about it. It also explains the best time of day to eat protein and why.

Does THE ZEEBRA Approach Work?

THE ZEEBRA is a commonsense approach. Although it may seem very different from many psychiatry practices. The brain and body are viewed as a whole, as we also include the effects of nutrition, disease, and other bodily influences on mental health. At last we have an objective and truly balanced approach to finding relief from depression.

Chapter 8

T – Take Care of Yourself

First and most important, THE ZEEBRA approach encourages you to take care of your body.

It may seem odd to begin an "antidepression program" by saying that you have to take care of your physical body. Because of the strong relationship between physical and mental health, certain physical diseases and health habits can set the stage for depression. The fact that so many lifestyle choices and diseases contribute to depression points to the need to take good care of the body as well as the mind.

In some cases, the link between physical disease and mental disorder is obvious. A brain tumor, for example, can cause personality changes, while severe dehydration can trigger confusion. In many other cases, the links are subtle and, therefore, often overlooked.

It's impossible to cover in this book all the physical diseases, habits, and factors that cause or worsen depression. This chapter focuses on simple yet major physical factors, some of which you can address on your own, without the aid of a health care professional. They include diet, digestion, sleep, refined sugar, and stress.

Diet and Depression

Diet has long been linked to physical illnesses such as diabetes and heart disease. And low levels of certain dietary elements, including the B vitamins, omega-3 fatty acids, and zinc, have been linked to an elevated risk of depression. But not just individual nutrients matter. The entire diet can influence mood and have a profound effect on your mental well-being.

A 2010 study published in the *American Journal of Psychiatry* compared regular diet to mental disorders in 1,046 women aged 20 to 93. Specifically, the researchers looked at the effects of a "healthy" diet of vegetables, fruit, meat, fish and whole grains to that of an "unhealthy" diet of refined grains, fried foods, sugary products, and beer. They found that the unhealthy diet was linked to a higher level of depressive and anxiety disorders. Another study, also published in 2010, looked at the effects of diet on 7,114 teens. The results were no surprise; those who ate "poor" diets of unhealthy and processed foods were more likely to say they had depression than those eating "good" diets that more closely followed government dietary recommendations.

According to a report published in 2015, depression in America cost society nearly $210 billion in 2014, factoring in costs related to treatment as well as lost productivity. With the numbers expected to rise, scientists are beginning to pay more attention to how simple dietary changes can play a key role in the prevention of mental disorders such as depression. Most recently, the International Society of Nutritional Psychiatry Research urged a shift in the current treatment model to focus more on nutrition as more research demonstrates the positive clinical impact observed from dietary changes.

One 2014 study involved 13,486 Iranian children who were evaluated for junk food consumption that included sweets, sweetened beverages, fast foods, and salty snacks. Students were given questionnaires to assess for symptoms of depression, anxiety, aggression, and feelings of worthlessness. Researchers found that increased junk food consumption was significantly associated with psychiatric distress. Daily consumption of salty snacks and sweetened beverages was also associated with displays of violent behavior.

Another study conducted later that year echoed the same findings. Researchers reviewed twelve studies exploring the link between diet quality and mental health in children and adolescents. Adolescents whose diets consisted mainly of processed foods exhibited significantly higher incidences of depression and other mental health disorders than the children consuming good quality diets.

Dietary intake impacts various biological mechanisms, including how our bodies regulate inflammation. Evidence suggests that diets high in saturated fats and refined carbohydrates can affect proteins that are important in brain development, such as the brain signaling molecule brain-derived neurotrophic factor (BDNF). Patients with depression commonly have low levels of BDNF. When levels of BDNF increase, patients often experience improvement in their symptoms.

Given that everyone is biochemically unique, it's impossible to create a single diet that gives everyone the best chance of enjoying excellent mental health. But I can say for sure that the standard American diet—filled with fried, refined, sugary junk foods, genetically modified foods, artificial flavorings and colors, and gluten—is best avoided. On the other hand, a diet rich in fresh organic vegetables and fruits, whole grains, and moderate amounts of fish, meat and poultry is much more likely to promote good mental, as well as physical, health.

Digestion and Depression

Digestion might seem like a simple process: chew the food well enough, mix it with stomach acid and a few enzymes, and that's all there is to it. That's the general idea, but it's a much more complex process that depends on hundreds of events taking place at just the right time and in the right "strength." This is an area in which I see a lot of problems and a lot of room for fast and big improvement among my patients.

Digestion begins with the sight, smell, or even thought of food, as the brain sends "get ready" signals to the digestive system. While food is being chewed, it mixes with enzymes in the saliva that begin to break down fat and starch. Once swallowed, food travels down the esophagus and into the stomach, where it is bathed in hydrochloric acid, an acid so powerful that a single drop can burn a hole through a piece of wood. But hydrochloric acid does more than dissolve food into its parts. It is also needed, among other things, to absorb vitamin B_{12} and minerals and to make an enzyme called pepsin, which is needed for the digestion of protein. For these and other reasons, hydrochloric acid is very important for digestion.

We often mistakenly blame too much hydrochloric acid for the painful symptoms of gastroesophageal reflux disease (GERD), commonly called heartburn or acid reflux, and take pills such as Prilosec, Nexium, Maalox, and Tums to cut back on acid levels. These pills can indeed reduce heartburn symptoms, but they can harm good digestion. (Ironically, what doctors typically think is heartburn caused by too much acid may be triggered by *low* acid levels.)

After being processed in the stomach, the food moves into the small intestine. Here, it is covered in sodium bicarbonate to neutralize the hydrochloric acid, and fat, protein and carbohydrates are broken down into even smaller parts before being absorbed through the intestinal wall. Most of the absorption of vitamins and minerals also takes place here.

Digestive Enzymes

Digestive enzymes begin breaking down food as soon as it enters the mouth, continuing their work in the stomach and small intestines until the food has been broken down into tiny pieces that move into the intestinal wall and are absorbed into the body. Many enzymes work at specific "stations" in the body, and each must do a good job, or the process fails. The body uses zinc, protein, vitamin C, and other nutrients to make these enzymes, which means that good nutrition leads to good digestion, and good digestion helps ensure that all the needed nutrients are absorbed.

The reverse is also true: Bad nutrition can lead to bad digestion, and bad digestion worsens the problem by causing bad nutrition. Once someone is caught in the negative feedback loop, it's very hard to break out. More likely, the downward spiral of poor digestion equals poor nutrition equals worse digestion equals worse nutrition continues, slowly growing worse with time. This becomes worse with age, as the production of stomach acid declines naturally.

For many patients with digestive problems, digestive enzymes in the form of a pill are available and can be very helpful. They can, among other things:

- rapidly improve digestion, which automatically improves absorption and nutritional status
- reduce or get rid of gas, bloating, and certain other symptoms of poor digestion
- support the development of healthy intestinal bacteria
- protect against inflammation in the intestines

There are a number of digestive enzymes, including bromelain from pineapple, papain from papaya, and trypsin from animal sources. A good, broad-spectrum supplement contains a variety of enzymes designed to digest specific parts of food. Thus, it should include enzymes such as amylase to digest carbohydrates and sugars; cellulose for vegetable and vegetable fibers; lipase for fats; and protease for proteins and the peptides that make up protein molecules.

The dosage depends on the person, and different people have different needs, depending on diet, lifestyle, and biochemical individuality. I recommend working with a health professional who understands digestive enzymes and is familiar with the different brands and products. Start with the dosage on the product label, adjusting up or down until the best dose is discovered. (The best dose may change over time as one's nutrition, health, and lifestyle changes.) The dosage may also vary depending on the size and type of meal being eaten.

Because everyone is different, some people respond rapidly, noticing improvements in digestion and fewer gastrointestinal symptoms almost right away, while others may not see any improvements for days or weeks. It's important to stick with the initial dose for a few weeks before adjusting it and to work with a health professional who truly understands nutritional medicine.

Even if someone is eating a perfect diet, if he or she lacks the acid and enzymes needed to digest and absorb it, the nutrients in the diet may go to waste. That's why digestive enzymes can be so helpful, even in those eating healthful diets.

Plentiful supplies of digestive enzymes and powerful stomach acid are not the only things required for good digestion. A surprising number and variety of bacteria are also needed.

We tend to think of all bacteria as being harmful, but the right bacteria in the intestines perform a number of chores, including helping break down food, synthesizing nutrients, and guarding against infection and illness. These helpful bacteria are called probiotics, and they should far outnumber the unfriendly bacteria (pathogens) that can trigger inflammation, allergies, and disease. Unfortunately, a number of factors can harm the probiotics, allowing the unhealthy bacteria to reproduce and spread, damaging the intestines, interfering with nutrient absorption, and triggering depression, fatigue, constipation, diarrhea, and other gastrointestinal symptoms.

That's why many otherwise healthy people can benefit from probiotic supplements. Exciting new research is beginning to demonstrate just how powerful probiotics can be in aiding the treatment of depression. Probiotics are discussed in greater detail in Chapter 15.

Sleep and Depression

Difficulty sleeping is a common symptom of depression, as is, in a smaller number of depressed people, sleeping too much. But the sleep–depression connection doesn't move in only one direction, from depression to poor sleep. Poor sleep quality can both contribute to and result from depression.

> "I am so depressed," Tanya told me during her first visit to my office. This thirty-two-year-old woman had tried several antidepressants over the past three years, with continued depression and fatigue. She was having difficulty caring for her two children and was less productive at work. As I listened to Tanya, what was most striking was her three-year struggle with chronic insomnia. On an average night, she slept a combined five hours, spending most of the night tossing and turning and watching late-night infomercials. Rather than prescribe an antidepressant, I focused my treatment on nutritional supplements and medication to help her sleep better. Sleeping eight hours per night and waking fully rested was all Tanya needed. She stopped her sleep medications after four weeks, and within three months, she felt like herself again. Although she had come to my office because of depression, she was never prescribed an antidepressant.

Both the body and the brain need sleep to refresh and restore top functioning. A lack of sleep, or disturbed sleep, can lead to increased irritability and tension, which can set the stage for depression or make existing depression worse. Not getting enough sleep can also encourage people to engage in poor dietary habits such as eating highly refined, carbohydrate-rich foods, which can also make depression worse.

Each night, millions of people struggle to fall asleep or sleep through the night. A 2013 study conducted by the Centers for Disease Control and Prevention found that 4 percent of adults in the United States resort to sleeping pills or sedatives to help them fall asleep or sleep through the night.

Many people are also not sleeping nearly enough, and the problem is growing worse. A 2013 survey revealed that 40 percent of Americans were getting less than the recommended minimum of eight hours of sleep per night, with an average of 6.8 hours. Researchers also observed a rise in insomnia and other sleep disorders in the past decade. Sleeping problems can be caused by a number of factors, including physical disease, poor sleeping habits, and even nutritional imbalances (a fact that surprises most patients and psychiatrists alike).

Several recent studies have demonstrated that higher incidences of depression are observed in patients who report insufficient sleep. In one 2015 study, researchers followed 12,063 same-sex twin pairs born in Finland and found that consistently poor sleep increased their risk for depression 2.5 times. Moreover, it increased their risk of disability retirement.

Sleep is critical for brain development in the adolescent population, and children between the ages of 5 and 12 years need about 10 to 11 hours of sleep each night. Researchers note aberrations in brain maturation, neurotransmitter and hormone metabolism, and neuronal networks in adolescents who report sleep disturbances. One study involving children aged 9 to 16 found that sleep problems predicted increases in the prevalence of generalized anxiety disorder, depressive symptoms, and other behavioral disorders.

A 2014 meta-analysis reviewing 23 studies found that adolescents aged 12 to 20 years with major depressive disorder reported significantly more sleep disturbances, including more wakefulness in bed and interrupted sleep, resulting in poor treatment outcomes.

It is no surprise that adequate, high-quality sleep plays an important role in your recovery from depression. Sleep is our own body's natural defense mechanism, allowing us to recharge and heal our brain.

Sleep difficulty may be caused by a disease

A major contributor to sleeping difficulties is sleep apnea, a disorder that causes a person to stop breathing at night, up to a minute or even longer each episode, tens or even hundreds of times during a night. The problem may be caused by collapse of the soft tissue at the back of the throat during sleep, failure of the brain to maintain normal breathing, or a mix of the two. If untreated, sleep apnea can cause or contribute to heart disease, sexual problems, weight gain, and other problems, including depression.

People with sleep apnea are five times more likely to become depressed than those without the disease, and 20 percent of those who are depressed also have sleep apnea. Studies show that simply treating sleep apnea can relieve depression in some people, so it's important that people with depression are checked to make sure they don't have the disorder, or, if they do have sleep apnea, to ensure it is being treated properly. Symptoms of sleep apnea include:

- Waking up feeling tired in the morning
- Feeling tired during the day
- Memory problems
- Tossing and turning while sleeping
- Choking or gasping while sleeping
- Snoring loudly
- Headaches in the morning or at night
- Going to the bathroom more than once or twice
- Swelling of the legs
- Chest pain or sweating during sleep

Many people think that sleep apnea strikes only the obese. That's incorrect, for normal-weight and thin people can also have it. I remember a slim and fit forty-three-year-old man with complaints of depression who was found to have severe sleep apnea that required the use of a continuous positive airway pressure (CPAP) machine and mask through the night to keep oxygen flowing through his lungs. The CPAP helped him sleep and resolved his symptoms of depression.

A host of factors can worsen sleep problems, including stress, caffeine, alcohol, many prescription and over-the-counter medicines, hormonal imbalances, allergies, asthma, hyperthyroidism, chronic pain, and many nutritional deficiencies, the most common of which are magnesium and zinc.

Restless legs syndrome is another disorder that can make it difficult to sleep. The syndrome causes a powerful, sometimes irresistible, urge to move the legs, which is often worse at night or when lying down. Restless legs syndrome can make it difficult to fall asleep and stay asleep.

Improving sleep with good sleep hygiene

Medications can help many people solve sleep problems, but I like to start, whenever possible, with more natural methods such as improving sleep habits, referred to as sleep hygiene.

A recent survey conducted in Japan proposed that individuals suffering from sleep disturbances spend more time in bed preparing to fall asleep as a sleep habit that can help improve sleep hygiene. Many people can also solve their sleep difficulties by trying these bedtime actions:

- Go to bed and get up at the same times every day
- Avoid caffeine after lunch
- Make sure your bed, pillows, and bedding are comfortable and supportive
- Set the thermostat so that your bedroom is slightly cool throughout the night
- Use blackout curtains, get rid of TVs or radios with lights, and otherwise make your bedroom as dark as possible
- Use the bed for only sleep and sex
- Don't use the bed for work, watching television, or anything else that causes your brain to link the bed to other activities
- Develop a prescribed ritual, which might include reading, bathing, deep-breathing exercises, yoga, or other relaxation techniques
- Avoid computers, electronic games, texting, and similar activities before bedtime
- It's also important not to try too hard. If, after following these rules, you don't fall asleep within 20 or 30 minutes, get out of bed, go to another room, and read until you're sleepy

Improving sleep with natural remedies

Ideally, you should try to sleep without taking a pill every night. But if improving sleep habits doesn't solve the problem, you may want to try natural remedies such as melatonin, magnesium, valerian, inositol, 5-hydroxytryptophan (5-HTP), glycine, or gamma-aminobutyric acid (GABA) under the direction of a health professional. It's important to keep in mind that natural remedies are not regulated the way drugs are, so not all brands are made using high-quality ingredients and meeting manufacturing standards.

Melatonin for sleep. Melatonin, a hormone produced by a part of the brain known as the pineal gland, works with the body's built-in "clock" to regulate sleep and wake cycles. Ideally, the clock signals the body to produce more melatonin during the evening, keeping the levels high through the night, and then to reduce melatonin as morning arrives. As melatonin levels rise, you become sleepier; and as they fall, you become more awake and alert. It's also interesting to note that the body needs the mineral zinc to manufacture melatonin. Zinc plays a key role in preventing depression.

The sleep produced by melatonin supplements is remarkably normal, especially compared with the "drugged" sleep of some people taking sleeping pills. One example involves a fifty-six-year-old female patient who had struggled with sleep problems for nine years. I prescribed 1 milligram of melatonin, and she was quickly back to sleeping "normally again," as she described it.

I have found that taking 1–3 mg of melatonin helps many people go to sleep within 30 minutes. The hormone is cleared from the body fairly quickly, so it doesn't linger and make one feel tired or sluggish during the day. Although it has been used by millions of people in numerous countries for many years and is considered safe when used as prescribed, it can cause side effects such as drowsiness, stomach upset, headaches, and even symptoms of depression, so it should be used with caution and only as needed.

Magnesium for sleep. Although it's perhaps better known for working with calcium to cause the body's smooth muscles to contract and relax at the appropriate times, the mineral magnesium is also important for sleep. Considered an "antistress" mineral, magnesium supplements can reduce levels of cortisol in the body and prevent nighttime muscle cramps, both of which can help improve sleep.

Magnesium is also one of the first minerals to disappear from food when it is processed and one of the first to leave the body when a person is stressed. Between the large amounts of processed foods we eat and the stress of modern life, as well as the fact that magnesium supplies are depleted by alcohol, caffeine, and certain medications, many people do not have optimal levels of magnesium in their bodies. A shortage in magnesium ties directly into depression, as symptoms include irritability, nervousness, anxiety, apathy, mood swings, insomnia, and depression.

Case studies of individual patients have shown that taking 125–300 mg of magnesium (either magnesium glycinate or magnesium taurate) per meal and at bedtime help relieve the symptoms of major depression. I have found that 200–300 mg of magnesium glycinate or citrate before bed helps those who have trouble falling asleep as well as those who fall right to sleep but wake up three hours later and cannot fall back to sleep. It may take a few weeks for patients to experience the benefits of magnesium. The only major side effect of magnesium supplementation is loose stools. As with every aspect of THE ZEEBRA approach, everyone is different, and you need to find the right dose that works for you.

Valerian for sleep. Many herbs have been promoted as sleep aids, but the only one I've consistently found to be useful is valerian, which has been called the "herbal Valium" because it helps reduce anxiety while improving sleep. Valerian was used in a four-week study involving thirty people with sleep disorders. Some of the research subjects took valerian for four weeks, and the remaining were given a placebo. Neither the patients nor the researchers knew which patients were given the herb as opposed to the placebo, a procedure termed a *double-blind study.* The study found that valerian reduced the amount of time needed to go to sleep in people with sleep disorders. Another study showed that valerian improved sleep—even in people who had been taking Valium, Librium, Klonopin, or other benzodiazepine medications.

I've found that 300–500 mg of valerian before bed can help people enjoy better sleep. Valerian does not work right away and needs to be taken for a few weeks for best results. The herb's side effects may include headache, restlessness, sleeplessness, and irregular heartbeat. Anyone taking valerian should watch for these side effects.

Inositol and 5-HTP for sleep. Made by the body as well as by intestinal bacteria, the vitamin inositol has many duties, including helping transmit nerve signals and preventing the buildup of fat in the liver and other organs. I have treated many patients who reported improvements in chronic sleep difficulties using inositol.

Research has supported the use of inositol in depression and obsessive compulsive disorder (OCD). Researchers who reviewed the results of seven randomized controlled studies involving patients suffering from bipolar disorder (BPD), major depressive disorder (MDD), and premenstrual dysphoric disorder (PMDD) all found that subjects who took inositol were more likely to feel relief from their symptoms. They also observed a better response to inositol supplementation in the group of patients with PMDD.

I have found that patients with obsessive thoughts in the evening find relief with 1 teaspoon (about 2.8 grams) of inositol around 8 p.m. and then 1 teaspoon before bed. This tends to decrease the obsessive thinking, enabling them to more easily "turn off" the thoughts that interfere with sleep.

Another natural remedy for insomnia that I recommend to my patients is 5-HTP, which is an early form of the neurotransmitter serotonin and is then chemically changed to make melatonin. Among other duties, 5-HTP helps increase serotonin levels, as many popular antidepressants strive to do. Several studies have suggested that taking 5-HTP can help reduce anxiety, and I've found that it can also help improve sleep quality. I recommend 50–200 mg of 5-HTP 30 to 60 minutes before bedtime. However, you should not take 5-HTP if you are currently taking a prescription antidepressant.

Glycine for sleep. Glycine is an amino acid produced in the body and it is considered an inhibitory neurotransmitter. As an inhibitory neurotransmitter, it calms down neurotransmitters so that they don't fire rapidly with excessive electrical force. Glycine also helps relax blood vessels and lower the core body temperature, both of which enhance sleep onset.

In one study, patients who suffered from mild sleep deprivation were given 3 grams of glycine or placebo. The glycine-supplemented group reported increased sleep quality and decreased symptoms of fatigue after waking. Another study echoed glycine's ability to ward off fatigue and daytime sleepiness. Ten healthy male volunteers were restricted to 5.5 hours of sleep for three consecutive nights and were given 3 grams of glycine or placebo. Subjects were evaluated using a visual analog scale, and the group receiving glycine reported a significant reduction in fatigue and sleepiness.

Glycine is safe and can be extremely effective for patients suffering from mild sleep disturbances. I typically recommend 3 grams of glycine 1 hour before bedtime. Glycine can also be combined with magnesium and melatonin.

GABA for sleep. GABA is also a useful sleep aid for many patients. GABA, a neurotransmitter, helps brain cells calm down and become less excited. By reducing brain cell excitability, GABA is known for its ability to act as a natural tranquilizer, reducing stress and anxiety while increasing alertness. People with low levels of GABA often experience anxiety, depression, irritability, headache, and hypertension.

I typically recommend mixing 500–750 mg of GABA with a cup of water and drinking half of the mixture 30 minutes before bed. If you wake up in the middle of the night, take the other half. It is important to take a small test dose of GABA before trying the higher dose, as a few patients become agitated on GABA. First, try 100–250 mg of GABA and, if you feel relaxed or have no reaction, which is most common, increase the dosage to 500–750 mg at night before bed.

A brief note on supplements

Supplements are sold without prescription in vitamin stores, supermarkets, and drugstores, as well as on the Internet. The fact that they seem to be available everywhere may give a false sense that they are absolutely safe. However, they do have side effects, can be harmful if you use too much of them, and may interact with other supplements, medications, and health conditions. Remember, it's important to use them under the direction of a health professional experienced and trained in integrative medicine. For more information on where to obtain high-quality supplements from a trusted source, please refer to the Resources section.

Sugar and Depression

The second major physical factor that can contribute to depression is eating and drinking too much sugar. Common sense tells us that what we eat affects our energy levels and mood. We often eat to feel better—scarfing a chocolate brownie, perhaps, after a rough day at work—and it works. We do feel better—for a little while. Knowing that food can improve the mood for the better, it's not surprising to learn that it can also do the reverse. One of the biggest food offenders is sugar.

The brain runs almost only on glucose, the form of sugar in the blood. When blood glucose levels run low, mood can be affected in major ways. Signs of a lack of glucose to the brain include weakness, irritability, anxiety, headaches, fainting and, yes, depression. Low blood glucose results from eating too little (as in dieting, fasting), not eating often enough (as in skipping meals) or, ironically, eating too much sugar. The problem can be particularly bad when a person eats a high-sugar food like a candy bar by itself, without foods that contain protein or fiber. It's easier for the body to break down sugar than to break down complex carbohydrates (e.g., whole grains, fruits, vegetables). So the glucose from that candy bar hits the bloodstream a lot faster and in larger amounts than the glucose from, say, a piece of rye bread. And when it hits, blood glucose levels soar, spurring a surge of the hormone insulin throughout the bloodstream.

Insulin and sugar cravings

Insulin is a hormone that helps move glucose either into hungry cells, where it's used for fuel, or into fat cells, where it's stored for future use. But a problem occurs when insulin "overdoes it" and clears too much glucose from the bloodstream, causing blood sugar to drop to very low levels, along with a decline in mood. Depressed, irritable, fatigued, weak, and—guess what?—craving sugar, those with low blood sugar usually want to gobble up more sugar, but that just starts a vicious cycle that keeps the problem going. Eating more sugar spurs the release of more insulin, which clears away more blood glucose and sets the stage for further bouts of low blood sugar and poor moods.

Mood disturbances caused by low blood glucose can be a particular problem for those who have insulin resistance, a condition in which glucose has difficulty entering the hungry cells—even when blood sugar levels are normal to high. You can think of insulin as the "key" that "unlocks" the hungry cells and allows glucose to enter and "feed" them. In certain circumstances, most notably obesity, lack of exercise, aging, genetic factors, or hormonal changes, the insulin "key" no longer "unlocks" the cells properly, so less glucose can enter, and it takes longer for the cells to get their fill. In severe cases, the cells begin to starve, while blood sugar levels go sky high, otherwise known as full-fledged diabetes.

When the cells resist the effects of insulin, blood levels of both insulin and glucose rise, negatively affecting kidney function and increasing blood fats, including triglycerides and cholesterol. As the hungry cells keep demanding fuel, sugar cravings can become irresistible. Exhausted, depressed, shaky, and hungry, a person with low blood sugar may feel like she could eat a horse—especially if it were sugarcoated.

To avoid the mood-lowering effects of low blood sugar, it's important to include foods containing protein and complex carbohydrates with every meal or snack or whenever blood sugar starts to slip. Because these foods contain fiber and protein, the digestion process takes longer than it does with simple sugars, so glucose is released more slowly and evenly into the bloodstream.

Remember that fruits and, to a lesser extent, vegetables, also contain natural sugars that can drive up blood glucose levels, so they, too, should be eaten with some complex carbohydrate or a small amount of protein (e.g., cottage cheese).

Getting a handle on your sugar intake

Because sugar can play many roles in causing and/or maintaining depression, it's important for anyone at risk to cut back on sugar as much as possible. In *Beat Sugar Addiction Now!,* author Jacob Teitelbaum, MD, promotes a step-by-step approach for breaking sugar cravings and limiting sugar. Obviously, all forms of sugar can't be avoided all the time, but the amount of sugar in the diet can be limited just by following a few simple rules.

Tips for cutting back on sugar

Following are some easy ways to cut back on sugar without feeling deprived:

- Use less sugar in cooking. Try cutting out one-quarter of the sugar in a recipe and see if it still tastes good. If it does, cut back a little more the next time and repeat until you find out how much sugar you can get rid of without ruining the finished product. Many recipes contain plenty of unnecessary sugar.
- Try xylitol, a safe and natural sweetener that comes from birch tree bark and corn husks. Xylitol is a sugar alternative that does not raise insulin or blood sugar levels. I urge you to use pure xylitol crystals, as they are free of fillers and other additives. I caution against the use of other sugar alternatives, such as artificial sweeteners.
- Throw away or store the sugar bowl so you won't add sugar to your foods at the table.
- Try using small amounts of cinnamon, cardamom, ginger, nutmeg, and other spices for a "sweet" flavor without adding sugar or to replace some of the sugar in certain recipes.
- Eat plain popcorn rather than candy or cookies for snacks.
- If you like jelly and jam, try the low-sugar versions.
- If you really need to eat cookies, stay away from the worst offenders: chocolate chip, chocolate covered, or sandwich-style. Try plain graham crackers, ginger snaps, or vanilla wafers instead.
- Eat fresh fruit instead of canned, whenever possible.
- If you do eat canned fruit, make sure it's packed in fruit juice or water rather than syrup.
- Cut back on sugary desserts, sweet baked goods, ice cream, and other sweets.
- Instead of frosted layer cake, try plain angel food cake with fresh fruit.

Sugar-containing foods and drinks

Most of the sugar in our diets doesn't come from the sugar bowl or even desserts. It's hidden in a wide array of foods, including things such as ketchup, salad dressing, and barbeque sauce. Be aware of the sugar content of foods and limit your intake, particularly in the morning.

One of the biggest offenders is artificially sweetened carbonated soft drinks, which can contain up to 44 grams of processed sugars per 20-oz can. In 2014, a group of researchers investigated whether there was a link between mood and soft drink consumption. They assessed aggression and suicidal thoughts and behavior in 16,410 high school students across the United States. The results showed that the students who consumed more soft drinks also reported feeling more depressed, hopeless, and aggressive.

In addition, refined foods such as white bread, white rice, instant potatoes, or cornflakes can act like sugar in the system because the body quickly breaks them down into glucose. Therefore, it's wise to treat these foods as if they were straight sugar and eat them only with high-protein, high-fiber foods that slow the release of glucose into the bloodstream.

The many faces of sugar

Although sugar is sometimes listed as such on food labels, most of the time it isn't listed simply as "sugar." Sugar hides in processed foods under a number of different names, including the following:

- Brown sugar
- Concentrated fruit juice
- Corn syrup
- Dextrose
- Fructose
- Glucose
- High-fructose corn syrup
- Honey
- Lactose
- Maltodextrin
- Maltose
- Molasses
- Raw sugar
- Sucrose

If one of these sugar additives is listed in the first four ingredients on the label (which means it's one of the main ingredients), it is a high-sugar food. Look for a healthier, low-sugar alternative.

I'm sure you can think of many other ways to eat and drink less sugar; these suggestions are just a start. The important thing is to become aware of the massive amounts of sugar that are in many of our foods and find pleasant, doable ways to cut back. You can do much to improve mood just by eating less refined sugar.

Stress and Depression

Another factor that can lead to depression is stress. Stress is a perfectly normal response to the problems life throws our way. It's normal. In fact, millions of years ago, the body developed a set response to stress that prepares us to either fight or flee in order to protect ourselves. This stress response involves rapid changes in body processes: Blood is moved to the muscles, blood-clotting is "put on alert" in case we're injured, fat and glucose are released into the bloodstream to "feed" the muscles, the pupils dilate, and other changes occur that are designed to turn us instantly into a fighting and/or running machine.

In days past, the stressor was often a large and hungry animal, or perhaps an enemy soldier, intent on killing or capturing us. In such situations, a massive, all-out physical response to allow us to fight or run like heck made sense, for the stakes were high, and the price of failure was great. It didn't matter that repeatedly triggering the side effect damaged the immune system and otherwise harmed the body over time, for surviving the immediate threat was much more important.

Today, however, stress is rarely a matter of life or death. Yes, there are times we have to jump out of the way of an oncoming car or fend off a physical attacker, but most modern stress comes in the form of chronic psychological or social conflicts. Unfortunately, our bodies haven't adapted to modern society by developing a softer stress response more useful in twenty-first century life—and less damaging to the body. Thus, millions of people are unknowingly harming their bodies and setting the stage for emotional distress by repeatedly triggering the stress response.

A recent survey found that 72 percent of people who have daily stress and anxiety claim that it interferes with their lives. Of those people, 40 percent experience persistent stress, while 30 percent are taking prescription medications that help them manage stress-related problems.

Even for healthy subjects, chronic stress predisposes these individuals to increased levels of inflammation, which has been correlated with depressive symptoms. In fact, stress can activate dormant genes that can affect future offspring. A group of researchers exposed pregnant female rats to two stressors twice daily. Gestational stress activated genes that made their offspring more prone to mood disorders. In human studies, they found that mothers who reported maternal stress during pregnancy resulted in an increased risk of moderate to severe depression in their eleven-year-old children in a follow-up study.

The best solution is to learn to control the response to ensure that it is not turned on every time you get upset. The best way to prevent a full-blown fight-or-flight response is to simply say "no" and tell yourself that there is no one to fight and nowhere to run, and it's not worth the damage to your mind and body to trigger the stress response.

There are many ways we can learn to control our emotions and the fight-or-flight response, including relaxation techniques, psychotherapy, meditation, and the "burning off" of anger and energy by exercising. (I talk more about this in Chapter 19.)

I am not alone in promoting stress reduction in our busy, complicated lives. In her book, *The Super Stress Solution*, Roberta Lee, MD, vice chair of the Department of Integrative Medicine at Beth Israel Medical Center, describes a four-week approach to building stress resistance and resilience. Lee emphasizes nutrition, sleep, and exercise to combat stress and restore physical and mental balance.

There's not enough room in this chapter—or indeed in the entire book—to discuss all that we need to do to ensure a healthy body. But if you make sure you're getting eight hours of quality sleep every night, adopt a healthful diet, and keep your stress low, you've gone a long way toward developing the good physical health that supports good emotional health.

Chapter 9

H—Hormones and Herbs

Chapter 8 covered physical contributors to depression that you can control by making lifestyle changes: sleep problems, poor diet, and stress. The second part of THE ZEEBRA approach is H for hormones and herbs. Hormone disturbances are an often-missed and hidden factor contributing to depression, while certain herbs have been shown to fight depression symptoms.

Fatigue, dry skin, high cholesterol, constipation, irregular periods, and acne. Any of these and many more physical problems may be the reason why someone is depressed and why standard antidepressant treatment fails—no matter how many medications are prescribed.

The link between these seemingly unrelated problems and depression is hormones, substances produced by the body to regulate certain cells and organs. Some hormones, such as testosterone and estrogen, are well-known, while others are not. But whether well-known or not, many hormones can affect mood. Psychiatrists often overlook the link between depression and certain hormones, despite published studies showing that everyone being tested or treated for depression should have their hormone levels checked.

If a particular hormone level is low, the treatment options are to replace it with either a synthetic (human-made), natural (animal-based), or bioidentical (exact match) hormone. Because some hormones, such as melatonin and DHEA, are thought to be safe, they can be sold over the counter. Other hormones, such as testosterone and estrogen, require a doctor's prescription. Hormone replacement therapies are controversial and not well studied. You will want to learn about each option.

In the meantime, it's important to understand how too-high or too-low levels of a few key hormones can trigger depression. In the second half of the chapter, I discuss the herbs curcumin, St. John's wort, and rhodiola.

The Thyroid and Depression

The thyroid is a small gland, shaped something like a butterfly, that wraps around the voice box and windpipe (larynx and trachea). It has several duties, including controlling the heart and respiratory rates, but it doesn't do these things on its own. Instead, the thyroid sends out hormones, or chemical messengers, that tell other parts of the body what to do. In fact, every cell in the body depends on having enough thyroid hormones.

I like to think of the thyroid as the manager of a large factory, constantly yelling orders—telling that department to speed up and that one to slow down, ordering that a certain machine be left on longer than planned and another one be turned off sooner than expected. This manager has to be aware of everything that is happening in the factory, understand how to keep everything running, and be able to give orders at a moment's notice. Should the thyroid not run well, things start to go wrong.

The thyroid talks with the rest of the body via hormones such as thyroxine (T_4) and triiodothyronine (T_3). The biggest communication problems are either too little hormone production, called hypothyroidism, or too much, called hyperthyroidism. Thyroid hormones are

Symptoms of Low Thyroid Levels (Hypothyroidism)

Depression	Acne
Anxiety	Eczema
Memory and concentration problems	Hair loss
Low sex drive	Infections that keep coming back
Constipation	Irregular menstrual periods
High cholesterol	Severe premenstrual syndrome
Gum disease	Ovarian cysts
Obesity	Endometriosis
Hypoglycemia (low blood sugar)	Fluid retention
Muscle aches and pains	Fatigue
Dry skin	Intolerance to cold
	Lower sweat production

responsible for regulating body metabolism and are needed for the production of cellular energy.

Hypothyroidism and hyperthyroidism don't trigger a specific disease that is obviously linked to thyroid problems, the way that the measles virus causes measles or the way damage to certain parts of the liver triggers type 1 diabetes. Instead, hypothyroidism and hyperthyroidism trigger a variety of symptoms that often seem unrelated to the thyroid and to each other. Therefore, it may take some time for the real problem to be diagnosed. In the case of hypothyroidism, up to 50 percent of patients are never diagnosed at all. And many of those who are diagnosed are not given good treatment. This is a shame, for even a small imbalance of thyroid hormones can set the stage for depression.

Low thyroid and depression

Doctors have known for years that the symptoms of low thyroid include depression and fatigue, which often clear up if the thyroid problem is properly treated.

> Janet, a forty-three-year-old teacher, asked her doctor to check her out for "something" medical. For two years, she had tried many antidepressants but was still depressed. Coinciding with her persistent depression was slow-but-steady weight gain (including puffiness in the face) and acne. As she suspected, her thyroid was running in low gear and not producing enough hormone. As she had hoped, her symptoms began disappearing soon after she started taking thyroid hormone.

Dr. Mark Starr, author of *Hypothyroidism Type 2: The Epidemic*, promotes the thyroid–depression connection in his book. He describes the relationship between low thyroid function and many chronic health conditions, including depression.

Most doctors and psychiatrists are aware of the thyroid–depression link, yet the thyroid levels of most depressed patients go unchecked. Many patients referred to me for testing and treatment of depression have not had their thyroid levels checked, and far too many patients have been told that they do not have thyroid disease because of a single blood test.

Faulty testing equals faulty diagnosis

Even when doctors and psychiatrists do check the thyroid, the tests they use are not very good. A doctor who suspects a thyroid problem does not check the levels of thyroid hormone directly by measuring the amount of T_3 and T_4 in the bloodstream. Instead, she uses the standard thyroid test, the thyroid-stimulating hormone (TSH) test. TSH is a hormone released by a part of the brain called the pituitary gland, which tells the thyroid gland that the body needs more thyroid hormones. TSH acts like a message to the factory manager, requesting either "More production!" or "Less production!"

The TSH test measures the amount of TSH in the blood. In a sense, the test asks the question: How much thyroid hormone does the pituitary think the body needs? If the TSH level is high, doctors think, it must mean there are lots of requests for more thyroid hormone. This, in turn, must mean that the thyroid is not making enough hormone. So the person with a high TSH has low thyroid production, or hypothyroidism.

On the other hand, if the TSH level is too low, doctors think, it must mean that the cells and organs aren't requesting much thyroid hormone—not even routine amounts. This, in turn, "proves" that the thyroid is hyperactive, pouring out too much hormone.

And if the TSH "request-for-hormone" level is considered just right—0.4 to 4.5 milli-international units (mIU) per liter (L)—everything must be okay. In short, a high TSH request means the thyroid is putting out too little hormone; a low TSH request means the thyroid is pumping out too much; and a moderate TSH request means the thyroid gland is working well.

This makes perfect sense—until you realize it's built on the never-tested assumption that the body always requests the right amount of thyroid hormone. But suppose the pituitary gland gets it wrong and requests too little or too much thyroid hormone? Every doctor knows that human physiology can easily get out of tune and do too much or too little of something. Why don't we ever ask whether the pituitary's request for more or less thyroid hormone is off kilter? Why do we assume that the request is exactly right and that the thyroid gland is working fine?

In addition to the possibility that the pituitary may make the wrong request, the thyroid might be sending out enough thyroid hormone, but for some reason, the body isn't able to use it properly. This is similar to what happens with type 2 diabetes: The pancreas releases enough insulin to control blood sugar, but the body's cells can't respond properly to that insulin. More and more insulin must be released over and above the proper amount, until the cells, flooded with insulin, finally respond. Could it be that the thyroid is making what seems like enough hormone but that the body can't use it properly and keeps asking for more? If that's the case, the pituitary gland looks at the amount of thyroid hormone in the blood, decides that all is well, and does not ask for an increase—even though the cells are screaming for more.

There's another problem: How much TSH is normal and healthy? Remember, either too much or too little TSH may mean that the thyroid is not working properly. But what's "just right?" Although the TSH test has been popular since the 1960s, no one has yet scientifically shown what the healthy TSH level or range should be. The truth is, we're just guessing.

Many integrative medicine doctors think of a TSH level of more than 2.5 mIU/L (remember, the upper limit of the optimal range is 4.5 mIU/L) as an accurate reflection of sluggish thyroid function. I've seen many patients with "normal" TSH levels who clearly had hypothyroidism, or a lack of thyroid hormone. I remember well forty-three-year-old Jane, who came to see me because of a "mild depression that started slowly a year or so ago," as she put it.

> Jane had already been to her family doctor, who tested her TSH and found it was normal. As I spoke with Jane, I learned that she had depression, fatigue, elevated cholesterol, constipation, acne, and dry skin. Her depression and fatigue blended together to her. These problems can all happen if there isn't enough thyroid hormone in the body.
>
> I also noted that Jane reported that she was always cold. So I ordered tests of her T_3 and T_4, finding that they were indeed on the low side. I referred Jane to an integrative medicine doctor, who treated her with replacement hormones. This treatment resolved Jane's depression and her skin and constipation problems, saving her the frustration of going on one antidepressant after another without relief.

With these three built-in complicating factors—the assumptions that the TSH request level is always correct, that the body can use all the thyroid hormone properly, and that we actually know how much is enough—

many people's thyroid problems may be misdiagnosed on the basis of the TSH test. And it's likely that many people with depression who might get better with thyroid hormone replacement are not offered this treatment.

Correcting thyroid levels to relieve depression

The concept of treating low thyroid hormone levels by giving more thyroid hormone is not new. Studies of the use of thyroid hormone to treat depression began in the late 1960s. In one of these early studies, depressed patients were given the antidepressant imipramine along with either T_3 or a placebo. Those taking the antidepressant plus T_3 in this double-blind study enjoyed a faster and better recovery than those taking the antidepressant plus placebo. This showed that replacing missing thyroid hormone helped relieve depression. A meta-analysis, or summary analysis, that used statistical means to combine the results of eight different studies found that T_3 increased the improvements seen with antidepressants given for treatment-resistant depression.

Other studies have supported these findings. For example, in a 2014 study on the link between thyroid hormone and depression, forty-four patients referred to a psychiatric hospital for treatment of depression had their blood drawn and their depression rated using two depression scales. The researchers found that T_3 and T_4 were both predictors of the level of improvement in depression symptoms.

It always fascinates me that psychiatrists have been using T_3 as a hormone strategy for treating depression, yet most other physicians use only T_4. It's important to have both checked. Another 2014 study found that T_3 seems to work better than T_4 for depression and that women tend to respond more than men.

I believe that everyone who is depressed or is being evaluated for depression should be checked for a thyroid shortage. Testing should go beyond simply the TSH test, which isn't enough and can be misleading. Patients should find a doctor who understands a comprehensive integrative approach that includes evaluating all symptoms of thyroid shortage, measuring the basal metabolic temperature, and testing the levels of T_3 and T_4 in the blood. If there's a sign of hypothyroidism, I recommend thyroid replacement therapy with T_3 and T_4. I have often seen results with the addition of natural dry thyroid replacement therapy that includes T_3 and T_4.

Special note on the thyroid and iodine

The thyroid uses iodine to create thyroid hormones, which means that a lack of iodine can result in thyroid shortage.

In areas in which diets are low in iodine, people are more likely to have goiter, a very swollen thyroid gland that makes the neck bulge out like a little tire sitting on the shoulders. People whose diets are low in iodine are also more likely to have the stunted mental and physical growth called cretinism, which arises when a pregnant woman deficient in iodine gives birth to a child who also lacks thyroid hormones.

Iodine shortage used to be a major problem in the northwestern United States, in Appalachia, and in the Great Lakes region, which were once known collectively as the "Goiter Belt." With the addition of iodine to culinary salt, the problem was thought to have largely disappeared in the United States. However, the problem persists and may lead to subclinical hypothyroidism, a minor version of the disease that's hard to detect because blood test results are still within the normal range.

Other nutrients, including tyrosine, zinc, and iron, are necessary for the thyroid gland and its hormones to function properly. If the standard American diet continues to stay away from naturally grown, nutritious foods and embrace processed, refined foods without trace minerals, thyroid problems are likely to increase. Some researchers describe an epidemic of thyroid disease in the United States. This is not just because of nutritional problems but also because of toxins in our environment.

Environmental toxins interfere with thyroid function

Scientists and medical professionals are increasingly aware of the dangers of environmental toxins. These toxins seep into our bodies through water, food, and air, often via harmless-looking objects such as plastic water bottles, baby teething rings, and air fresheners. Despite the innocent appeal of that water bottle, more and more evidence has shown that long-term exposure to these toxins can harm our endocrine and nervous systems.

Environmental toxins can especially harm the thyroid, which is part of the endocrine system. Some environmental toxins, including polychlorinated biphenyls, dioxins, phthalates, and polybrominated diphenyl ethers (PBDEs), have been shown to affect thyroid function. These chemicals interfere with the production, transportation, and use of thyroid hormones. These chemicals hurt our bodies in many different ways, and many of them use their similarity to thyroid hormone to interfere with its normal function. Their similarity to thyroid hormone allows them to connect to thyroid receptors and change the way the thyroid normally functions.

The best way to avoid toxin damage to the thyroid is to limit exposure to environmental toxins by:

- Using natural cleaning products, when available
- Limiting exposure to pesticides, insect repellants, air fresheners, and other aerosol (spray) chemical products
- Eating organic foods
- Using glass, ceramic, or metal containers (rather than plastic) for food storage

I can't emphasize enough how important it is to check for thyroid shortage. A few blood tests, a history, and a physical exam more than outweigh the money and time lost on wasted studies with antidepressants that can't work because they're not resolving the real problem: a too-low supply of thyroid hormone.

DHEA and Depression

Dehydroepiandrosterone (DHEA) is a hormone produced by the adrenal glands. It does several things on its own and is also used by the body to make testosterone and estrogen. The body's production of DHEA rises to its highest level in a person's mid-twenties and slowly declines as the years pass.

DHEA is the most abundant steroid hormone used by the body. Like all steroid hormones, DHEA is made from cholesterol. Without adequate cholesterol, you cannot keep high enough levels of DHEA or other steroid hormones. When under stress, the adrenal glands make more hormones, including DHEA. After DHEA is secreted into the bloodstream, it changes chemically in the liver into DHEA-sulfate (DHEA-S). DHEA-S is the form measured and monitored in the blood.

DHEA has been used as an antiaging supplement, with some people arguing that putting more DHEA into the body helps the body make more sex hormones, strengthens the immune system, and otherwise helps keep us young. But this is still a controversial idea.

A different line of research has looked into the use of DHEA as a treatment for depression. In a study published in *Biological Psychiatry*, researchers tested the effects of DHEA in fifteen people with midlife depression. The results were very good, with 60 percent of those receiving DHEA responding to treatment, compared with only 20 percent of those who got the placebo. (It's expected that at least 20 percent of people in any depression study will respond to a placebo.) Thus, a new treatment is typically compared with a placebo to make sure it's really effective and much more effective than a placebo. A similar study published in the *Archives of General Psychiatry* in 2005 also found that DHEA was an "effective treatment for midlife-onset of major and minor depression." The results of these and other studies make sense when you consider that DHEA levels are lower in adults with major depression than in those who are not depressed. This was confirmed by a 2014 study in which researchers studied the depression scale scores of twenty-four patients with major depression and twenty-four healthy people. They found that DHEA levels do indicate improvement in depressive symptoms in patients with major depression. Another study in 2015 reached similar findings. It found that low levels of DHEA are linked to depression and that DHEA levels decrease with advancing age. DHEA may be more effective in men than in women. One 2013 study also found that higher DHEA-S levels lowered the risk of depression in men but not in women.

Although DHEA is not a magic bullet for depression and should be taken only under the supervision of a doctor skilled in its use, it can be helpful for patients with low levels of DHEA-S.

Psychiatry is constantly in search of a magic pill. Even though research has shed a little light on the relationship between DHEA and depression, few acknowledge the core concept of THE ZEEBRA approach and biochemical individuality. Measuring DHEA is a perfect example of the search for physiological imbalances leading to personalized treatments for patients with depression. If a simple blood test reflects low levels of DHEA-S, careful supplementation should be done. If blood levels are optimal, supplementation is not likely to help. I recommend a relatively low dose: 5–10 mg for women and 10–25 mg for men. These doses raise DHEA levels. I have also often seen improvement in mood as well as allergies, high cholesterol, headaches, and fibromyalgia symptoms with DHEA.

Sex Hormones and Depression

Testosterone

Australian researchers looked at 3,987 men aged seventy-one to eighty-nine, assessing their moods and levels of free testosterone. (Some of the testosterone in the bloodstream is bound to other substances, while the rest is unbound, or "free." It's the free testosterone that's biologically active.) The men were placed in five different groups according to their free testosterone levels. The researchers found that those in the lowest testosterone group were almost twice as likely to be depressed as those in the group with the highest testosterone levels.

A 2014 study looked at levels of testosterone and DHEA in thirty-eight female hospitalized patients, nineteen of whom had high anxiety, versus sixty-five healthy people. The levels of testosterone and DHEA were much lower in the hospitalized patients than in the healthy people. The study also found that levels were even lower in anxious patients with major depression versus patients who were not anxious.

In 2003, researchers from Harvard Medical School's McLean Hospital tested the effects of testosterone in men aged thirty to sixty-five who had both depression that did not respond to standard antidepressants and low or borderline-low testosterone levels. The twenty-three men in the study kept taking their prescribed antidepressants, but half were also given a testosterone gel to rub directly onto the skin, while the other half were given a placebo gel. The results were impressive. Those using the testosterone gel had much greater improvements in their depression scores, measured by standard depression scales, than those using the placebo gel.

This was a small study, but it suggested that testosterone may relieve depression (either by itself or with standard antidepressants) when used in men with low testosterone levels. And as the researchers pointed out, there is a "large and probably underrecognized population of depressed men with low testosterone levels."

In a 2012 study of 762 men with low testosterone prescribed a 1 percent testosterone topical gel, researchers found that men with moderately severe to severe depressive symptoms reported a decrease in symptoms, from 17.3 percent to 2.1 percent. At twelve months, a depression scale showed a meaningful improvement in depression symptoms of 5.62 points.

In 2014, researchers looking at sixteen studies about the effect of testosterone on mood found that testosterone was an effective treatment, either alone or with other therapies, for dysthymia and mild depression in middle-aged men with low testosterone levels.

These and other studies do not mean that testosterone is a magic antidepressant. Instead, they suggest that:

- Low testosterone levels are linked to depression
- In some men, depression cannot be relieved until testosterone is raised to a normal level
- Antidepressants cannot raise testosterone to a normal level, which helps explain why they do not help some men

So it is critical to check the testosterone levels of depressed male patients of any age. If they are low or borderline low, I try to understand why. I've been surprised many times at the low levels I've seen in many patients, including some men in their thirties and forties.

Rather than prescribing testosterone right away, I use natural means to raise the level of hormone. I have patients:

- Monitor zinc levels, which are important for testosterone synthesis
- Exercise regularly to strengthen muscles, which helps the body keep testosterone levels up
- Reduce stress to reduce cortisol, a stress-induced hormone that can encourage the breakdown of muscles and thus reduce testosterone levels
- Cut back on or avoid soy and other foods containing large amounts of phytoestrogens, which can "counteract" testosterone
- Eat plenty of the omega-3 fatty acids known as EPA and DHA, which are found in salmon and other cold-water fish. The body can use essential fats to produce testosterone and other hormones.
- Monitor cholesterol and DHEA levels, which are required for the synthesis of testosterone
- Try supplementation with tribulus, an herb that enhances testosterone synthesis

If natural means of raising testosterone are not enough, I refer patients for hormone therapy. Hormone therapy should be done under the supervision of an endocrinologist, a physician who specializes in the endocrine glands, which produce hormones. The endocrinologist can rule out a pituitary gland tumor or another disease that may be interfering with testosterone production and can monitor the effects of the additional testosterone. This is important, for some of the side effects of testosterone use can be harmful. They include headaches, gum pain and swelling, breast growth, changes in the size and shape of the testicles, nausea, depression, and dizziness.

Estrogen and progesterone

There's no doubt that the female hormones estrogen and progesterone influence mood. Many women can sense the changes as they move through their menstrual cycle and again as they approach and go through menopause.

A 2014 study of the effects of estrogen on brain-derived neurotrophic factor (BDNF) found that estrogen affects depression through interactions with BDNF and the body's system for regulating serotonin. BDNF's role is to support the survival of neurons and the growth of new neurons and their connections. Another study showed that estrogen can affect mood by degrading, or reducing levels of, MAO, the enzyme that breaks down serotonin.

Hormonal influences on mood in women are much more complex than they are in men, and there is no simple formula such as "more estrogen = less depression in certain women." Instead, the key is to balance the hormone levels, a tricky process that should be done only under the supervision of an endocrinologist.

There is considerable controversy surrounding hormone replacement therapy for women. Conventional hormone replacement therapy with synthetic hormones was the standard of care until studies by the Women's Health Initiative, a fifteen-year research program involving forty medical centers and more than 160,000 women across the country, received national attention. The Women's Health Initiative was created to address health concerns in women who have gone through menopause. Most notable was its study of estrogen-plus-progestin hormone therapy in women who had gone through menopause. The study was ended three years early when the researchers found that the risks of the therapy outweighed the benefits. On the combination hormone therapy, women had increased risks of invasive breast cancer, coronary heart disease, stroke, and pulmonary embolism compared with women taking only placebo pills.

Due to these concerns, I have consistently preferred to use natural hormones rather than synthetics. Although few research studies support the benefits of natural hormones, the potential side effects of synthetic hormones far outweigh the benefits. As with all nutritional and natural therapies, further research on natural and bioidentical hormone therapy is unlikely because this type of treatment cannot be patented and therefore will not make large profits for drug companies. Make sure you work with a trusted doctor experienced in the use of natural or bioidentical hormones before considering any type of hormone replacement therapy.

Herbs

St. John's wort, Curcumin, and rhodiola have been used with some success in people with depression.

St. John's wort

St. John's wort is a perennial herb with yellow flowers originally hailing from Europe and blooming primarily in the summertime. The scientific name for St. John's wort, *Hypericum perforatum*, literally translates to "above a ghost," and legends and folklore say that the herb has magical powers to ward off evil spirits. The use of St. John's wort dates back to 400 BC, when the ancient Greeks and Romans used it to treat various ailments, including melancholia, snakebites, upset stomachs, and superficial wounds. Today, millions of people use St. John's wort as a natural antidepressant to treat mild to moderate depression. Yet its effectiveness remains under constant debate. However, in countries such as Germany, St. John's Wort is licensed to treat anxiety, depression, and sleep disorders. It is also used as a pain reliever for individuals suffering from intense pain caused by nerve damage, as it has antispasmodic and anti-inflammatory properties.

A review conducted by Cochrane researchers evaluated twenty-nine studies involving 5,489 patients with mild to moderate depression that compared treatment with St. John's wort extract for four to twelve weeks with placebo or standard antidepressants. Overall, participants given the St. John's wort extract experienced improvements superior to placebo and had fewer side effects compared with antidepressants. One 2009 study evaluated 440 patients who were treated with 500 mg of St. John's wort for as long as one year and concluded that it was a safe and effective treatment for long-term use and noted its ability to prevent relapses in depression.

Although it is unclear exactly how St. John's wort works, scientists suspect that it is able to elevate levels of the neurotransmitters responsible for mood, such as serotonin, dopamine, and norepinephrine—similar to the effects from SSRIs. Research studies have focused primarily on two active ingredients found in the plant: hypericin and hyperforin. Hypericin has been shown to have antiviral activity and has been used in therapy against cancer and in HIV in stored blood. Hyperforin has been found to activate a particular receptor in the liver that activates the production of an enzyme used to metabolize medications.

St. John's wort can be used as a single agent to treat mild to moderate depression. Most of the published research studies used a dosage range between 300 and 1,200 mg. I typically recommend 300 mg three times daily for patients suffering from mild depression, with noted improvement in symptoms. Although the herb is considered generally safe, there are still risks to consider before starting St. John's wort. There is considerable variation in the amount of active ingredients in herbal supplements, based on preparation, including how the supplement is cultivated, harvested, and stored. These variations can trigger unwanted side effects such as dizziness, nausea, and elevated blood pressure, so it is advisable to obtain St. John's wort supplementation from a trusted, high-quality source.

Over the years, my use of St. John's wort has decreased as I have focused on individual testing and targeted nutritional therapies. Anyone who is considering St. John's wort supplementation should consult with a medical professional, as it can potentially interfere with the effectiveness of several common medications such as birth control pills, blood thinners, heart disease drugs, and some cancer drugs. I would also advise caution while using St. John's wort with antidepressants. Individuals with bipolar depression or a family history of bipolar disorder should not take St. John's wort, as it can trigger manic episodes and psychosis.

Curcumin

You may know curcumin as turmeric, the main herb used in curry. The active ingredient found in curcumin stimulates blood flow, acts as an aromatic stimulant, relieves pain, and has antimicrobial properties. Researchers believe that curcumin plays a role in inflammatory pathways and helps regulate our stress response system. Because these pathways are involved with depression, curcumin has been an area of interest in the treatment of depression. Studies have shown it to be a safe and effective drug when used either alone or with an antidepressant.

In a 2013 study, forty patients aged twenty to sixty who were depressed for the first time were given antidepressants plus either 500 mg of curcumin a day or placebo. The researchers found no difference between curcumin and placebo in improvement of depression; however, patients who took the curcumin were more likely to get more rapid relief of the depressive symptoms.

That same year, researchers looking at curcumin as an antidepressant concluded that curcumin has properties that may make it an effective treatment. Curcumin may exert its effects by degrading the enzyme MAO, which breaks down serotonin. Curcumin protects against oxidative stress and mitochondrial damage. It also regulates the level of neurotransmitters in the body, promotes the birth of new neurons in the hippocampus, and decreases inflammation.

Curcumin has been shown to be effective in the treatment of major depression. In a 2014 study, fifty-six patients with major depression were given 500 mg curcumin twice daily or placebo for eight weeks. While it took four weeks to work, it was found to be much more effective than placebo in relieving symptoms. Also in 2014, researchers studying the effectiveness and safety of curcumin in patients with major depression found that curcumin had similar effects as the antidepressant fluoxetine in treating major depression.

As a psychiatrist who mostly treats patients in whom past treatments didn't work, I rarely use curcumin as a sole agent. I recommend curcumin as an adjunct to all patients struggling with depression. Curcumin can be used with medications or with an integrative nutritional program. I feel strongly about the benefits, without any risks, and have included curcumin in my NeuroMood Pure Pack for depressed patients. The Pure Mood Pack is a convenient, once-daily supplement with essential nutrients such as curcumin, vitamin D_3, fish oil, CoQ10 enzyme, taurine, and all of the essential B vitamins.

Curcumin dissolves in fat and therefore should be taken with meals that contain a bit of fat for more efficient absorption.

Rhodiola

Rhodiola rosea is a perennial green-yellow flower that grows on sea cliffs and mountains in cold regions of the world. It is used in traditional Chinese medicine and is known to help prevent altitude sickness. Rhodiola is commonly used in eastern Asian and eastern European countries for relieving mental and physical ailments. Currently, rhodiola is recognized by the Russian Ministry of Health as both a medicine and an herbal tonic that supports mood and wards off fatigue. Due to its mood-boosting properties, rhodiola is also recognized as an effective therapy for depression.

In 2012, researchers showed that rhodiola was effective in reducing depressive symptoms, boosting mood, reducing fatigue, and treating an addiction to opioids in male and female patients taking 340–680 mg a day. Rhodiola is able to assist in normalizing the stress response in the body by increasing the body's resilience.

In one 2012 study, rhodiola helped reduce signs of nicotine withdrawal in animals, perhaps by increasing serotonin and serotonin receptors. Other experts have proposed that rhodiola works by affecting levels of endorphins and serotonin in the brain by degrading the enzymes MAO A and MAO B, which break down serotonin.

When researchers profiled gene expression in human cells, rhodiola extract affected 1,062 genes, 50 of them linked to behavior and 62 of them linked to psychological disorders. The researchers concluded that rhodiola may improve emotional behavior in many different disorders.

Rhodiola can be an important nutritional therapy for the treatment of depression. Drs. Richard Brown and Patricia Gerbarg describe the many uses of rhodiola in the popular book *The Rhodiola Revolution.* Rhodiola can enhance mood, concentration, and energy levels. I would caution use in individuals who have anxiety and bipolar disorder, as this herb may be too stimulating. I typically use 100 mg per day to start and slowly increase up to 400–600 mg maximum daily for depression. Some individuals notice improvement at 100 mg, while others may need more. It's important to keep in mind that the effects of herbal supplements are gradual and that increasing dosages slowly, typically every seven days, is critical to safely minimize the risk of possible side effects while maximizing the therapeutic effect.

Chapter 10

E—Exclude

In some cases, finding relief from depression involves not just adding medications, exercise, sleep, or supplements but removing substances from the diet. In THE ZEEBRA approach, "exclude" refers to getting rid of foods that lead to or worsen depression. Changing the diet isn't very high-tech or glamorous for the growing numbers of patients with celiac disease or food intolerances and food allergies, but improvement in depression can be dramatic. When the underlying connection between diet and depression is ignored, there is little hope for relief with antidepressants.

Depression is multifaceted, and a thorough assessment should include digestive issues. If they are present, they must be resolved before treatment for depression to be effective. Common digestive disorders contributing to depression include celiac disease, difficulties with incompletely digested proteins such as casomorphin and gliadorphin, and food allergies and intolerances.

Celiac Disease and Depression

Once considered a relatively uncommon problem affecting young children, celiac disease is now recognized as a serious ailment that can strike at any age. It affects about 1 in 130 Americans, or about 2.25 million people. And many women with celiac disease (37 percent in one study) report depressive symptoms.

It begins as a "bad reaction" to a certain part of wheat and develops into a self-destructive assault on the digestive system, but the effects of celiac disease are not limited to the stomach. The health consequences of celiac disease may affect every organ system, including the brain. In a depressed person with celiac disease, depression can be resolved only when the celiac disease is treated.

In celiac disease, the body mistakenly decides that a protein called gluten, found in wheat, rye, and barley, is a dangerous toxin. Responding just as it would to harmful bacteria, a virus, or other invader, the immune system sets out to destroy the gluten. That by itself is not too bad, for humans can live quite well without any gluten at all. Unfortunately, in the battle to destroy gluten, the immune system heavily damages the surrounding area, the small intestine. Like the buildings and fields where a real-life war takes place, the small intestine can be so badly damaged that it cannot do its job of absorbing nutrients. Unable to properly break down food into component parts that can be absorbed into the bloodstream, the small intestine lets vitamins A, B_6, B_{12}, D, E, and K, as well as folic acid, and minerals such as iron, zinc, magnesium, and calcium, pass right through the bowels and out of the body. Essential fats, as well as tryptophan and other essential amino acids, are also poorly absorbed.

The intestinal damage can cause first-wave symptoms soon after eating, including abdominal cramps and distention, pain, gas, and vomiting. Second-wave symptoms include diarrhea and constipation. These first- and second-wave symptoms can be so disagreeable in some people that they try to eat as little as possible, potentially leading to serious malnutrition and weight loss.

> A college student had abdominal distention, pain, and constipation so severe that she was literally afraid to eat. Her family doctor and the psychiatrist to whom she was referred diagnosed anorexia. But no matter how much she protested that "eating makes me physically hurt," they kept referring her to mental health professionals for eating disorder treatment. When she was sent to me for a second opinion, I determined that she had celiac disease, with multiple nutritional deficiencies related to this disease. When we removed gluten from her diet, she was able to return to college and restore weight.

Patients with celiac disease can develop a surprising variety of third-wave problems that may not heal. Although these problems may appear entirely unrelated, they are all linked to the intestinal damage that makes it difficult to absorb different nutrients. No matter how much food the person eats, he or she is always malnourished, lacking certain essential nutrients. Depending on which ones are missing, the results can include problems such as:

- Anemia
- Anorexia
- Arthritis
- Dermatitis herpetiformis (blistered, itchy skin rash)
- Edema (swelling caused by fluid retention)
- Fatigue
- Infertility
- Joint pain and inflammation
- Migraine headaches
- Missed menstrual periods
- Numbness and tingling of the hands and feet
- Osteoporosis
- Seizures and other neurological problems
- Stunted growth
- Tooth decay and discoloration

If the absorption of zinc, tryptophan, the B vitamins, or certain other nutrients necessary for mental health is hindered, the result may be depression and/or anxiety. These nutrients are necessary to create essential chemicals in the brain, such as serotonin, a shortage of which has been linked to depression. Researchers who looked at eighteen studies on depression and eleven studies on celiac disease found that depression is more common, more severe, or both in adults with celiac disease. The relationship between celiac disease and depression is commonly seen in children. One study found that teens with celiac disease had a 31 percent risk of a major depressive episode, compared with a 7 percent risk in healthy children. Another study of twenty-two subjects with irritable bowel syndrome found that ingestion of gluten induced feelings of depression.

The difficulty with diagnosis

Researchers have long been aware of a connection between celiac disease and depression. Research articles and studies on the two have been published in the scientific literature for years. Reports of depression among celiac disease patients appeared in the 1980s, and in 1982, Swedish researchers reported that "depressive psychopathology is a feature of adult celiac disease and may be a consequence of malabsorption." A 1998 study reported that about one-third of those with celiac disease also have depression. More recently, a 2007 study compared 13,776 people with celiac disease with 66,815 controls without the disease. This study found that celiac disease was linked to depression, with about 40 percent of those with celiac disease developing depression.

Different studies report slightly different conclusions regarding the numbers of celiac disease patients who are also depressed, but the point is clear: depression and celiac disease are linked, and it is critical to assess for and treat celiac disease in depressed patients. The celiac–depression link is not often discussed or well-known among psychiatrists and mental health professionals.

The symptoms triggered by celiac disease vary widely from patient to patient. Variations may depend on how strongly the immune system reacts to gluten, how much intestinal damage has occurred, which part of the intestines has been harmed, the overall quality of the diet, any coexisting physical or psychiatric disorders, and any treatment the patient has received. Neither antidepressants nor other medications can stop or cure celiac disease. Often, medications may worsen other nutrient absorption problems, making the situation worse.

Take the case of Larry, a twenty-five-year-old physical therapist who began our first meeting by announcing that he had been diagnosed with attention-deficit hyperactivity disorder (ADHD), anxiety, and bipolar disorder. Over the previous five years, he had taken more than ten different medications without any relief from his symptoms. When I saw Larry, he was taking several medications, including Adderall, a stimulant, three times a day for attention problems; Xanax, a tranquilizer, to treat anxiety from the Adderall; and Seroquel, an antipsychotic, to help him sleep.

During my first meeting with Larry, I noticed he lacked iron. A twenty-five-year-old male who routinely eats meat should not lack iron. Further blood testing, and later, a biopsy, confirmed celiac disease. It took almost two years, but Larry no longer takes any psychiatric medications and no longer has three psychiatric diagnoses. Larry's symptoms of irritability, anxiety, and insomnia had been managed with medications, but nobody sought the true cause. If we find the cause, which in this case was celiac disease, we can better direct our treatment and, in some cases, find a cure.

It is easy to confuse celiac disease with anorexia, a disease that makes its victims—typically girls and women—believe that they are horribly fat and refuse to eat, even as they waste away. Both diseases attack nearly every organ and organ system of the body, causing overlapping symptoms such as the following:

- Abdominal pain
- Anemia
- Arthritis
- Behavioral changes
- Bowel gas
- Constipation
- Depression
- Diarrhea
- Fatigue
- Irritability
- Joint pain
- Memory loss
- Mood swings
- Osteoporosis
- Reproductive issues (infertility and miscarriages)
- Skin lesions
- Weakness
- Weight loss

It's also possible to have celiac disease without any stomach symptoms at all—no bloating, pain, gas, diarrhea, or other obvious indicators that something is wrong in the intestines. This makes the diagnosis even more difficult, even when the patient carefully lists each and every symptom for the doctor. As soon as a physician hears "migraines," "tingling of the hands," "difficulty conceiving," "arthritis," "skin rash," or any number of other symptoms, she likely refers the patient to a specialist. This is helpful for most people but can be harmful for those with celiac disease because it may send them down the wrong track, with a neurologist searching for a brain or nervous system explanation for migraines or tingling, a fertility specialist looking for a sex-organ–based reason for infertility, and so on. Each specialist prescribes the latest treatments for problems related to his or her specialty, but these work for only awhile or don't work at all, because the underlying problem—an intolerance to gluten—is not being addressed.

Making the diagnosis

Diagnosing celiac disease is difficult, which is why the disease is often misdiagnosed as anorexia, chronic fatigue syndrome, diverticulitis, irritable bowel syndrome (IBS), Crohn's disease, or iron-shortage anemia. Perhaps it's most important for a doctor to be aware of the diverse and often confusing symptoms of celiac disease. Otherwise, he might send a patient to several different specialists. In that case, the celiac disease is "chopped up" into several different disease categories, each of which is considered an entity unto itself instead of part of a whole.

Once celiac disease is suspected, a doctor can look for high levels of antibodies such as anti-gliadin, anti-endomysial, and anti-tissue transglutaminase. These are specialized proteins made by the immune system that tag gluten as the enemy so that it might be easily identified by the fighting cells of the body's internal defense system. A simple blood test reveals the presence of antibodies to gluten, which suggests the possibility of celiac disease. However, the only way to be sure of a correct diagnosis is to perform an endoscopy (insertion of a narrow, flexible tube into the intestines) and snip out a small piece of the intestinal lining for examination in the lab. This can confirm the diagnosis of celiac disease and reveal the extent of damage to the intestines.

Managing the disease

There is no treatment for celiac disease—no medication, vitamin, surgery, or procedure that can get rid of the disease and the damage it has already caused. Over time, the intestinal damage heals if the body is able to restore enough nutritional support.

Although celiac disease cannot be treated, it can be managed. The way to do that is to stop eating all foods containing gluten, including wheat, rye, and barley, and anything made from them. Removing these items from the diet would be challenging enough for many people, but the task is more complex than that because gluten, used as a thickening and stabilizing agent, shows up in many foods. Obvious ones include:

- Baking mixes
- Beer
- Bread
- Cakes and pies
- Pretzels
- Cereal
- Cookies and crackers
- Pastries
- Doughnuts
- Muffins
- Pasta

A number of not-so-obvious foods that contain gluten include:

- Ice cream
- Ketchup
- Soy sauce
- Licorice
- Sauces (thickened with flour)
- Salad dressings
- Chutneys and pickles
- Instant cocoa
- Processed meats
- Meat substitutes (such as veggie burgers)
- Spices (with anticaking agents)

Other foods, such as oats, must be avoided because they may accidentally be contaminated with gluten if they are processed in the same factory as gluten-containing foods. Even some lipsticks and lip glosses contain gluten.

Vegetables, fruits, and meat are gluten-free, so they can be eaten without restriction. A number of grains and starch sources are acceptable; these include rice, potatoes, corn, and tapioca. Gram flour, made from chickpeas, is also free of gluten, but gram flour should not be confused with graham flour (as in graham crackers), which is made from wheat.

As people are learning how to eat gluten-free, it's a good idea to assume that all processed and packaged foods contain gluten until proven otherwise. Sometimes the label specifically mentions gluten, while other times the gluten comes in forms such as glucose syrup, malt flavoring, vegetable protein, vegetable starch, and modified food starch. Gluten in food is often not on the label, which includes only the ingredients, not gluten that may be used to make the food. It's in this process that gluten from one food may work its way into another food.

I advise patients to look for foods that are specifically labeled gluten-free. Ideally, this means that the food contains no gluten and that none was added during processing. It also means that the food was processed and packaged in facilities that do not handle any foods containing gluten or with added gluten and that the packages were carefully sealed to ensure that no gluten got in during shipping or storage.

But problems with the current labeling regulations allow some gluten to remain in certain foods and allow food makers to determine how safe their foods are. So even a product labeled gluten-free may contain some gluten.

If you have celiac disease, removing gluten from your diet is the only way to stop ongoing damage to your intestines and to give your body the chance to heal.

Supplements for celiac disease

Unless a person is diagnosed with celiac disease very early on, there's a good chance that he or she has nutritional problems. That's why I recommend nutritional supplements to replace nutrients the body needs. This includes taking at least a multivitamin with iron, EFAs, and digestive enzymes. Testing commonly reveals individual needs for further nutrients, including iron, folate, magnesium, and amino acids.

In addition, 1–3 g of omega-3 fatty acids such as EPA and DHA can help reduce intestinal inflammation and assist healing.

I've seen people do remarkably well once their celiac disease is diagnosed and they begin a gluten-free diet. The physical symptoms that accompany eating often vanish, and many other problems resolve or begin to improve. The fatigue that is often coupled with celiac-related depression usually vanishes as well.

Just as I encourage every patient with depression to be tested for celiac disease, I also encourage doctors to test depressed patients for the presence of two peptides, casomorphin and gliadorphin.

Casomorphin, Gliadorphin, and Depression

Before the body can absorb food, it must break it down into tiny snippets that are digestible and recognized by the immune system as safe. The breakdown process begins as food is chewed and continues as enzymes in the stomach attack the food. For these enzymes to work, plenty of stomach acid must be available to activate them.

After the partially digested food moves from the stomach to the small intestine, the acid is neutralized. Different enzymes continue to chop the food into smaller and smaller pieces, releasing amino acids, vitamins, fatty acids, and other parts of the food so that they can pass through the intestinal wall and into the blood vessels in the intestinal wall. By the time protein from food reaches the bloodstream, it has been broken down into peptides, particles composed of only ten to twenty amino acids, which the body can reconfigure and recombine to create larger molecules, neurotransmitters, hormones, and more.

Although it may seem simple, the digestion–absorption process is complex and depends on the presence of just the right amount of stomach acid, numerous enzymes, and other factors. Should there be a problem with any of them, the process does not work well. For example, if there isn't enough stomach acid to activate the stomach enzymes, or if the acid isn't strong enough, food may pass from the stomach to the small intestines partially undigested. If the intestinal wall has been damaged, even properly digested nutrients may not be absorbed.

In some cases, problems arise due to the incomplete digestion of proteins that still manage to pass into the body. This is what happens when people are unable to completely digest the protein called casein, which is found in milk, cheese, and other milk products, and gluten, which comes from wheat, rye, barley, and certain other grains. Casein is broken down into a substance called casomorphin, and gluten is broken down into gliadorphin. Casomorphin and gliadorphin are products of incomplete breakdown that have been processed enough to slip into the body. But once inside, they can behave in unfortunate ways. Dr. David Perlmutter describes the destructive effects of indigestible gluten on brain function in his best-selling book *The Grain Brain.* He explains how even healthy grains can wreak havoc and how diets that are rich in gluten can cause inflammation and other neurological disorders.

Both casomorphin and gliadorphin are morphine analogs. This means they are chemically similar to morphine and may trigger morphine-like effects in the body. We don't fully understand how these two substances function in the body, but some experts think that they cross the blood–brain barrier and interact with parts of the brain that control behavior and feelings.

Casomorphin and gliadorphin were first found in higher concentrations in the urine of people with autism. Other research has linked the incomplete digestion of these proteins and related neuropeptides to a variety of conditions, including ADHD, childhood psychosis, dyslexia, Down syndrome, celiac disease, postpartum psychosis, Rett's disease, and severe depression. The appearance of excess peptides in people with a range of psychiatric disorders has led some researchers to believe that these peptides are unique carriers of information in the brain that may worsen many psychiatric disorders.

Levels of casomorphin and gliadorphin rise due to a shortage or inadequate functioning of an enzyme called DPP IV (dipeptidyl peptidase IV), which is responsible for snipping the casomorphin and gliadorphin proteins into small pieces. If there isn't enough DPP IV, casomorphin and gliadorphin are left intact and absorbed into the body. A number of things can cause DPP IV activity levels to fall. These include a shortage of zinc and other nutrients, certain antibiotics, interferon, gelatin, yeast from the *Candida* genus, and too-high levels of mercury, heavy metals, and pesticides in the body.

Researchers have measured levels of DPP IV activity in the blood of depressed and nondepressed patients, finding that there is much less activity in those with major depression and treatment-resistant depression than in healthy controls. Researchers think that a drop in DPP IV occurs during the severe phase of a depressive episode in certain people, making a lack of DPP IV both a cause and a result of depression.

More research is needed to fully understand the link between casomorphin and depression, but it's likely that a large number of depressed patients are suffering from the incomplete digestion of casein and gluten. On the scale of human evolution, casein and gluten are relatively new proteins in the human diet. Milk, cheese, and other milk products were not historically a big part of the diet because local agricultural economies did not domesticate animals until relatively recently, in the past several hundred years. Wheat, barley, and rye became widespread in the diet some ten thousand years ago with the spread of grain-based agriculture. Ten thousand years is not a lot of time for the human body to adapt and develop ways to prevent the absorption of casomorphin and gliadorphin.

Fortunately, most of us have little difficulty with gluten or casein. But an unknown number of people have difficulty completely breaking down the proteins, and the resulting casomorphin and gliadorphin may lead to psychiatric symptoms.

> Kathy had struggled with obsessive-compulsive disorder (OCD) and depression for most of her life. Her OCD started in childhood with obsessive worrying about germs, hurricanes, and the size of her head. As she got older, her OCD continued but interfered less with her life than her overwhelming depression. Depression limited her ability to succeed in school and at work, and, eventually Kathy ended up on disability. After urine testing showed elevated levels of casomorphin, Kathy dedicated her life to changing her diet, removing casein, taking nutritional supplements, and finding new hope for the possibilities of psychotherapy.
>
> According to Kathy, "All of a sudden, I had some understanding as to why I was feeling so out of control and depressed. No one ever looked for what was causing my problems." Kathy continues therapy but has started working part-time, has renewed connections with her friends, and is hopeful about the future. Her symptoms of OCD and depression have gone from "a nine on a scale of one to ten to a three."

Our understanding of casomorphin and gliadorphin is still evolving, but if there's any chance that they may be causing or contributing to someone's depression, it's worth checking with a simple urine test. If either of these substances is causing a problem, the most effective treatment is simple: stop eating the offending foods. In addition, supplemental DPP IV enzymes can be taken to increase DPP IV levels. This helps with digestion of any casomorphin or gliadorphin that is accidentally eaten.

Food Allergies and Depression

Food allergies must also be investigated and ruled out as a factor in depression. Food allergies are a difficult subject to deal with, for there is confusion about exactly what a food allergy is and whether people are truly allergic to one or more foods and how much.

Many people do have severe allergic reactions to foods, especially eggs, shrimp, and other shellfish. Their immune systems mistake harmless food for a dangerous enemy and launch a full-blown attack on the "invader," damaging the body during the battle. The result can be stomach pain, diarrhea, nausea, itching, eczema, difficulty breathing, nasal congestion, dizziness, and swelling of the lips, face, throat, and tongue. In some cases, the allergic reaction may be so severe that it causes anaphylactic shock, resulting in a significant drop in blood pressure, rapid heart rate, dizziness, airway constriction, and loss of consciousness. If medical treatment is not given quickly, an anaphylactic reaction can be life threatening.

These immediate hypersensitivity reactions are called IgE-mediated food allergies because immunoglobulin E is overactive. Most people with these types of food allergies know they have them because the reactions are usually severe. Another type of food allergy causes more nonspecific symptoms that can occur twenty-four to seventy-two hours after ingestion of the offending food. These reactions are called delayed hypersensitivity reactions and IgG-mediated food allergies because immunoglobulin G is primarily overactive. These reactions may include fatigue, depression, anxiety, stomach problems, and headaches. Many patients with IgG-delayed hypersensitivity reactions struggle with chronic unexplained health problems, including depression.

People with food allergies or food intolerances tend to have more depression than their healthy peers. It is unclear which psychological changes occur due to nutritional deficiencies and/or inflammation. In many cases, the depression improves when the food allergies are treated.

Although there is insufficient research, years of clinical experience have convinced me that food allergies contribute to many psychiatric illnesses, including ADHD, anxiety, and particularly, depression. The medical profession has minimized and dismissed this association for many years. A simple blood test can help determine food sensitivities. Although testing is not always 100 percent reliable, it does serve as a guide. Elimination diets, used to determine sensitivity to offending foods by introducing new foods one at a time, are another way of determining if you are sensitive to particular foods.

Other Gastrointestinal Problems and Depression

Besides celiac disease, other stomach problems are also linked to depression. People with either ulcerative colitis or Crohn's disease, both forms of inflammatory bowel disease (IBD), have been found to have higher rates of depression than the general public. A study published in the medical journal *Gut* found that about one-third of patients seeking treatment for IBD also had depression and anxiety. A Canadian study found that patients with IBD or other bowel disorders had depression rates triple those of the general population. It's clear that many patients who have ulcerative colitis or Crohn's disease also have depression.

Some of those who have ulcerative colitis or Crohn's may have psychiatric symptoms, such as depression and anxiety, without any of the normal physiological symptoms of abdominal pain, diarrhea, and weight loss. Depression or anxiety present before or, in some cases, without any physical symptoms, can lead to a delay in diagnosis and treatment of the underlying stomach problems.

Depression also plays a role in the course of Crohn's disease. Individuals with Crohn's disease have symptoms in bouts rather than continuously. Some studies have found that people with higher depression scores suffer more flare-ups of symptoms than those with lower depression scores.

It's important to consider all gastrointestinal disorders affecting nutrient absorption, including ulcerative colitis and Crohn's disease, when treating depression.

Chapter 11

Z—Zinc and Other Minerals

The idea that a daily nutritional supplement containing zinc and other minerals could relieve or even prevent depression is shocking to most psychiatrists. That reaction is equally shocking, for a great deal of research has been published in well-regarded scientific journals on the importance of zinc and other minerals for mental health. But psychiatry has largely ignored these findings in favor of medications with limited effectiveness and frequent side effects.

In this chapter, I review the scientific research supporting the use of zinc and other minerals for the treatment of depression. The key message is this: Minerals are important to healthy brain function and mood, as they play important roles in the functioning of neurotransmitters that regulate mood. I like to think of minerals as the raw materials of a healthy and happy outlook.

Zinc and Depression

Zinc is one of the most important minerals for mental health, a sort of metabolic spark plug that is everywhere in the body and that participates in some two hundred different enzyme reactions. Zinc, which is found in abundance in the brain, has a variety of duties, including:

- Helping make DNA and proteins
- Helping the immune system fight off viruses and bacteria
- Helping wounds heal
- Regulating neurotransmission in the brain
- Making it possible to taste and smell
- Making sex and reproduction possible
- Helping make enzymes needed to digest fats, carbohydrates, and protein

Zinc is found in a number of foods, including oysters, poultry, red meat, beans, whole grains, and nuts. The recommended daily intake of zinc for adult men and women is 11 mg/day and 8 mg/day, respectively, depending on age and the presence or absence of pregnancy or lactation.

Those at greatest risk for zinc shortage are vegetarians, because they don't eat the red meat and poultry that are the best sources of zinc; alcoholics and patients with eating disorders, because they absorb less of the mineral; and those with ulcerative colitis, Crohn's disease, or other conditions that interfere with zinc absorption. A number of medications can deplete the body's zinc supplies. These include aspirin; benazepril (Lotensin), which is used to treat high blood pressure; cholestyramine (Questran), which is used to reduce cholesterol; and ofloxacin (Floxin), which is used to treat pneumonia, bronchitis, and other infections.

A lack of zinc can lead to delayed growth in children and infants, hair loss, diarrhea, loss of appetite, weight loss, difficulty tasting food, acne, fatigue, elevated cholesterol, increased infections, memory impairment, impotence, and other problems. A lack of zinc has also been linked to anorexia, impaired cognitive function, and other behavioral disturbances.

Numerous studies have linked low blood levels of zinc to depression in both men and women. A study performed by a team of researchers from Belgium, the United States, and Italy confirmed that zinc levels are lower in people with major depression. This study also found that levels are particularly low in people with treatment-resistant depression, raising the possibility that measuring zinc levels before starting treatment may help identify those least likely to respond to standard medicine and who need the most individualized care.

Low zinc levels have also been found in females with postpartum depression. One study examined sixty-six women on the third and thirtieth days following childbirth, checking both their zinc levels and the depth of their depression. On analyzing the results, the researchers found a link between the severity of depressive symptoms and decreased zinc in the blood.

Another study examined zinc levels in female university students. After screening a random selection of young women, the researchers selected twenty-three with moderate or severe depression and compared them with twenty-three healthy students. Participants filled out food questionnaires and had blood samples taken to determine how much zinc they consumed and the amount of zinc in their blood. The results were clear-cut and dramatic: Both daily intake of zinc and zinc levels in the bloodstream were about one-third lower in the depressed women than in the healthy women. More than 20 percent of the depressed women had blood levels low enough to be considered lacking in zinc, whereas none of the healthy women did.

In 2013, researchers showed that the lower the zinc concentration in depressed subjects, the more severe the depression, and vice versa. Similarly, a 2014 study found that low dietary zinc intake is linked to more cases of depression in both men and women. In a group of one hundred psychiatric patients, 41 percent were found to lack zinc, compared with only 14.4 percent in a group of healthy people.

What is the zinc–depression link?

How could a mineral influence mood that much? We don't know exactly how, but there are several theories. An obvious one is that zinc levels are low in depressed people simply because depression reduces both appetite and interest in eating. Thus, depressed people are likely to eat less and to eat fewer healthful foods, resulting in lower zinc levels. According to this argument, low zinc is a *result* of depression, not a cause. However, studies with depressed patients have not found any link between decreased appetite and zinc levels. So while depression may reduce the appetite, it is most likely not the cause of very low zinc levels.

Other explanations offer biochemistry as the link between zinc and depression. One theory holds that the body's inflammatory response system is activated when depression strikes. According to this theory, the body treats depression like a physical enemy that can be destroyed in the same way viruses or bacteria are destroyed. The inflammatory response triggers many biochemical changes, including lowering the amount of albumin, a protein that transports zinc through the bloodstream. The shortfall of zinc in the blood, then, may be due to fewer "zinc buses" available to move it around. So while there may be enough zinc in the body, it can't get to the places it needs to go.

Another possibility is that the liver might be snatching up all the zinc it can to make more substances needed for the inflammatory response. It's as if the body were saying, "Right now, it's more important to use zinc to create the substances that fight off invaders, so it's okay to let the mood suffer."

These and other ideas have all been supported by studies with animals and humans, but we have not yet found the exact link between zinc and depression. Although it's not known exactly how zinc works in depression, one study suggests that it works by inhibiting N-methyl-D-aspartate (NMDA) receptors in the brain. NMDA receptors control the activity of the powerful excitatory neurotransmitter glutamate. Glutamate is responsible for sending signals between nerve cells, and under normal conditions, it is important in learning and memory. However, when there is too much glutamate in the brain, it can lead to overstimulation, resulting in progressive damage to the function of neurons, which is commonly associated with depression. The science of the zinc–depression link is complex and involves numerous biochemical pathways that may take years to untangle.

Can zinc relieve depression?

We can effectively use zinc for depression, even though we don't know precisely how it works. This is true of a surprising number of medicines. Exactly how they effectively treat an illness is often a mystery. Indeed, aspirin was first made in the 1890s and soon became one of the most popular medications in the world. But it wasn't until the 1970s that medical scientists realized that it worked by interfering with the making of inflammation-producing substances called prostaglandins.

Animal studies reinforce the idea that zinc has antidepressant properties and that it works well in combination with certain standard antidepressants. Consider the following:

- Lab animals given citalopram (Celexa) had significant increases in zinc blood levels.
- When given citalopram or imipramine, lab animals showed increased zinc levels in the hippocampus and decreased levels in other parts of the brain.
- Multiple courses of electroconvulsive therapy (ECT), a treatment for advanced cases of depression, triggered changes in the hippocampus that suggest an increase in the activity of zinc in that area of the brain.
- Supplemental zinc has an antidepressant effect in lab animals subjected to stress.
- Low doses of citalopram (Celexa) and imipramine (Tofranil) are ineffective as antidepressants in lab animals stressed by being forced

to swim for long periods. But these medications become effective antidepressants when low doses of zinc are added.

- Chronic treatment with antidepressants and ECT causes zinc levels to increase in the brains of rats.
- In laboratory animals, a zinc-deficient diet triggers depression-like symptoms, including anorexia and anxiety. Giving zinc-deficient animals fluoxetine (Prozac) reduces their despair.

The results of these and other animal studies suggest that zinc levels are linked to depression and that the mineral has antidepressant effects. New evidence is showing that zinc makes standard antidepressants more potent in humans. This was demonstrated in a study of fourteen people with major depression who were randomly assigned to take either 25 mg of zinc daily or a placebo, along with their standard medications (SSRIs and tricyclic antidepressants). The study was double blind, which means that neither doctors nor patients knew who was receiving the zinc until the end of the study. The HDRS and the Beck Depression Inventory were used to measure the depth of the patients' depression. Depression was assessed at the beginning of the study and two, six, and twelve weeks after treatment began.

The results were interesting: At the end of the study, the patients taking zinc had much less severe symptoms of depression according to the Hamilton and Beck scores. Depression severity scores fell faster in the group given the placebo and antidepressant initially. But by week six, scores were much lower in the zinc-plus-antidepressant group, and they remained lower for the rest of the study. Although this was a small study, the important findings reinforce the argument that zinc strengthens the effects of standard antidepressants.

The researchers who conducted this study followed up with the first large-scale clinical study of "added zinc therapy." For this second study, sixty adults aged eighteen to fifty-five with major depression were randomly assigned to receive either imipramine plus 25 mg of zinc daily or imipramine plus a placebo for twelve weeks. This was also a double-blind study, with the mood measured with different depression scales. Overall, adding zinc to the standard medication improved both the speed and strength of the medication. Even more interesting, the volunteers who were most affected were those who had not been helped by the standard

Zinc Taste Test

There is no single, widely accepted blood test for zinc status. Instead, doctors measure zinc levels in the blood, blood cells, and even hair in an attempt to determine exactly how much zinc a patient has available for use.

I have found that the single best method for assessing zinc status is the zinc taste test, which is based on the fact that the sense of taste depends on having enough zinc in the body.

It is safe for anyone to try the zinc taste test, because the solution used in the test has a very dilute concentration of zinc.

For the test, a liquid zinc sulfate supplement is kept at room temperature for two hours. The patient does not eat, drink, or smoke for an hour before the test to make sure there are no competing flavors in the mouth. The patient takes a small drink of the zinc solution (1 tsp), swirls it around in his or her mouth for ten seconds, and then either spits it out or swallows it. The patient records the taste according to the categories listed below:

Responses

Category 1: Has no taste or tastes like water

Category 2: Has no taste at first but after a few seconds has a dry, mineral, bicarbonate, "furry," or sweet taste

Category 3: At first has a definite but not strongly unpleasant taste, which tends to get stronger over time

Category 4: Has an immediate unpleasant, strong, or metallic taste, which may linger for a half hour or more

Interpreting the Results

A category 1 or 2 response indicates a zinc shortage that will likely benefit from zinc supplementation.

A category 3 or 4 response suggests that zinc status is adequate. Supplementation of zinc should be used as part of a preventive nutritional strategy.

medications alone. This suggests that, for many of those who are not helped by standard medications, zinc may be the missing ingredient in their treatment regimen, either in combination with antidepressant medication or on its own.

Recent research shows that zinc deprivation can result in behavioral disturbances, including dysphoria, impaired cognitive function, learning disabilities, and neurological disorders. In one study, researchers found that zinc levels in depressed participants were 22 percent lower, on average, than those of healthy volunteers.

Zinc may also be helpful in individuals who don't have a diagnosis of major depression yet have low moods. This idea was investigated by a team of Japanese researchers who enlisted thirty premenopausal women in a double-blind study comparing the effectiveness of zinc with that of a vitamin pill. Volunteers were randomly assigned to take either 7 mg of zinc or a multivitamin pill daily for ten weeks. Their blood was checked before and after the study, and their mood was monitored using standard depression and mood scales. At the end of the ten-week period, the women taking zinc enjoyed a big decrease in their depression-dejection and anger-hostility scores compared with the vitamin group. In addition, blood levels of zinc rose in the zinc group but not in the vitamin group. The researchers concluded that zinc supplements may be an effective treatment for depression and anger.

Studies have shown that zinc supplementation, either alone or as an add-on to other therapies, can be beneficial in the treatment of depression. One systematic review of randomized, controlled trials published in 2012 examined the efficacy of zinc supplementation for reducing or preventing depressive symptoms. All the controlled trials included in this review found that zinc was an effective adjuvant therapy to standard antidepressant treatment.

Research has shown that people with major depression have zinc levels that are 12 to 16 percent lower than those who are not depressed. A recent analysis reviewed seventeen studies that measured blood zinc levels in 1,643 depressed people and 804 healthy controls. The authors of the study found that zinc concentrations were lower in the depressed patients. Zinc deficiencies also set off a cascade of other biological actions that impair cognitive function and disrupt mood regulation. The severity of depressive symptoms was also associated with greater zinc deficiencies.

Scientific evidence clearly suggests that zinc is needed for good mental health. Unfortunately, zinc research will continue slowly, at best, for no major drug company will spend tens of millions of dollars studying a mineral it cannot patent and sell for profit. However, psychiatrists and patients interested in natural treatments for depression should understand how to assess and treat zinc shortages.

If the results of the zinc taste test are in category 1 or 2, I generally recommend 30 mg of zinc supplementation taken three times daily—90 mg maximum per day. If the results of the zinc taste test are in category 3 or 4, a multivitamin that contains at least 15 mg of zinc should be adequate.

Although it is safe to take zinc at home, I believe that it is best as part of a comprehensive nutritional and medical treatment plan. Not all depressed people are zinc deficient, and not all respond to zinc supplementation.

When twenty-eight-year-old Gabi came to my office, she was on three antidepressants and had a fourteen-year history of depression. She believed that the medications "kept [her] going" but did not improve her mood.

During our first meeting, I noticed many signs and symptoms of a lack of zinc in Gabi: She thought the zinc taste test solution tasted like water. She also had adult acne and white spots on her fingernails. Routine blood work showed that she had low levels of alkaline phosphatase. This enzyme, made primarily in the liver, needs zinc for optimal function. Due to its zinc-dependent function, alkaline phosphatase can be used as a functional measure of zinc shortage. As zinc is added back, alkaline phosphatase levels increase.

As Gabi started taking liquid zinc, she noticed improvement in her mood and participated in the other protocols described in this book. It was almost a month before Gabi started to notice a strong metallic taste during the zinc taste test, which indicated that she had enough zinc. Over the course of a year, Gabi was taken off antidepressants, and she no longer struggles with the darkness of depression.

Anyone who continues to have symptoms of depression should be assessed for a zinc shortage. And unless the zinc levels are on the high end of normal, patients should be given zinc supplementation and encouraged to eat ample amounts of zinc-containing foods.

Copper and Depression

With zinc, the problem is too little; with copper, it may be too much *or* too little.

Copper is a micronutrient, which means the human body needs it in relatively tiny amounts. Found mostly in the heart, liver, brain, and kidney, copper has a variety of functions, including helping in the growth or maintenance of red blood cells, bones, nerves, and the brain. It also helps make the prostaglandins needed to regulate heartbeat and blood pressure; plays a part in getting the energy out of fats, protein, and carbohydrates; and helps the body fight free radicals. Copper is found in liver and other organ meats, shellfish, whole-grain cereals and breads, dark green leafy vegetables, peas, poultry, nuts, and beans.

Check the Copper!

Every patient's copper level should be checked. If it is high, remove sources of accidental ingestion or absorption. Possible ways that you may ingest or absorb too much copper include:

- Absorbing copper from dental fixtures
- Drinking water from copper pipes
- Eating food cooked in copper cookware
- Being exposed to copper at work (a problem for plumbers, machinists, welders, and others who work with copper)
- Using certain birth control pills or a copper intrauterine device (IUD)

On the other hand, if the copper level is low, supplementation may be necessary. The problem may be dietary, especially if you are on a strict diet or a crash weight-loss diet. Celiac disease, short bowel syndrome, or any other diseases that interfere with copper absorption can lead to low levels. Elderly persons are also more likely to lack copper. However, the most common cause of low copper is taking too-high doses of zinc supplements (more than 100 mg per day) without professional monitoring. Too much zinc can decrease copper levels and cause depression. The delicate balance between zinc and copper reinforces the need for patients to have mineral levels and supplementation monitored by a health professional.

A lack of copper can lead to anemia, high blood pressure, diarrhea, difficulty breathing, lowered immune function, electrocardiogram (ECG) abnormalities, and other problems. A lack of copper may be caused by a poor diet, digestive or intestinal disorders that interfere with nutrient absorption, chronic diarrhea, and even excess zinc, because copper and zinc compete to be absorbed in the intestines. A number of medications can interfere with copper absorption. These include delavirdine (Rescriptor), used to treat HIV infection; ethambutol (Myambutol), used to treat tuberculosis; and penicillamine, used to treat rheumatoid arthritis. Elderly persons, vegetarians, athletes, people who do difficult physical work, pregnant women, and premature infants are most likely to lack copper. Healthy adults eating a varied diet are not likely to lack copper.

Too much copper and depression

Too much copper can be a problem, because the mineral is an important component of enzymes involved in depression (monoamine oxidase, dopamine-beta-hydroxylase, and tyrosine hydroxylase). These enzymes stimulate and regulate the production of dopamine, one of the most important neurotransmitters in the brain.

We've known for many years that depressed patients may have high blood levels of copper. For example, one study compared copper levels in the blood of thirty-five depressed people to those of thirty-five healthy people. Copper levels were much higher in the depressed group than they were in the nondepressed group, and they declined when the patients had recovered from their depression.

Ongoing research continues to expand our knowledge of the link between copper and depression. For example, a 2007 study compared copper levels in seventy-eight women with postpartum depression to those in nondepressed women, as well as to levels in women who had had a form of depression other than postpartum depression. Copper levels were very much elevated in the women with postpartum depression compared with the nondepressed women and the women who had once had other forms of depression.

A study published in 2010 in the *Journal of Affective Disorders* reported that copper levels were higher in thirteen people with depression than in thirteen healthy people.

We don't know why copper levels rise in depressed people. We do know that copper is necessary for the neurotransmitter dopamine to change into norepinephrine, so excess copper may upset the normal balance of brain chemicals. Other theories include the possibility that excess copper interferes with the making of cellular energy or the sending of signals through the nervous system. It may also be that both high copper levels and depression are the results of something else, perhaps an inflammatory reaction in the body or a lack of zinc.

Many years may pass before all the biochemical pathways linking too-high copper to depression are identified and fully understood. In the meantime, high copper levels in depressed patients should be recognized and treated. Often, the treatment may be simply adding zinc supplements and, if possible, finding the source of the extra copper. Some studies have shown that high copper levels in depressed people return to normal (or near normal) with standard antidepressants, further suggesting that normalizing copper levels may be a treatment for depression in some patients.

Low copper and depression

There is also the problem of not having enough copper. Although there is not as much research into the problem of low copper as high copper, over the years, I have found low copper levels to be a big problem. I've been surprised by the number of times I have found low copper levels in depressed patients and have been pleased to see those patients' moods improve when copper levels were returned to normal. The link between low copper and depression is likely dopamine. Copper is needed to make dopamine, so a lack of copper may lead to low levels of the mood-balancing neurotransmitter.

> I remember well a young woman named Megan who was referred to me by her family doctor for the treatment of depression. As we talked about her diet, I learned that this twenty-seven-year-old accountant ate a balanced and healthful diet, filled with fresh vegetables, fruits, and whole grains, plus modest amounts of fish and red meat. Her nutrient levels should have been ideal, but testing of her serum copper and red blood copper showed that her copper levels were below normal. Fortunately, she responded well to supplemental copper, 4 mg per day. Her copper levels rose, and her depression lifted.

Magnesium and Depression

I have discussed how magnesium aids in sleep, but the mineral plays many other roles in the body, including a role in depression. Magnesium is an essential nutrient found in relatively large amounts throughout the body. About 54 percent of the body's magnesium resides in the bones, with an additional 27 percent in the muscles and 19 percent in the heart and liver. Relatively little magnesium is found in the blood (only about 1 percent), but stable blood levels of magnesium are very important, and the body regulates them tightly. The mineral takes part in more than three hundred biochemical reactions, contributing to good health in many ways, including the following:

- Maintaining a healthy immune system
- Keeping the bones strong
- Regulating blood pressure
- Making proteins
- Ensuring that the nerves work properly
- Keeping the heart beating steadily

A lack of magnesium can cause irregular heartbeat, nausea, lack of appetite, seizures, fatigue, muscle weakness, poor coordination, and other problems, including personality changes. It may also worsen psychological problems such as depression and apathy, irritability, nervousness, anxiety, excessive emotional reactions and frequent mood changes, decreased memory and concentration, migraines, fatigue, and ADHD. Very low magnesium intake is linked to depression, especially in young adults.

Those at risk for a lack of magnesium include people with Crohn's disease or other illnesses that interfere with nutrient absorption, alcoholics, diabetics with poorly controlled disease, and senior citizens. Certain medications can interfere with the body's ability to absorb and/or use magnesium. These include diuretics such as furosemide (Lasix) and bumetanide (Bumex), as well as antibiotics such as gentamicin.

Magnesium is found in dark green leafy vegetables, nuts, whole-grain breads, beans, and peas. It is one of the first minerals to be stripped from foods as they are processed. Refined grains have only a fraction of the magnesium found in whole grains. It is also one of the first minerals to be cleared from the body during stress, which means that everyone with chronic stress—even if it's low-level stress—is at risk for a shortage.

Many Americans lack magnesium. According to studies, "substantial numbers of U.S. adults fail to consume adequate magnesium in their diets." More exactly, about two-thirds of Americans consume less than the recommended dietary allowance (RDA) of magnesium (420 mg for men; 320 mg for women). This is not surprising, as the processed foods that make up so much of the modern diet are relatively low in magnesium. In addition, magnesium and other minerals are often removed from water used for drinking and cooking. Consumption of dietary magnesium has decreased over the past century to a shocking degree, with estimates of daily magnesium consumed decreasing from roughly 500 mg per day in the early 1900s to less than 300 mg per day today.

A dietary shortage of magnesium should be of great concern to those with mood problems, as a lack of magnesium can trigger depression. This has been shown by clearing magnesium stores in mice, which then show an increase in anxiety and depression-like behaviors. In humans, the risk of depression increases when magnesium intake is low. In addition, patients with treatment-resistant suicidal depression or those who have attempted suicide often have low magnesium levels in their cerebrospinal fluid (CSF). However, blood levels of magnesium that are too high can also occur in depressed patients. This sounds confusing until you remember that the body tries to keep the blood magnesium level within a very narrow range. When magnesium stores or activity gets out of sync, as appears to happen in depression, the body may raise the blood levels too high. So high blood magnesium may also be a marker of depression.

Exactly how these changes in magnesium levels in the brain, CSF, or elsewhere set the stage for depression is unknown. One theory is that a lack of magnesium allows an excess of calcium to flow into certain areas of the nervous system, damaging the nerves and causing symptoms similar to those of depression. A lack of magnesium may also reduce brain levels of the neurotransmitter serotonin.

Knowing that depressed people tend to consume less magnesium and that there is less magnesium in the CSF of depressed patients, it's fair to ask whether giving supplemental magnesium can relieve depression. This question has not been studied in depth, but as far back as 1921, a published study described how treatment with magnesium was successful in 220 out of 250 people with what was then called "agitated depression."

One clinical study compared magnesium with the standard antidepressant medication imipramine. For this study, twenty-three senior citizens with type 2 diabetes, depression, and low blood levels of magnesium were randomly assigned to receive either 450 mg of elemental magnesium or 50 mg of imipramine daily for twelve weeks. At the end of the study period, depression ratings were equally improved in both groups, indicating that magnesium is an effective treatment in depressed people who lack magnesium.

This study opens the door to the type of personalized treatment that I promote: All patients should be tested for a lack of magnesium. Their dietary and supplemental intake of the mineral should be analyzed, and any factors that may deplete the body of magnesium (such as stress) should be investigated. If the dietary magnesium intake is low or if the blood levels are not safely within the normal range, you should be urged to eat a magnesium-rich diet and take magnesium supplements.

In addition, factors that may be depleting the body of magnesium should be addressed. For example, in the case of stress-induced magnesium loss, the individual could try meditation or take stress-management classes. Magnesium-depleting medications should be switched to those that do not interfere with the mineral and so on. Such a plan must be devised on an individual basis, because each patient is unique. Simply recommending the averages calculated from large groups of people may lead to inadequate treatment.

Four common symptoms of a lack of magnesium are:

- Insomnia
- Anxiety
- Constipation
- Muscle spasms

If a patient has any of these symptoms, I recommend 300–600 mg of magnesium (magnesium glycinate or magnesium citrate) per day. The dose of magnesium can be adjusted based on improvement of the symptoms. Chronic constipation may disappear in as little as a few weeks.

Lithium and Depression

Another mineral related to depression is lithium. Most people know that lithium is a medication used to prevent and treat the manic phase of bipolar disorder. What many don't realize is that lithium isn't made in the lab. It is a natural metallic element listed in the periodic table of elements, along with hydrogen, nitrogen, sodium, potassium, and others. Lithium can be found in every organ and tissue, and the U.S. Department of Agriculture has determined that it is an ultratrace element that appears essential for human health. Research indicates that lithium helps stabilize mood, regulate neurotransmitter signaling, and protect brain cells from early death and performs other duties. The typical American adult takes in 650–3,100 micrograms (μg) of lithium each day, primarily from grains, vegetables, and water.

Like many other elements, lithium influences human biochemistry. As early as the 1870s, it was used to treat mania at New York's Bellevue Hospital Medical College. Although it proved successful as a medication, it was eventually set aside and ignored by the mental health community. But in 1949, an Australian psychiatrist rediscovered it as a helpful treatment for mania, and it was approved for that purpose in the United States in 1970.

Research into lithium's potential antidepressant effects began as far back as the 1960s. In 1981, a paper published in the *British Journal of Psychiatry* reported that adding lithium to the standard antidepressants of eight volunteers who had not been helped by standard medications produced "remarkable relief of their depression within 48 hours." Through 2010, more than forty studies showed the value of lithium augmentation in treating depression; ten of these were double-blind, placebo-controlled research studies (the gold standard).

A meta analysis of the ten double-blind studies, which used statistical methods to combine these results and produce a larger, more robust look at the subject, found that adding lithium to standard antidepressant medications produced much better effects than using the medications alone. Lithium plus standard medication had a response rate of 41.2 percent, compared with a 14.4 percent response rate for placebo plus standard medicine.

Research also indicates that lithium may be helpful in treating aggressive behavior. Violent criminals have been found to have low levels of lithium in their hair (an indication of reduced lithium throughout the body). An investigation into the drinking water in twenty-seven Texas counties found that the incidence of rape, suicide, and homicide was much higher in counties with water containing little or no lithium than in those with water containing larger amounts (70–170 μg/L).

Lithium has clearly been shown to be helpful in reducing suicide and suicide attempts in people with mood disorders. A meta-analysis published in the *Journal of Clinical Psychiatry* in 2007 "statistically married" eight separate studies involving 329 people with major depressive disorder. It found that lithium reduced the risk of suicide and suicide attempts by 88 percent. These findings expanded on a 2005 meta-analysis published in the *American Journal of Psychiatry*, which found that "lithium is effective in the prevention of suicide, deliberate self-harm and death from all causes in patients with mood disorders." A 2010 study compared the levels of lithium in tap water to the suicide rate in eighteen different cities in Japan. It found that the lower the lithium, the higher the suicide rate; likewise, the higher the lithium, the lower the suicide rate.

We don't know how lithium lifts and stabilizes mood. Lithium influences the actions of numerous enzymes, hormones, vitamins, and other substances in the body, so it may act in multiple ways. Lithium increases the activity of the important brain enzyme MAO, and it may help the body use vitamins B_{12} and folate.

New research has shown that lithium may stabilize mood by fighting the effects of inflammation in the brain. The study involved feeding rats either a diet containing lithium chloride or a diet free of lithium for six weeks. At the end of six weeks, inflammation-inducing bacteria were introduced into their brains, which were then analyzed. The researchers found that lithium reduced levels of the inflammatory compound arachidonic acid and increased levels of the anti-inflammatory compound 17-hydroxy-docosahexaenoic acid (17-OH-DHA). Extra or unwanted inflammation can damage sensitive brain cells, which can contribute to depression. Lithium lowers damage-inducing inflammation. Some research also points to the ability of low-dose zinc to protect against Alzheimer's disease, although further research is needed.

Lithium as a prescription medication is used long-term in doses of 600–1,800 mg/day. At these doses, side effects are common, and some are permanent, including kidney damage and thyroid damage. These side effects limit the use of lithium at prescription strength.

In my practice, I use lithium in doses found naturally in food and in supplements from health-food stores. I have had great success stabilizing mood in patients with lithium in the form of lithium orotate at doses of 5 –20 mg. The doses are so low that I have rarely seen any side effects, and blood tests are not required to monitor levels. Lithium orotate has been particularly helpful in patients who have a family history of alcoholism, bipolar disorder, or depression.

> David's experience illustrates the danger of high levels of lithium. David is a forty-year-old patient with bipolar disorder who has been treated with lithium for many years. After he developed kidney damage, he was unable to continue taking lithium, and no other medication helped. David remained depressed for two years before coming to see me. David got his life back on 10 mg of lithium orotate, and fortunately, the damage to his kidneys has not worsened.

Although the psychiatric community tends to view lithium strictly as a medication, I prefer to view it as nature's mood stabilizer, necessary for most people only in the small amounts that can be gotten from food and water. Refer to the "Resources" section for more information on the beneficial effects of low-dose lithium.

Chromium and Depression

Chromium is another trace element linked to depression. Humans require small amounts of chromium for good health, although we can't fully explain everything it does in the body. The mineral is found in a wide variety of foods, but most foods contain relatively small amounts, making it difficult to meet the necessary daily dietary intake of 50–200 µg per day. In addition, body stores of the mineral can be cleared by infection, exercise, physical trauma, diets containing large amounts of simple sugars, and other forms of stress.

Chromium is often recommended to help balance insulin use and cholesterol levels. It has been shown to stabilize blood sugar and energy levels. It can get rid of sugar cravings by increasing the ability of insulin to move sugar into cells. Chromium also helps lower body-fat levels, total cholesterol, triglycerides, and low-density lipoprotein (LDL, or "bad cholesterol") while raising high-density lipoprotein (HDL, or "good cholesterol.")

As for chromium and depression, a 2000 paper published in the *International Journal of Neuropsychopharmacology* described what happened when eight patients with difficult-to-treat major depressive disorder, dysthymic disorder, or bipolar disorder were given chromium supplements. In every case, the patients enjoyed "dramatic improvements in their symptoms and functioning." None of the patients had ever had a satisfactory response to standard antidepressant therapy. With chromium, they all enjoyed the lifting of their depression. This news was encouraging but limited, because the eight patients were individual case studies rather than one large, placebo-controlled clinical study. Since then, larger studies have shown promising results.

In 2015, researchers found that chromium had antidepressant effects by decreasing immobility and enhancing swimming in a forced swim test in rats under chronic, unpredictable mild stress.

Researchers from Duke University Medical Center enlisted fifteen people with major depressive disorder, atypical type. The study participants were randomly assigned to receive either 600 μg of chromium picolinate or a placebo daily for eight weeks. At the end of the study period, 70 percent of those taking chromium responded to treatment, compared with 0 percent of the placebo group. Although this was a small study, the researchers concluded that chromium shows "promising antidepressant effects" against this form of major depressive disorder.

A larger study involved 110 people with either major depressive disorder or dysthymia. The participants were randomly assigned to take 400 μg of chromium picolinate per day for two weeks and then 600 μg per day for another six weeks, or a placebo for the entire eight weeks. The HDRS was used to measure the severity of the patients' depression at the beginning and the degree of improvement at the end of the study. Among those who began the study with carbohydrate cravings, chromium was shown to be better than placebo in reducing both depressive symptoms and cravings.

As with so many medications and supplements, we don't know exactly how chromium works against depression. It is known to increase insulin sensitivity, and depression has been linked to insulin resistance. Perhaps restoring insulin sensitivity also enhances the activity of serotonin and noradrenaline. This large study reinforced the theory that chromium is an effective antidepressant for patients with carbohydrate cravings. These findings also reinforce my conviction that each patient must be treated as an individual; chromium may be an effective treatment for some, while another approach may be needed for others. We must break away from the one-medication-fits-all concept of psychiatry and view the patient as an individual with unique biochemistry and unique needs.

Most primary care physicians and psychiatrists do not check chromium levels in their patients. I believe we should do so routinely. If the levels are low or low-normal, we should recommend chromium supplements. Chromium picolinate at a dose of 400–600 μg per day is usually enough to build up a good level of chromium.

Iodine and Depression

An essential trace mineral found naturally in food and in the human body, iodine is used to make the thyroid hormones T_3 and T_4. The thyroid gland "snatches" iodine in the blood and incorporates it into these hormones. The human body needs relatively small amounts of this mineral. But should it run low, the thyroid enlarges in size as it tries harder and harder to get the iodine it needs, eventually growing large enough to be a visible goiter. And, of course, no matter how large the thyroid grows, if there simply is not enough iodine available, it cannot make the precious hormones.

Iodine is found in ocean water and in soil, although the amount in the soil varies from region to region. It's also found in iodized salt, which is a major source of the mineral for many people.

We have long known that problems with the thyroid gland and thyroid hormones can trigger psychiatric symptoms and that even mild problems with thyroid function can increase the risk of a psychiatric disorder. We also know that, in up to 25 percent of those with depression, there is a weak response to a "request" for more thyroid hormone from the pituitary gland. In addition, researchers have found that when thyroid hormone is added to standard antidepressant therapy, the response can be better than that seen with the medication alone. This suggests that iodine levels should be monitored in depressed patients and, if low, pushed up to well within the normal range.

There is not a large body of scientific evidence showing that simply taking iodine relieves depression. But I remind you that many factors contribute to and maintain depression. As I pointed out in chapter 8, the standard tests for a lack of thyroid shortage may be misleading, so it's not enough to perform a standard TSH test and assume that everything is okay. Instead, I suggest a full thyroid screening (checking free T_3 and T_4 levels), plus monitoring iodine intake and levels. For a certain number of people, simply bringing iodine up to an adequate level and restoring proper thyroid function can go a long way toward resolving depression.

Iron and Depression

Finally, let's look at the mineral iron. It's rare that a psychiatrist or physician considers a lack of iron a potential cause of depression. However, this connection is common. Iron is important for regulating cell growth and serving as part of the hemoglobin molecule within red blood cells, which carries oxygen through the blood. A shortage of iron results in a lack of fresh oxygen being brought to body cells, leading to fatigue, a weakened immune system, and many psychological problems, including poor attention. Signs of iron shortage include weakness, fatigue, digestive problems, fragile bones, difficulty maintaining body temperature, increased infections, and poor performance at work or school.

Iron is found in red meat, fish, poultry, beans, lentils, iron-fortified cereals, and other foods. An iron shortage is caused by low consumption of these foods and/or high consumption of foods rich in iron inhibitors (such as fiber and phytate). Worldwide, a lack of iron is the No. 1 nutrient shortage. Those at greatest risk for a shortage include:

- Pregnant women (more iron is required during pregnancy)
- Older infants
- Toddlers
- Teenage girls
- Women of childbearing age (especially if they have heavy menstrual bleeding)
- Those with celiac disease or other stomach disorders that interfere with iron absorption

How does a lack of iron affect depression? It can depress mood, as was shown in a 2007 study involving 192 young women in Tehran. Of these women, seventy-seven were depressed, and 125 were not. After measuring iron levels, the researchers found that the average iron level in the depressed women was much lower than in the healthy women.

Iron-shortage anemia also affects the emotions of women after they have given birth. This was shown in a 2005 study involving depressed South African women (some of whom did not have enough iron and some of whom did) who had just given birth. Some of the new mothers were given daily doses of vitamin C and folate; others received vitamin C, folate, and 125 mg of iron. The women and their babies were monitored, with testing ten weeks after birth and again at nine months. Among the women who lacked iron, iron supplementation resulted in a 25 percent improvement in depression and stress scales over the course of the study.

One 2014 study suggested that people with emotional disorders such as anxiety may lack vitamins and minerals and may need more supplementation than healthy people. The next year, researchers showed that high doses of iron given in stressful situations decrease depressive-like behavior. In a 2012 study of 1,875 people older than sixty-five in England, researchers found that subjects with depression were more likely to have an iron shortage, but this link was accounted for by physical health status.

Depressed mood and other behavioral problems linked to low iron status can show up even before iron levels are low enough to fall into the iron-shortage anemia category. But physicians and psychiatrists often overlook emotional problems that begin to surface as iron levels drop into the low-normal range and don't become alarmed until levels fall far enough to qualify as a "real problem."

I recommend that all patients have their iron and ferritin levels checked—especially women with heavy menstrual bleeding. Levels of ferritin, a protein that binds to iron, are checked because most of the iron stored in the body is bound to ferritin. If levels of both iron and ferritin are low, more iron-containing foods should be eaten and/or iron supplements should be taken. I like to see ferritin levels close to 100 µg/L and iron levels higher than 50 µg/dL. Low levels of iron and depression often coexist in older people, although the lack of iron may be more to do with their physical health or the presence of chronic disease.

I generally recommend starting supplementation with a form of iron called ferrous bisglycinate, which does not cause the typical side effects of iron supplementation, including nausea, constipation, and stomach upset. I also recommend taking 10 mg of ferritin supplements twice per day until iron and ferritin levels return to normal.

However, use caution when supplementing, because too much iron can be harmful. Iron supplements should not be taken by men or postmenopausal women unless there is a clear indication of a shortage, because neither group has an ongoing means of disposing of excess iron.

Take-Home Message

In this chapter, I've looked at a lot of studies examining the link between depression and zinc, copper, magnesium, lithium, chromium, iodine, and iron. The key points to remember are:

- Minerals and other nutrients influence brain function and mood.
- Doctors should always consider the possibility of excess or inadequate amounts of trace minerals (or an imbalance) when assessing patients for depression.
- Everyone with depression should be evaluated for a lack of trace minerals.
- Everyone is unique, and each person's needs must be assessed individually.
- Taking too much of any trace mineral sets up imbalances among minerals, and supplementation should always be done under the guidance of a health professional.

Many Americans eat too much food but do not eat nutrient-dense whole foods. There may be plenty of calories, but too many of us lack the nutrients we need for top mental and physical health. Although vitamins and vitamin shortages receive considerable attention today, I believe our trace mineral shortages have more effects on mental health—in particular, depression. Fortunately, in many cases, our nutrient status can be corrected fairly quickly and easily. Restoring the balance in any of these trace minerals can even help resolve long-standing depression that has not responded to medication and psychotherapy.

Chapter 12

E—Essential Fatty Acids and Cholesterol

The human brain is a fatty organ that simply does not work unless it is given plenty of essential fatty acids, cholesterol, and other naturally occurring fatty substances called lipids. If you were to wring the liquid out of a brain and analyze what's left, you'd find that about 60 percent of its dry weight consists of fat, and at least 25 percent of its white matter is made from fatty acids. But despite its high fat content, the brain doesn't look like a steak, with chunks of fat that can be sliced off and thrown away. Instead, the fat is part of every brain cell, where it takes different forms and performs many tasks that keep us alive, healthy, and—we hope—happy.

Fatty Acids, the Building Blocks of Fat

Fats belong to a larger group called lipids, which also includes sterols such as cholesterol. When we talk about fats in the body, we're usually talking about fatty acids, which are organic compounds made up of chains of carbon and hydrogen atoms that promote and maintain the health of the body in countless ways. Fatty acids are to fat what amino acids are to proteins: the building blocks. Just as different amino acids can be combined to make different proteins, different fatty acids can be joined together in specific combinations to create different kinds of fat.

The body uses many fatty acids, most of which it can make on its own by taking fats from the food we eat and recombining them in different shapes. But the body cannot make two fatty acids—linolenic acid and linoleic acid—which makes them "essential" fatty acids that must be obtained from food sources.

Fatty acids, both those we can make and those we must get from food, are needed to make and maintain every single cell in the body. They also help promote the health of the nervous system, immune system, skin, and joints, and they normalize appetite, burn body fat, make hormones, and control inflammation. But perhaps even more interesting and more relevant to this book is the link between fatty acids and depression. Before we go further, let's take a look at the fatty acid itself: what it is, how it's named, and how it affects the body.

What's a fatty acid?

A fatty acid is basically a line of carbon atoms, each of which is hooked to the one in front and in back of it, except for those at the head or tail of the line. Think of a train, with each car hooked to two others (one in front and another in back), except for the engine and the caboose. Every carbon atom in the chain (except those on each end) has an "arm" on either side. At the end of each arm is a "hand" that can hold onto a hydrogen atom. When all of the carbons in the line are holding onto two hydrogen atoms, the fatty acid is considered *saturated*. Unable to hold any more hydrogen atoms, it is completely full, like a very wet sponge.

But if a carbon atom lets go of a hydrogen atom, meaning that it now holds onto just one hydrogen atom, the fatty acid is considered either *monounsaturated* or *polyunsaturated*, depending on how many times this occurs in the line of carbons (*mono* for once; *poly* for more than once.) If the first missing hydrogen atom occurs on the third carbon atom in the line, the configuration is called an *omega-3* fatty acid. If it occurs on the sixth carbon atom, it's called an *omega-6* fatty acid. This may not seem like much of a difference, but in the three-dimensional world of biochemistry, the position of a single atom can make a world of difference by allowing a molecule to interact with others or preventing it from even getting close.

Omega-3 fatty acids are found in fish, fish oil, flaxseed oil, and walnuts, while omega-6s are found primarily in corn, soy or sunflower oil, margarine, eggs, and meat. Both play important roles in brain function; thus, both are necessary components of a balanced diet. However, because omega-6 fatty acids can promote inflammation under certain circumstances, while omega-3s can help quell inflammation, it's important to have the proper ratio of omega-6s to omega-3s. The recommended ratio is 4:1. Shockingly, the standard American diet is not only low in omega-3s, it can contain as many as twenty-five times more omega-6s than omega-3s, skyrocketing the ratio from 4:1 to 25:1. The omega-6 fatty acids are certainly healthful and necessary, but not in that amount.

Way too many omega-6s coupled with a shortage of omega-3s is believed to contribute to a large number of diseases and conditions, including depression, allergies, angina (chest pain), arthritis, behavioral disorders, cancer, diabetes, dementia, heart disease, reduced immune function, hyperactivity, inflammatory conditions, autoimmune disorders, obesity, psoriasis, schizophrenia, stroke, and vision disorders. The imbalance between omega-6s and omega-3s is primarily due to our typical diet, which is extremely heavy in foods containing omega-6 fatty acids, especially oils used in cooking, fried foods, processed foods, and junk food. The decrease in overall levels of omega-3 fatty acids in the diet is, in part, the result of eating cage-raised cattle and farm-raised fish, which contain as many as five times *fewer* omega-3s than wild fish.

Not only is the omega-6:omega-3 ratio skewed, but we also take in fewer EFAs than we need, even though our diets are high in fats. So although we have too much fat in our diets, we can't seem to get the right kind of fat in the proper ratios to enjoy healthy lives.

Essential fatty acids and depression

Two specific omega-3 EFAs are important to brain health: EPA and DHA. Both fuel the brain and help control the chronic inflammation of degenerative brain diseases, such as Alzheimer's disease. EPA plays a major role in the maintenance of nerve cell membranes, while DHA is the main structural fatty acid in the brain's gray matter and in the retina of the eye. DHA also improves the sending of brain signals and, thus, communication between brain cells.

When it comes to the brain, you are indeed what you eat, for diet affects the levels and kinds of fat that the brain contains. Experiments with animals have shown a difference in the contents of their brain fats after only a few weeks on experimental diets. And in humans, inadequate omega-3s during early neural development (in the embryonic/fetal stages) resulted in lower levels of DHA in the brain.

But does the level of EFAs in the brain have an effect on brain function? A great many studies suggest that it does. Babies bottle-fed without DHA supplements or born to mothers who don't have enough omega-3 may not develop good sight and cognitive ability. A lack of omega-3 may render children less likely to sit still and pay attention in school. Too few omega-3s later in life may increase the risk of memory problems, dementia, and stroke. And low levels of DHA and other omega-3s have been linked to depression and bipolar disorder.

DHA is found in high amounts in the area of brain cells where the mood-altering neurotransmitters are stored. It also may help regulate mood by increasing levels of serotonin, a neurotransmitter that relieves depression. Several studies have found links between low blood levels of omega-3 EFAs and depression. Consider the following examples:

As the EPA content of red blood cells decreases, the severity of depression increases, and vice versa. Similar results were found for EPA and DHA levels in fat tissue. Mildly depressed people were found to have 34 percent less DHA in their fat tissue than nondepressed people.

Low blood levels of EFAs may be related to postpartum depression. A mother transfers a significant amount of EFA to her developing fetus, and her EPA levels have to be restored after the baby is born. The longer this process takes, the greater the risk of postpartum depression.

Compared with healthy people, patients with bipolar mood disorder have lower levels of EPA, DHA, and alpha linolenic acid, a plant-based omega-3 that the body uses to make EPA.

Suicide attempts are correlated with low plasma levels of DHA, as well as with a high ratio of omega-6s to omega-3s. Adequate intake of omega-3s has been linked to reduced depressive symptoms, especially in women. In a study of pregnant African-American women in the third trimester living in low-income settings, consuming the fatty acid DHA was linked to less perceived stress and reduced levels of stress hormones. A 2013 study of 1,746 African-American and white adults aged thirty to sixty-five in Baltimore found that higher levels of omega-3 fatty acids were linked to a lower risk of depressive symptoms.

If low levels of EFAs are correlated with depression, will increasing the intake of EPA and/or DHA reverse the condition? Many, but not all, studies say yes. For example, a study published in the medical journal *Lancet* compared the intake of fish (a key source of omega-3 fatty acids) with the rates of depression in different population groups. The study found that higher fish consumption was linked with lower levels of depression, and vice versa.

Here's a sampling of the positive results found in other depression/omega-3 studies:

- Consuming fish or seafood is correlated with protection against postpartum depression, bipolar disorder, and SAD. A 2014 study found that consumption of omega-3 fatty acids helped reduce depressive symptoms better than placebo.
- A Norwegian study showed that women who had low levels of omega-3 fatty acids in late pregnancy had higher depression scores three months after giving birth than women with normal levels. The researchers concluded that fertile or pregnant women—especially those at risk for postpartum depression or with other risk factors—should eat more seafood or take an omega-3 fatty acid supplement.
- In a double-blind, placebo-controlled study, depressed people who took 9.6 g of DHA and EPA per day for eight weeks had improvement in mood, with decreased scores on the HDRS.
- Improvement in symptoms of major depressive disorder was seen in six- to twelve-year-old children given EPA and DHA supplementation, as measured by the Children's Depression Rating Scale, Children's Depression Inventory, and Clinical Global Impression rating scale.
- In 2012, researchers studying 132 psychiatric patients aged sixty and older who had previously had major depression found that omega-3 levels were associated with better cognitive function and immediate recall.
- Omega-3 fatty acids were compared with fluoxetine (Prozac) in a 2008 study involving sixty people with major depressive disorder. The study subjects were randomly assigned to take 1,000 mg of EPA, 20 mg of Prozac, or both, every day. By the end of the eight-week study, EPA proved to be as effective as Prozac in treating major depressive disorder, although the combination of the two was even better.

Not all omega-3 studies have yielded positive results. Sometimes EPA, DHA, or some combination of the two doesn't seem to be particularly helpful. This happens often when a new treatment is being researched, and it can lead to conflicting claims of efficacy. Are omega-3 fatty acids helpful in treating "straight" depression, depression with anxiety, bipolar depression, postpartum depression, or other forms of the illness?

To advance our understanding, Canadian researchers conducted the largest "effectiveness" study to date, enlisting 430 adults with a major depressive episode lasting at least four weeks. A little more than half of them also had an anxiety disorder. The subjects were randomly assigned to take either a combination of EPA and DHA or a placebo. Then the severity of their depression was tracked for eight weeks. The results were interesting: The omega-3 fatty acid supplements were somewhat more helpful than placebo in treating depression overall. But the omega-3s produced a "clear benefit" among those who simply had a major depressive episode without anxiety. This study suggests that, while not everyone with depression benefits from omega-3s, those who have certain types of depression may enjoy substantial relief. As the research progresses, we'll no doubt learn who will most likely benefit from omega-3 fatty acids in cases of depression.

Exciting new research has shown that individuals with specific markers of inflammation are most likely to benefit from fatty acid supplementation. In 2015, researchers found that EPA supplementation was able to enhance mood in a subgroup of 155 participants diagnosed with major depressive disorder who also had high levels of at least one of the four markers of inflammation in their blood. The results from this study support the idea that addressing underlying physiological problems, such as inflammation, can be extremely helpful in augmenting the treatment response in individuals who would otherwise be unresponsive to other therapies.

The core concept of THE ZEEBRA approach is individualized treatment. If you have low levels of EFAs, determined via testing or via the presence of symptoms described previously, supplementation is most likely to help.

> A young woman named Julie had depression for ten years. As I reviewed the thick files sent to me by her various physicians, I was struck by the fact that she intermittently complained of dry skin, fatigue, allergies, and being thirsty all the time. These, along with depression, are symptoms of an omega-3 fatty acid shortage, so I asked Julie about her diet. She explained that she tried to eat healthy foods, but her diet was unbalanced. Testing her levels of nutrients revealed very low levels of omega-3s in addition to other nutrient shortages. Within a few months of correcting her diet, Julie's dry skin cleared. She stopped feeling thirsty all day, and she started to notice an improvement in her mood and energy levels.

Add essential fatty acids to your diet

Although eating enough fat is not a problem for most Americans, getting enough of the right kind of fat is. Here's what you can do to help ensure that you're giving your body enough EFAs, particularly EPA and DHA:

- Eat seafood at least twice a week, especially salmon, mackerel, herring, sardines, halibut, and albacore tuna. Grill or bake the fish without adding oils, and avoid deep-frying, as this can destroy the omega-3s.
- Eat wild rather than farmed fish; the farmed kinds usually have far fewer omega-3 acids than their wild cousins.
- Eat meats from grass-fed animals whenever possible, as these contain a higher omega-3:omega-6 ratio.
- Eat foods containing omega-3s, such as walnuts, pecans, pumpkin seeds, sesame seeds, tahini, hummus, tofu, and fresh spinach.
- Check levels of EFAs to determine the proper ratios for supplementation.
- Take an omega-3 supplement. These may come in different forms, labeled as omega-3, fish oil, EPA, DHA, essential fatty acids, or cod liver oil. Be sure to read the label carefully, for it can be confusing. If you have not been tested for EFA levels, look for a supplement that contains EPA, DHA, and gamma-linolenic acid, which supplies all the EFAs.

Although omega-3 fatty acids are good for mental and physical health, overdoing it is not recommended. Beyond a certain point, omega-3 fatty acids disrupt the ratio between omega-6 and omega-3 fatty acids and perhaps push certain necessary fats out of the diet. Too-high amounts of omega-3 fatty acids can cause the blood to thin, leading to excessive bleeding and delayed clotting time. Be sure to check with your physician before taking omega-3 supplements, particularly if you are taking blood-thinning medications.

My recommendations

A wealth of scientific literature supports the use of omega-3 fatty acids for depression, and many of my colleagues are prescribing higher dosages of omega-3s for their patients. I've been testing levels of EFAs in my patients for almost twenty years and have been struck by individual differences in EFA levels that are often not predicted by dietary intake.

I'm a strong advocate for individual laboratory testing to develop a personalized program for each patient. The omega-3 fatty acids are so important that it's fine to take up to 3 g per day for as long as three months without testing or while waiting for tests to be ordered and performed. That's enough to fix a shortage without upsetting the level of omega-6 fatty acids and, possibly, other substances. But beyond the three-month period, I recommend no more than 2 g per day.

Interestingly, many patients I see lack omega-6 fatty acids after EFA testing. This is common when high doses of omega-3 supplements are taken for months without monitoring or testing. This is surprising to many, because usually the problem is an elevated level, especially in relation to the omega-3 fatty acids. I routinely recommend both omega-3 and omega-6 fatty acids from the outset, especially for those with eczema, rashes, or other skin conditions that suggest a lack of omega-6 fatty acids. In these cases, I often suggest that patients take omega-6 fatty acids in the form of borage oil or evening primrose oil (which can be rubbed right on the skin).

A final word

EPA and DHA, the two key EFAs, are not magical cures for depression; neither are fish, fish oil, or cod liver oil. However, there is enough scientific evidence and practical experience to show that too-low levels and ratios of EFAs may interfere with moods. Psychiatrists and other doctors should ensure that their patients understand the importance of taking in enough EFAs in a ratio of 4:1 (omega-6 to omega-3). Unless you are taking blood-thinning medications, there is no risk of significant side effects.

With so many patients still suffering from depression despite standard treatment, it is worthwhile to address EFA status as a potential factor in this complex disorder.

Cholesterol and Depression

Most people are aware that elevated cholesterol levels are a risk factor for heart disease. The U.S. government and health organizations have been pounding that message home for decades, and cholesterol has developed a reputation as a dangerous substance. But cholesterol is also a valuable and needed part of human chemistry for top brain function. The brain is the most cholesterol-rich organ in the body.

Technically speaking, cholesterol is a waxy steroid metabolite in body cells that is moved through the body in the bloodstream. It is absolutely essential for life. Cholesterol ensures that cell walls function properly. It is changed into vitamin D, is used to make sex and stress hormones, and serves as a major part of the coating of nerve cells, making it crucial to a functioning nervous system.

The body makes cholesterol as needed, with the bulk of the production in the liver. Relatively little cholesterol, about 15 percent, comes from the food we eat. The body responds to cholesterol absorbed from food. If more is eaten, less is made internally. If less is eaten, the body makes more.

The lipid hypothesis, proposed by German pathologist Rudolf Virchow in 1856, received renewed attention in the latter half of the twentieth century. It argues that high levels of total cholesterol and LDL (bad cholesterol) set the stage for heart disease by damaging the interior linings of the arteries. On the other hand, HDL (good cholesterol) can protect the arterial linings by carrying cholesterol away, so higher levels of HDL are considered good.

Low cholesterol and depression

Several studies have linked low cholesterol levels to an increased risk of depression. Consider the following examples:

- In a 2000 study published in *Psychosomatic Medicine*, researchers compared cholesterol levels with depressive symptoms in men aged forty to seventy. They found that men with long-term low total cholesterol levels "have a higher prevalence of depressive symptoms" than those with higher cholesterol levels.
- Women with low cholesterol levels are also vulnerable to depression. In 1998, Swedish researchers reported the results of their examination of cholesterol and depressive symptoms among 300 healthy women aged thirty-one to sixty-five in and around Stockholm. Women in the lowest cholesterol group (the bottom tenth percentile) had many more depressive symptoms than others. A 2001 study published in *Psychiatry Research* that looked at primary care patients in Ireland found that low levels of cholesterol were linked to higher ratings on depression rating scales.

- Italian researchers measured the cholesterol levels of 186 patients hospitalized for depression and found a link between low cholesterol and depressive symptoms.

This research is supported by other studies, including a 2008 meta-analysis that found that higher total cholesterol was linked to lower levels of depression. Another very interesting study looked at levels of HDL in depressed people and found that low levels of HDL were linked to "long-term depressive symptomatology." Another study, this one in pregnant women, found that low HDL levels were linked to higher scores (indicating depression) on the Edinburgh Postnatal Depression Scale.

Low cholesterol and suicide

Suffering through a depressive episode can be very difficult, and one of the great fears is that someone in the throes of depression will not see any point in continuing to live.

Early evidence of a link between low cholesterol and suicide came from the Multiple Risk Factor Intervention Study, a large-scale, long-term look at different health factors involving hundreds of thousands of volunteers. Data from the study was analyzed by researchers from the University of Minnesota, which found that people with total cholesterol levels lower than 160 mg/dL were more likely to commit suicide than those with higher cholesterol levels. Other studies are equally alarming:

- A 2008 study looked at forty men hospitalized due to bipolar disorder. Twenty had attempted suicide at some point in the past, and the other twenty had not. Both cholesterol and blood fat levels were lower, on average, among those who had attempted suicide.
- A paper published in the *Journal of Clinical Psychiatry* in the same year reported the results of an examination of cholesterol levels in 417 patients who had attempted suicide at some point, 155 hospitalized psychiatric patients who had not, and healthy controls. Results of the study suggested that low cholesterol may be linked to suicide attempts.
- The suicidal method of choice, self-inflicted fatal gun wound versus pills, for example, may also be related to cholesterol levels. A 2008 study published in *Psychiatry Research* compared nineteen people who had attempted suicide using violent methods with sixteen

> who had attempted to kill themselves nonviolently, as well as with twenty healthy controls. The researchers found that "violent suicide attempters had much lower total cholesterol and leptin levels compared with those with nonviolent suicide attempts."

The strong link between low cholesterol and suicide is highlighted in a 2004 study that concluded that a low total cholesterol level can be an indicator of suicide risk. This study, involving suicide attempters with major depressive disorder, nonsuicidal depressed patients, and normal subjects, found large differences in cholesterol levels among the groups.

The average total serum cholesterol level was 190 mg/dL among normal subjects, 180 mg/dL in the nonsuicidal depressed group, and 150 mg/dL among the suicidal depressive patients. This study showed that the total cholesterol level can be used to gauge possible suicide risk (less than 180 mg/dL) and probable risk (150 mg/dL and lower). A 2013 study of fifty-one adult patients who were hospitalized after attempting suicide showed that their total cholesterol was much lower than cholesterol in a group of healthy patients.

Suicide is not the only type of violence linked to lower cholesterol levels. Homicide and other violence committed against others are also linked to low cholesterol. Swedish researchers compared one-time cholesterol measurements in nearly eighty thousand men and women aged twenty-four to seventy with later arrests for violent crime. The researchers reported that "low cholesterol is linked to increased later criminal violence."

What's the cholesterol–depression link?

The studies linking low cholesterol to depression, suicide, and violence looked at the serum cholesterol level, which is the amount of cholesterol in the blood. But what about the amount of cholesterol in the brain?

Canadian researchers were the first to examine this question in a 2007 study published in the *International Journal of Neuropsychopharmacology*. The researchers measured and compared the cholesterol content in different parts of the brains of forty-one men who had committed suicide and twenty-one men who had died of other, sudden causes that had no direct impact on the brain. The results were interesting: When the suicides were categorized as violent or nonviolent, those who had committed violent suicide were found to have less cholesterol than the others in the gray matter of their brains. This was seen specifically in the frontal cortex, a part of the brain that handles "executive functions," including processes involved in planning, cognitive flexibility, abstract thinking, starting appropriate actions and stopping inappropriate actions, and selecting relevant sensory information. The frontal cortex essentially controls the ability to make good decisions.

As is the case with so much of psychiatry, we don't know exactly why a low cholesterol level is linked to depression. Cholesterol is a critical precursor to many essential physiological molecules in the human body that directly and indirectly affect our moods and optimal brain function. Some researchers think that that low levels of cholesterol change brain chemistry, suppressing the production and/or availability of the neurotransmitter serotonin. Cholesterol is also essential for the synthesis of all steroid and sex hormones, including DHEA, testosterone, estrogen, and vitamin D.

Another hypothesis, based on the knowledge that cholesterol has a role in inflammation, suggests that the link between low cholesterol and depression is chronic, low-grade inflammation. More ideas have been proposed, and future research will no doubt find the missing link between low cholesterol and depression.

A dangerous trend

In the meantime, it's important that we become aware of a dangerous trend. For years, I've been looking into the depression–low cholesterol link, and I'm becoming increasingly alarmed as more and more people are put on statin medications that cause their cholesterol levels to plummet.

> Daniel, a forty-two-year-old executive, came to see me for depression and anxiety. After struggling with depression in college, he had been doing well until that year. Reviewing his laboratory tests, I shared with him my concern about his total cholesterol level of 125 mg/dL. A year before, he had been placed on a statin for "preventive" reasons when his cholesterol levels reached 200 mg/dL. As his cholesterol levels declined with the statin, so did his mood. His physician agreed to stop Daniel's statin. Within three months, Daniel's cholesterol levels normalized, and his depressed mood "miraculously" disappeared without medications.

One drug company has received FDA approval to begin advertising its statin as a preventive measure for *people who do not even have high cholesterol levels*. If they have elevated levels of inflammation in their body plus another risk factor for heart disease, such as high blood pressure, they are considered as eligible candidates for the medication.

Currently, about 80 million Americans can be prescribed statins, according to the old criteria. The new criteria for prescribing statins increases the number of Americans eligible for these medications by about 6.5 million people. Many of my patients have been pressured by their family doctor or cardiologist to take statins or other cholesterol-lowering medications, even if their cholesterol is only slightly high or in the higher ranges of normal. Doctors often prescribe cholesterol-lowering medications to patients with normal cholesterol levels, especially if they have diabetes, a family history of heart disease, or another cardiovascular risk factor. That may be reasonable from the point of view of cardiology, but it is not so wise from a psychiatric perspective. The "cholesterol culture" calls for pushing cholesterol numbers down further and further, without thinking about potential psychological consequences.

I believe all psychiatrists should look at the cholesterol levels of all patients with depression. If total cholesterol is less than 165, the psychiatrist should suspect that low cholesterol may be a contributing factor to depression. If it's 140 or less, I recommend that the cholesterol level be pushed back up above 165. For some patients, raising cholesterol levels is simply a matter of adjusting their cholesterol medication and allowing cholesterol levels to rise naturally. For others, it requires changing their diet to include eggs and other cholesterol-rich foods. This should be done with the patient's personal doctor to ensure that heart risk factors are properly monitored.

Too Important to Overlook

Cholesterol and EFAs are intimately linked to depression, although the links are not immediately obvious and often require a bit of detective work. Understanding the consequences of shortages in essential fats and cholesterol is important for the effective treatment of depression. Whether it is drug induced, genetic, or a result of dietary patterns, low cholesterol prevents our brains from functioning their best. Low cholesterol may contribute to the development of depression and stand in the way of successful and sustained recovery from depression.

Chapter 13

E—Exercise and Energy

"Yes, I know it's good for me," Marissa said when I suggested that she start exercising. "I think about it a lot, and I keep paying my health club fees, but I don't have the energy. I just don't have the energy."

Marissa is like many patients with depression. Patients have a hard time summoning the motivation and energy needed to exercise, even though they know it helps reduce symptoms of depression. Even some doctors are reluctant to prescribe exercise, knowing that their depressed patients likely lack the motivation. However, I believe that it is vital for everyone with depression to exercise. Which exercises you do is not nearly as important as simply doing something, whether it is walking, swimming, weight lifting, dancing, bike riding, gardening, tai chi, or aerobics. In fact, research has shown that even modest levels of exercise can help. And while most studies have focused on aerobic exercise, there's evidence that resistance training (weight-bearing exercises) can be just as effective.

Exercise can benefit everyone: men, women, teens, and children. It may be espccially important for people with certain chronic health problems; indeed, one study showed that patients with heart disease, who often have depression, can find relief from their depressive symptoms with exercise. However, always ask your doctor before beginning an exercise program.

Later in this chapter, I describe specific supplements I recommend to help patients gain the energy they may need to get started. But first, let's take a look at the antidepressive effects of exercise.

Science Supports Exercise

The idea that exercise can help relieve the symptoms of depression is not new. If you look through the online National Library of Medicine, you'll find studies on the psychological effects of exercise dating back to 1970. Here are some findings:

- Studies have suggested that exercise may be even more effective at relieving depressive symptoms in people with major depressive disorder than in those with other types of depression.
- In 2013, researchers assigned forty-eight alcohol-dependent, inactive patients to a twelve-week, moderate, group exercise program or simply advised them to exercise. The patients who undertook the group exercise program reported far fewer drinking and heavy drinking days than those who had simply been told to exercise.
- A Columbia University Department of Epidemiology researcher looked at data on exercise habits and mental status taken from 8,098 subjects participating in the National Comorbidity Survey. The 60.3 percent of adults in the survey who exercised regularly were much less likely to have major depression and anxiety disorders than those who did not.
- The National Institutes of Health assessed the effects of exercise in 5,451 men and 1,277 women aged twenty through eighty-eight. This study looked specifically at walking, jogging, and running as exercise, ranking the participants according to how often they exercised. Those who exercised more were less likely to have depressive symptoms, but it didn't take running a marathon to chase away the blues. In fact, the "dose response" peaked at eleven to nineteen miles per week, which amounts to 1.6 to 2.7 miles per day.
- Thirteen teens with depression and low levels of physical activity completed fifteen supervised exercise sessions and twenty-one independent sessions. Researchers wanted to see if depressed teens would exercise and, if they did, if it made them feel better. In the end, the teens all completed the program and showed a large reduction in depressive symptoms. Another study showed that aerobic exercise helped protect against depression in middle school girls.
- Depression during pregnancy may be more common than depression after pregnancy. A 2015 study of 167 pregnant women and exercise revealed that a supervised exercise program of three fifty-five- to sixty-minute sessions each week reduced depressive symptoms more than in pregnant women who did not exercise.
- In 2014, researchers following eleven thousand people aged twenty-three to fifty found that physical activity was linked to fewer symptoms of depression. They also found a link between the number of physical activity sessions per week and depressive symptoms; those

who exercised at least three times a week reported a lower average number of depressive symptoms than those who exercised less often. Similar results were obtained in a 2015 study in fifty patients hospitalized with major depression. The results showed that those who exercised in a group three times a week had significantly fewer depressive symptoms and a better quality of life.

- Duke University researchers compared the long-term effects of exercise with a standard antidepressant in a study of 156 adults with major depressive disorder. The volunteers were randomly assigned to either a four-month aerobic exercise program, treatment with sertraline (Zoloft), or both. At the end of the four-month period, results were similar in all three groups. In other words, exercise alone, Zoloft alone, or the two together were equally effective in reducing symptoms of depression. However, six months later, those who had exercised and seen improved symptoms of depression were less likely to get depressed again than those who had not exercised. The researchers noted that exercise is a feasible treatment for major depressive disorder and is linked to "significant therapeutic benefit."
- Weight lifting can also be an antidepressive exercise. A Harvard Medical School researcher examined the effects of weight lifting in senior citizens (average age, seventy-one). They were randomly assigned to either the exercise group, which performed ten weeks of supervised weight lifting followed by ten weeks of unsupervised weight lifting, or the control group, which did not receive any active treatment. Twenty weeks later, those who had been lifting weights had much lower depression scores than those in the no-exercise group. The volunteers were left alone for about two years and allowed to exercise or not exercise as they pleased. When they were retested, those who had originally been in the exercise group continued to enjoy lower depression scores, showing that exercise may have a long-term benefit.
- The antidepressant effects of yoga have long been reported, and several studies have shown that this mind-body exercise is effective. In one such study, young adults with mild depression were randomly assigned to yoga classes or a no-yoga control group. At the end of the five-week study period, those who had participated in yoga classes showed significant drops in depressive symptoms. A similar study evaluated the

mental health symptoms of professional musicians, who often have elevated stress and performance anxiety. Fifteen musicians practiced yoga and meditation. Another fifteen practiced yoga and meditation and participated in group classes and discussions emphasizing a "yogic lifestyle." A final group of fifteen, serving as the control group, practiced neither yoga nor meditation. Two months later, volunteers in the yoga and meditation groups enjoyed much less depression, general anxiety, and tension and anger than those in the control group.

- The ancient Asian movement form called tai chi is also effective in reducing symptoms of depression. This has been shown in studies of people with osteoarthritis and rheumatoid arthritis, senior citizens, and others. Part of tai chi's antidepressant effects may come from the exercise itself and part from the fact that it is usually practiced in a group, so participants benefit from social interaction.
- A 2013 study of 850 obese adults undergoing bariatric (weight loss) surgery showed that those who exercised regularly, even at low rates, were less likely to have been treated for depression or anxiety than those who did not exercise.

The antidepressant effects of exercise are so widely known that the June 2009 issue of *Current Psychiatry* even ran an article titled "Exercise Prescription," which reviewed the studies and recommended that psychiatrists help their depressed patients begin exercising and stay with it. (Only about 40 percent of patients receive counseling about exercise from their physicians.) Specifically, the article suggested that psychiatrists "counsel patients about exercise as a plan or prescription and discuss exercise at each visit." This is excellent advice because, as noted in *U.S. News & World Report*, exercise does the following:

- Reverses the harmful effects of stress
- Lifts depression
- Improves learning
- Builds self-esteem and improves body image
- Leaves you feeling euphoric, or joyful

Exercise may improve mood in ways similar to antidepressant medications by regulating neurotransmitters. University of Georgia researchers showed that exercise can activate genes that increase the level of the neurotransmitter galanin in the brain. In turn, galanin influences norepinephrine and reduces the body's stress response.

In 2013, researchers reviewing results from a number of studies found that four studies identified the positive effect of exercise on mood compared with standard treatment, no treatment, or placebo. They concluded that the promising findings point to a role for physical therapy combined with an antidepressant in the treatment of depression.

A healthy heart may also protect against depression. In 2013, researchers following 437 male and female students from six different middle schools during sixth and seventh grade found that cardiorespiratory fitness was linked to significantly less depression in girls by the seventh grade, regardless of preexisting depression or weight. The researchers also concluded that a fit heart may have a smaller but similar effect in boys.

Another study indicates that exercise can even help the brain heal from damage caused by early childhood trauma. Researchers from Australia's University of New South Wales separated newborn rats from their mothers for specific periods of time to cause high levels of stress. Once they were weaned, the young rats were randomly assigned to eat regular chow, eat a high-fat diet, exercise voluntarily on an exercise wheel, or both exercise and eat a high-fat diet for eleven weeks. Separating the young animals from their mothers caused measurable changes in the brain, which were reversed in the rats allowed to exercise over a long period (as well as in those who atc a high-fat diet). The researchers concluded that exercise benefited the mice after early-life stress from separation from their mothers.

How does exercise work?

We haven't yet identified the exact ways in which exercise relieves depression. Several possibilities include:

Physical factors

- Spurring the release of endorphins or other "feel-good" hormones
- Changing the levels or effects of norepinephrine, serotonin, or other brain chemicals
- Lowering the levels of cortisol, a stress hormone
- Increasing body temperature

Psychological factors

- Getting the mind off daily activities and stress

- Improving self-esteem as you accomplish exercise goals
- Improving self-image as you become stronger, more flexible, or slimmer
- Encouraging interaction with others (in some exercise activities)

The ultimate answer: Just exercise

Even though exercise has been proven to help relieve symptoms of depression, questions remain. Exactly which type of exercise is best? How often should one exercise, and how long and intense should each session be? Studies have looked at these questions and more without coming to definitive answers.

Meanwhile, start exercising! If you love to jog, jog. If you prefer ballet or yoga class, great. If you enjoy playing baseball or gardening, lifting weights or shooting baskets, do so. The most important thing you can do is get started. Yes, the studies show that a certain level of intensity is needed to get the antidepressant value, but many depressed people lack energy and motivation and are out of shape, which is why I say just start exercising. Even if the benefits are relatively small in the beginning, they'll begin to add up, making it easier to get to the next level over time.

Don't wait for the definitive study to answer all the exercise questions, and don't try to create the "perfect" exercise plan. Don't try to figure out exactly how many calories you're burning, and don't compare yourself to anyone else or to what you think you should do. Just get started. It is always helpful to discuss your plans for exercise with your primary care doctor.

How Can One Exercise without Energy?

Exercising improves brain chemistry and boosts energy, but if you haven't got the energy to begin with, how do you get started? Overcoming depression-caused inertia can be very difficult. "It's like I'm a car with no gas; I can't move," is how one patient described it. "I'd like to, but it ain't gonna happen."

Psychiatrists have long been aware that a great many of our depressed patients complain of a lack of energy. A paper published in the *Journal of Affective Disorders* used data from nearly twenty-two hundred patients with major depressive disorder to determine which physical symptoms were most common among those with major depressive disorder from a moderate to a more severe degree. The top five were as follows:

Complaint	Percent of Patients
Feeling fatigued, weak, or tired all over	78
Feeling not in as good physical health as friends	59
Not feeling well most of the time in the past few years	54
Feeling weak in parts of the body	45
Headaches	45

Psychiatrists have tended to dismiss these physical symptoms, hoping they will get better with medication and therapy. However, as you learned earlier, more than two-thirds of patients treated for depression continue to have symptoms such as fatigue. New research is looking into the physical symptoms of depression, including fatigue. The findings suggest that the body's mitochondria may be involved.

Mitochondria are tiny structures in the body's cells that serve as "cellular energy factories," making most of a cell's adenosine triphosphate (ATP), which acts as a form of "gasoline" for the cell's "engines." Mitochondria also participate in other cellular functions, such as regulation of cellular growth and death. Damage to the mitochondria can result in less energy available to the cells. This, in turn, can hamper their function. In 2008, a team of researchers from Sweden and the United States compared the mitochondrial function in muscle tissue and the "body complaints" of twenty-one people with major depressive disorder with that of ten healthy controls. This was the first time such a study had been done, and the results were interesting. It turns out that weakened mitochondrial activity translates into less cellular energy, which is linked to physical discomfort.

Could poor mitochondrial function be linked to psychiatric distress? The human brain, which requires a lot of energy, contains a large number of mitochondria. It would be no surprise to find that damage to the vital mitochondria may be a cause of depression and other psychiatric disorders. This idea has been looked at in animal studies, which show that stress interferes with mitochondrial energy production.

Understanding the importance of mitochondria for energy production in every cell of the human body offers us a new way to treat depression. It also gives us a way to deal with the never-ending fatigue and other physical symptoms linked to depression: Support the mitochondria. The strategy for doing so is threefold. First, keep the body as healthy as possible; second, use natural substances that are known to support the mitochondria; and third, use energy-boosting supplements to overcome fatigue so that you can start exercising. This breaks the terrible "depression, fatigue, can't move, more depression, more fatigue" cycle.

The entire THE ZEEBRA program works to strengthen the body and build energy. Better sleep garners energy, as does reducing stress, improving digestion, optimizing hormone levels, getting rid of foods that sap energy, and taking in generous amounts of all the necessary nutrients. Simply working through THE ZEEBRA recommendations will lead to better health and increased energy, which will be boosted even further with exercise. In addition, certain supplements help boost energy.

Overcoming "Antiexercise Inertia" with B_{12}

One of the key elements in THE ZEEBRA program, as far as energy is concerned, is vitamin B_{12}, otherwise known as cyanocobalamin. B_{12} works with other members of the B family of vitamins to perform a variety of tasks in the body, including strengthening the nervous and immune systems and helping maintain muscle tone and healthy skin. B_{12} plays a vital role in energy metabolism, and a shortage of the vitamin can lead to a lack of energy. A lack of vitamin B_{12} increases levels of homocysteine, a substance that can lead to or worsen heart disease.

Indeed, fatigue is one of the most common symptoms of a B_{12} shortage. (Another symptom is depression.) At one time, doctors regularly gave B_{12} injections to their patients who felt tired or run down. As was the case with many other natural remedies, B_{12} was pushed aside by a wave of new medicines and was never subjected to the extensive testing it deserves. Indeed, finding and treating vitamin B_{12} shortages is very important.

In a study of 259 patients in India with a vitamin B_{12} deficiency, sixty had neuropsychiatric symptoms. These symptoms were most severe in elderly men, in whom a lack of vitamin B_{12} was most prevalent.

I have found that B_{12} does indeed boost energy in people with low, low-normal, and even normal serum B_{12} levels. But there's disagreement about what optimal levels are. The normal range is usually given as 200–900 picograms per milliliter (pg/mL). That's quite a wide range, with the higher number being 4.5 times larger than the lower. Can we really say that someone whose level is 200 is as healthy as another person with a 900 level? Is 250 really just as good as 850?

Some doctors pick a middle range, saying that normal is 400 to 500. However, I have found that people have much better energy levels when their B_{12} is much higher, up in the 800 to 900 range. I talk more about vitamin B_{12} in the following chapter. For now, I simply want you to be aware that low levels of B_{12} can lead to low energy and that increasing the amount of B_{12} available to make energy can be very helpful, especially for senior citizens, vegans, and people taking acid-blocking medications for gastroesophageal reflux disease (GERD) or other reasons. Those taking acid blockers may have trouble absorbing vitamins. Vegans, who do not eat animal or dairy products, do not ingest B_{12}, which is found in foods of animal origin.

Other medications can also interfere with the body's ability to use vitamin B_{12}. These include amoxicillin and other antibiotics, as well as the colestipol used to reduce cholesterol levels.

Energizing the Cellular Energy Factories with Carnitine

While B_{12} helps with overall energy levels, a supplement called carnitine can especially help rev up the mitochondrial energy factories.

Carnitine is a natural substance made from amino acids and found in most cells in the human body. Its name comes from the Latin word for flesh (*carnus*) because it was first isolated in meat. One of carnitine's key functions is helping produce energy in the mitochondria. It does so by carrying fatty acids into the mitochondria, where they are "burned" to release energy.

Several studies have looked at the use of carnitine as an energy booster. One of these studies involved people aged one hundred or older, for they often have fatigue. Sixty-six of them were randomly assigned to receive either 2 g of carnitine (levocarnitine) daily or a placebo for six months. Those taking the carnitine showed less physical and mental fatigue than those taking the placebo. Carnitine supplements have helped restore energy levels in people with chronic fatigue syndrome, who have low blood levels of carnitine. Carnitine has also been used to treat fatigue related to cancer, adult celiac disease, and other illnesses.

We get some carnitine from food (the best sources are meat, milk, poultry, and fish), and some is made in the liver and kidneys from the amino acids lysine and methionine. Carnitine supplements come in different forms: L-carnitine, acetyl-L-carnitine, and propionyl-L-carnitine. The U.S. government has not set a daily minimum intake of carnitine, assuming we get enough from our food and internal production, and people are not generally tested for a carnitine shortage. Thus, we typically don't know if a patient is producing enough internally and, if she is, whether her body is able to transport and use the carnitine. Lacking simple tools to determine if someone lacks carnitine, I often recommend carnitine supplementation to patients with depression. Without it, a fifty-seven-year-old patient of mine named John stated, "I couldn't summon the energy to exercise if you held a gun to my head."

Many depressed people benefit greatly from carnitine. It gives them the energy boost they need to exercise and otherwise change their lifestyle to combat depression. It worked well for John, who after taking carnitine and other nutritional supplements for three months, told me, "You don't need a gun to get me to exercise anymore. You don't even have to tell me to do it. I look forward to my daily strolls."

To ensure they have generous supplies of energy-producing carnitine, I typically recommend that patients start by taking 500 mg twice a day and then work their way up, in a few weeks, to 1 g of carnitine before breakfast and another before lunch. Side effects of taking too much carnitine, which typically show up if you take 3 g per day or more, include nausea, diarrhea, and abdominal cramps. Keep in mind that medications such as carbamazepine and Depakote, used to treat mood disorders and seizures, and the chemotherapy agent doxorubicin can deplete the body of carnitine.

Strengthening the carnitine effect with CoQ10

The effect of carnitine is enhanced when it's taken with coenzyme Q10 (CoQ10), a natural, vitamin-like substance in the energy-producing mitochondria. As part of the "cellular energy factory," CoQ10 helps make ATP, the major source of cellular energy. In addition to boosting energy, CoQ10 has antioxidant properties and strengthens the immune system.

Several studies have shown that CoQ10 helps boost energy levels. In a double-blind, placebo-controlled study, seventeen healthy subjects (average age, 37.5) were randomly assigned to one of three groups: the 100 mg CoQ10, the 300 mg CoQ10, or the placebo group. They took their supplements daily for eight days, their ability to exercise on a bicycle was measured, and they switched to a new group. By study completion, all subjects had taken all of the substances (100 mg CoQ10, 300 mg CoQ10, and placebo), although neither they nor the doctors knew when they took each dose until the study ended. While taking either dose of CoQ10, the volunteers had less fatigue than when they were taking the placebo, and they were better able to exercise.

CoQ10 supplements are used to treat chronic fatigue syndrome, and I have found them to be very helpful in helping patients overcome depression-related fatigue. Studies have shown that CoQ10 supplements help improve athletic performance. In addition to carnitine, I often recommend that patients who complain of lack of energy take CoQ10, a fat-soluble molecule. It is available in two forms: ubiquinone and ubiquinol. Ubiquinol is the most active form of CoQ10 in the body and is made from ubiquinone. For the treatment of depression, I recommend ubiquinol in doses of 100 mg per day or ubiquinone in doses up to 200 mg per day. Because CoQ10 is fat soluble, it should be taken with food that contains some fat.

The body uses tyrosine and many nutrients to make CoQ10, and it is also found in food. Dietary sources of CoQ10 include whole grains, salmon and other oily fish, and organ meats such as liver. Medications such as the statins used to lower cholesterol, beta-blockers used primarily for heart rhythm disorders and high blood pressure, and imipramine (Tofranil) used for depression can deplete the body of CoQ10.

As discussed earlier, rhodiola can also boost energy levels and help strengthen the body to endure exercise and other fatiguing tasks. Rhodiola can provide support as you begin an exercise program. In one study, healthy adults were given 200 mg of rhodiola extract one hour before exercising and found that it significantly increased their endurance. Since rhodiola is naturally stimulating, I would start with a low dose of 100 mg per day and slowly increase it to 400 mg per day over several weeks.

Creating Cellular Energy with Ribose and Whey

The special sugar ribose, which is found in the body, produces the ATP that energizes cells. Ribose is an essential ingredient in the ATP-manufacturing process. But it is more than a building block, because its presence in the cells encourages the production of ATP. Thus, it serves as both a raw material and a "production manager," ordering the creation of more cellular energy.

The use of ribose as an energy-making supplement was tested in a study examining whether it (in the form of D-ribose) could improve energy levels in people with chronic fatigue syndrome or fibromyalgia. This was an open-label study, so both the participants and the doctors knew that all the volunteers were receiving the real thing and not a placebo. The forty-one volunteers took 15 g of D-ribose daily, and at the end of the study period, they showed a large improvement in energy, sleep, mental clarity, and well-being, and they had reduced pain intensity. The average increase in energy, as perceived by the participants, was 45 percent.

Ribose's energy-making properties can also be seen in athletes. Danish researchers had eight healthy athletes take either ribose or a placebo for three days after a week of heavy, on-again, off-again exercise. The level of ATP in the muscles of the participants fell by nearly 30 percent after the exercise period, but in those taking ribose, it returned to normal three days later. In those taking the placebo, ATP recovery took noticeably more time.

I typically recommend 5 g of ribose powder in addition to carnitine, CoQ10, and rhodiola. I also recommend that patients take free-form amino acids, the protein building blocks for neurotransmitter synthesis. Amino Replete, from a company called Pure Encapsulations, is a custom blend of free-form amino acids that can help give you the energy required to begin an exercise program that fits your lifestyle and interests.

Get Energized!

While some people with depression seem to get the energy they need to begin exercising, others need help from rhodiola, B_{12}, carnitine, CoQ10, ribose, or free-form amino acids. Whatever works for you is fine, as long as you begin exercising. And you needn't exercise for hours on end. New research shows that several smaller bursts of exercise are as effective for reducing the risk of heart disease as fewer, longer sessions. And I have found that, for my patients, smaller bursts of exercise help break the depression cycle and make more energy.

Get started!

Chapter 14

B – B Vitamins and Other Vitamins

An ample supply of vitamins and minerals is essential, not only for physical health but also for psychological well-being. But it's not just a matter of staving off terrible deficiency diseases such as scurvy or beriberi. Psychological health requires generous amounts of nutrients to make neurotransmitters, stabilize blood sugar, ease mood swings, improve sleep, and control inflammation.

> Nancy, a fifty-seven-year-old homemaker and grandmother, had been taking what she described as a "small dose of antidepressants" for three decades. "They helped, I guess," she told me. When I checked her diet and blood tests, I found she was moderately low in vitamin B_{12}—that is, she was at the low end of the recommended range. I suggested that she increase her B_{12} intake, but she said that there was no point in doing so if her level was in the recommended range. I pointed out that everyone is biochemically unique and that what was acceptable for the imaginary average person may be way too low for her. She agreed and increased her B_{12} intake. Soon after, her depression lifted.

This chapter focuses on vitamins that can affect your mood: the B vitamins and vitamin D, plus the neurotransmitter-regulating substance S-adenosyl-L-methionine, or SAMe. As you read through the chapter, you'll note that the recommended amounts are noted as either RDA (recommended dietary allowance) or AI (adequate intake). The Food and Nutrition Board of the National Academy of Sciences defines the RDA as the amount of a given nutrient considered enough to meet the requirements of 97 or 98 percent of healthy people in each sex and age group. AI, also defined by the Food and Nutrition Board, is believed to be an adequate amount. There is too little information available to predict the percentage of people for whom this amount is enough.

The B family of vitamins, which includes thiamine, riboflavin, niacin, vitamin B_6, vitamin B_{12}, folate (folic acid), and inositol, works as a team that performs several vital tasks in the body. Some of the most important jobs involve controlling the release of energy in the brain cells and making those all-important brain chemicals, the neurotransmitters. Niacin and B_6, in particular, help support the making of serotonin, a neurotransmitter that regulates mood, sleep, and appetite. The B vitamins also help regulate carbohydrate metabolism. They help stabilize blood sugar, ease mood swings, and improve sleep. In addition, they help the liver deactivate and dispose of old estrogen, which might otherwise build up to too-high levels, a suspected cause of mood changes.

The B vitamins are also critical to the Krebs cycle, the energy-making process that turns nutrients into energy. Without ample supplies of these vitamins, energy levels run low, contributing to the fatigue that is so common in depression.

Shortages of B vitamins can actually harm the brain, leading to depression, anxiety, irritability, and difficulty concentrating. Studies have shown that:

- Too little thiamine can interfere with the uptake of glucose in the brain, leading to mental fatigue and poor moods.
- A lack of folate can contribute to depression.
- A shortage of B_6, which is necessary to make serotonin and dopamine, can bring on depression and mental confusion.
- Too-low levels of B_{12}, which is needed to make red blood cells, can lead to problems moving oxygen through the body and can cause fatigue, mood swings, irritability, dementia, or mania.

Let's take a closer look at some of the key B vitamins to see how they influence mood.

Folate (Vitamin B_9)

Folate, commonly called folic acid, is required for normal cell development and the making of DNA and RNA. It's also needed for the formation of SAMe, which, in turn, is needed for neurotransmitter metabolism.

Folate may protect against colorectal, breast, and cervical cancers. It also protects the heart by breaking down homocysteine, a harmful substance linked to heart disease. High levels of homocysteine are also linked to weaker results on memory tests and poor thinking skills. For years, doctors have recommended that pregnant women take folate supplements to reduce the risk of fetal brain and spinal cord defects. This is because folate is needed to close the neural tube in the fetus, a tube that will become the spinal cord.

Folate and depression

The link between folate and depression has been discussed in the medical literature since the 1960s. As the decades have passed, ideas have been replaced by facts based on important research conducted by highly regarded academic institutions across the United States. Here's what they have found:

Folate affects depression in a number of ways. First, studies have found that many people with depression have lower levels of folate than those who are not depressed. Red blood cell folate levels are much lower in depressed patients than in those with other psychiatric disorders, and a recent study found that people whose diets contain greater amounts of folate report less depression. Thus, for some people with depression, the problem—and the solution—may be dietary.

Second, studies have also found that antidepressant treatments, including medications and ECT, do not work as well for people with low folate levels. One study looked at 213 adults with major depressive disorder who were treated with fluoxetine (Prozac) for eight weeks, finding that low folate levels were linked to a lack of response to the medication. This shows that a certain level of folate must be present if antidepressants are to be effective, and it may explain some kinds of medication failure in depression treatment.

Third, depressed people with lower levels of folate are more likely to get depressed again. That is, depression may lift with treatment, but it is more likely to return if there is not enough folate. This was shown by researchers from Massachusetts General Hospital in a study of depressed people who had improved after taking fluoxetine. The researchers checked patients' folate levels to determine prestudy levels and then monitored their progress for about seven months as they continued to take fluoxetine.

The baseline folate levels played a role in whether depression returned: 43 percent of those with low folate levels became depressed again, compared with only 3 percent of study subjects with normal folate levels.

Building on this knowledge, researchers explored the addition of folate to standard antidepressant treatment. In a ten-week study, men and women diagnosed with a new episode of depression were treated with daily doses of fluoxetine. In addition, they received either 500 µg of folic acid or a placebo every day. At the end of the study, the women (but not the men) who had taken folic acid with their medication were much happier than those on the placebo plus medication. The researchers noted, "Folic acid is a simple method of greatly improving the antidepressant action of fluoxetine and probably other antidepressant agents."

In a 2013 study of 554 depressed adult patients given L-methylfolate, 58.2 percent had a decrease in depressive symptoms three months later, 67.9 percent responded to treatment, and 45.7 percent went into remission from their symptoms. Subjects also reported a decrease in impairment in their work, home, and social lives.

Another study from psychiatrists at Massachusetts General Hospital also showed the benefits of taking folate with antidepressants. Patients with depression who had remained depressed despite taking SSRI antidepressants such as Prozac, Zoloft, Effexor, and Paxil were given a folic acid supplement to take with their medication for eight weeks. After eight weeks, the patients' depression improved.

The following summarizes the research on folate and depression:

- Low folate levels are linked to a higher likelihood of depression.
- Low folate levels are linked to poor response to antidepressants.
- Low folate levels map to a higher relapse rate.
- Folate supplementation makes antidepressants work better.

Folate, folic acid, and L-methylfolate

I have been using the words "folate" and "folic acid" interchangeably, as if they were exactly the same thing. But the truth is that they are different forms of the same vitamin, and as a result, the body handles them differently:

- Folate is the natural form of the vitamin in various foods.
- Folic acid is the human-made form of the vitamin used in supplements and fortified foods.

- 5-methyltetrahydrofolate (also known as L-methylfolate) is the natural, active form of folate used at the cellular level for DNA reproduction, the regulation of homocysteine, and other functions. L-methylfolate easily crosses the blood-brain barrier. One study with seventy-five subjects found that those who took 15 mg of L-methylfolate per day plus an antidepressant had a greater improvement in symptoms than those who took an antidepressant plus placebo.
- L-methylfolate, when given to seventy-five patients with antidepressant-resistant major depression, lifted depressive symptoms much more effectively than placebo in those with certain biomarkers. The findings from this 2014 study may someday allow doctors to identify patients with treatment-resistant depression and certain biomarkers who would likely respond to treatment with L-methylfolate.

The form of folate that people commonly take as a supplement is folic acid, the human-made form. This type of folate can exert activity in the body but not in the brain. To affect the brain and influence mental well-being, folate must first be changed into L-methylfolate. This form of folate can cross the physiological "wall" separating the rest of the body from the brain, the so-called blood-brain barrier. The blood-brain barrier surrounds and protects the central nervous system (the brain, spinal cord, and their fluids), allowing certain substances to cross it while fencing others out. Folate crosses the blood-brain barrier in the form of L-methylfolate. After entering the brain, this form of folate is changed into yet another form that helps create the mood-altering neurotransmitters serotonin, dopamine, and norepinephrine. Maintaining the proper amounts and ratios of these neurotransmitters is important for warding off depression.

Many people can easily and efficiently break down the folate they get from food and folic acid from supplements into the active forms needed for top body and brain function. But others do not, due to their unique genetics. For example, genetic mutations called *MTHFR* polymorphisms prevent the body from easily changing folate into the active form that crosses the blood-brain barrier. People with this genetic change may eat plenty of folate-containing foods and take folate supplements, but the amount of folate in the brain or brain area is still not enough. Not surprisingly, studies have found that people with a *MTHFR* mutation are more likely to become depressed than those without it and that people with depression are more likely to have a *MTHFR* mutation.

Determining if there is enough folate

No single test can determine if you have enough folate. You can measure folate levels in the blood, but they do not always accurately reflect folate levels in the CSF surrounding the brain. A blood level may be in the normal range, but because there is not enough folate in the brain, a person can have a "functional shortage." Another way to see if a person has enough folate is to measure the levels of the amino acid homocysteine. Folate helps break down homocysteine in the body; if a person doesn't have enough folate, homocysteine levels rise.

How much to take

For some depressed patients, especially those on severely restricted diets, simply adding folate-rich foods to the diet can make a difference. Good sources include asparagus, citrus fruit, fortified cereals, green leafy vegetables, and legumes (peas, beans, and lentils). Moreover, many brands of cereal and flour are fortified with folic acid.

But people can lack folate even if there's plenty of this nutrient in the diet. As stated earlier, some people have a genetic abnormality that prevents them from changing folate into a form that can cross the blood-brain barrier. Others may have trouble absorbing folate. In addition, birth control pills, antiseizure medications, antacids, certain antibiotics, alcohol consumption, and smoking can interfere with folate metabolism.

In many cases of depression, supplementation may be needed—particularly in older adults. I typically recommend folate in the form of L-methylfolate, the form of folate that crosses the blood-brain barrier, which is especially helpful for people with a *MTHFR* polymorphism. L-methylfolate can also be purchased over the counter in some pharmacies, vitamin stores, and health-food stores. A prescription-grade L-methylfolate is available as well. The good news is that, with a drug company backing a nutritional supplement, we are now beginning to see more research supporting the use of L-methylfolate for the treatment of depression. L-methylfolate can be used with antidepressants. For many, it can be a core supplement in a treatment plan that does not include antidepressants.

The results of studies exploring the relationship between folate and depression are clear and compelling. When supplementing, avoid human-made forms of folate such as folic acid; use L-methylfolate instead. Eat plenty of foods containing the natural forms of folate.

Folate in the form of L-methylfolate has been shown to have fewer health risks than the commonly used synthetic folic acid supplement. I recommend 3–5 mg of L-methylfolate per day for depression.

Remember that when you use supplements, your doctor should monitor you carefully to ensure that you are getting ample amounts, but never too much, according to your biochemical individuality.

Vitamin B_{12}

Vitamin B_{12} is not a single substance. Instead, it is a family of compounds made by bacteria, fungi, or other organisms. Best known for its role in forming red blood cells, B_{12} also works with B_6 and folic acid to make serotonin and dopamine. Low levels of this vitamin are linked to infertility, osteoporosis, heart disease, and stroke. B_{12} is also important for normal functioning of the central nervous system (brain and spinal cord).

People who are vitamin B_{12} deficient may have numerous neurological problems, including tingling in the hands and feet and difficulty with coordination and walking. If not recognized and treated, some of these symptoms can be permanent. A vitamin B_{12} shortage can also lead to a range of psychiatric conditions, including depression, anxiety, paranoia, hallucinations, memory loss, confusion, outbursts of temper, and behavioral changes.

Vitamin B_{12} and depression

Even slightly lower-than-normal levels of B_{12} may be linked to depression, fatigue, and poor memory in some people. And if levels drop further, a condition known as pernicious anemia can develop. A combination of vitamin B_{12} and folic acid is needed to make SAMe, which in turn is necessary for the use of the neurotransmitters that regulate mood. Studies have shown that up to 30 percent of those hospitalized for depression lack vitamin B_{12}.

In one study, researchers assessed vitamin B_{12} levels in nearly three hundred elderly people with depressive symptoms or clinical depression and compared them with those of people who were not depressed. They found that people with a vitamin B_{12} shortage were much more likely to be depressed than those with adequate B_{12}.

Another study assessed the vitamin B_{12} levels of 115 people with major depressive disorder and then followed them for six months, at which time researchers measured the levels again. Higher vitamin B_{12} levels were linked to better long-term psychological function. Those whose depression improved the most had the highest vitamin B_{12} levels in their blood after six months. Those whose depression had not improved at all had the lowest vitamin B_{12} levels.

Determining if there is enough vitamin B_{12}

Vitamin B_{12} blood levels of 200–600 pg/mL are generally considered normal, but "normal" is not high enough for many people. Even if this "normal" level were enough for physical function, the amount of vitamin B_{12} in the blood does not necessarily match the amount in the brain, so brain levels could be low even though blood levels are fine. Tests for blood and urine methylmalonic acid or homocysteine can also be used to gauge whether B_{12} levels are optimal. I recommend supplementation to anyone with a level less than 600 pg/mL.

How much to take

It's best to get ample amounts of B_{12} from foods such as beef liver, cheese, eggs, milk, fish, and yogurt. However, as with folate, some people may consume plenty of foods containing B_{12} yet still have a shortage because they cannot absorb the vitamin well. This can happen if the stomach is not producing enough hydrochloric acid to release B_{12} from the food. Hydrochloric acid levels fall with age and can be low due to the use of antacids and ulcer medications. B_{12} levels also decrease if the body fails to make enough intrinsic factor, a natural substance needed for B_{12} absorption. Intrinsic factor levels tend to fall with age, so many people who are middle-aged and older do not have enough. Without enough intrinsic factor, intestinal bacteria consume most of the available B_{12}, and the rest may be excreted.

I recommend that all depressed patients have their B_{12}, methylmalonic acid, and homocysteine levels checked. If B_{12} levels are low (less than 500 pg/mL) and homocysteine levels are high (more than 12 micromoles per liter [µm/L]), I recommend B_{12} shots of 1 mg to quickly increase levels as patients start taking daily supplements of a form of B_{12} absorbed under the tongue.

There are three forms of vitamin B_{12}: methylcobalamin, hydroxycobalamin, and cyanocobalamin. All three forms increase blood levels of B_{12}

and improve symptoms. My preference is hydroxycobalamin or methylcobalamin, if available.

Testing a patient's B_{12} level is simple and safe, and the rewards can be large for many patients. In my opinion, most doctors believe that a B_{12} shortage is a problem of elderly people. Yet I have seen B_{12} shortages in children, teens, and young to middle-aged adults with depression or anxiety. Get your levels checked.

Vitamin D

Vitamin D comes from two very different sources: food and sunlight. Cholesterol is the precursor to vitamin D. On exposure to ultraviolet light, cholesterol is changed to this vitamin in the skin and absorbed by the body. Vitamin D enables the body to absorb and use calcium and phosphorus and for the growth of bones and teeth. It is also very involved in brain function. Vitamin D receptors are found in both neurons and glial cells, brain cells that support neurons by providing nutrition and insulation.

Like other nutrients, vitamin D comes in different forms. They include vitamin D_2, known technically as ergocalciferol, which is made by plants and enters the human body when those plants are eaten, and vitamin D_3, also known as cholecalciferol, which the human body makes when the skin is exposed to sunlight.

Vitamin D was originally believed to be of use only in preventing rickets and osteomalacia, classic diseases of a vitamin D shortage, and other diseases of the bone. But research has shown that vitamin D does much more, influencing the health and function of tissues and organs throughout the body. Thanks to research conducted over the past several decades, we can now say with conviction that low levels of the vitamin are linked to psoriasis, muscle pain and weakness, high blood pressure, some forms of cancer, and autoimmune disease and other illnesses. One study even suggested that the link between levels of vitamin D in the blood and depression emerges first in childhood. As the scientific evidence grows, more health experts are calling for an increase in the recommended intake of vitamin D.

I have seen supplement fads come and go, but never have I been as impressed as I am by research about vitamin D effectiveness and importance to human health. An avalanche of solid scientific information shows that vitamin D is much more than a way to keep the bones strong. Although psychiatry has been slow to accept the importance of this vitamin, it is now clear that ample amounts of vitamin D are necessary for optimal mental health.

Vitamin D and depression

Health experts think there is a link between vitamin D and mood, because SAD arises in the dark times of the year when there is relatively little sunshine available to create vitamin D in the body. Researchers from the Washington University School of Medicine in St. Louis, Missouri, examined the relationship between vitamin D and depression in senior citizens. Both vitamin levels and emotional status were established in eighty research subjects, 59 percent of whom had abnormally low vitamin D levels. When vitamin levels and mood were compared, it was clear that a vitamin D shortage was linked to low mood.

Research suggests that low vitamin D levels are linked to major depression and that depression has increased during the last century as we have reduced our exposure to sunlight, leading to decreased vitamin D levels. Indeed, one study found that levels of vitamin D in the blood could predict scores on a depression test. Here's a look at some studies:

- In 2014, researchers who measured levels of vitamin D in patients with current or former depression found lower levels of vitamin D in those with current depression—especially those with the most severe symptoms—than in those with a former episode or healthy patients.
- Researchers studying 4,164 Australian adults without metabolic syndrome showed that lower vitamin D levels were linked to an increased risk of metabolic syndrome, characterized by a thick waist, high triglycerides, high fasting glucose, and insulin resistance, at five years.
- Researchers looking at levels of vitamin D in 2,752 children in southwest England found that higher levels of vitamin D were linked to fewer depressive symptoms at 13.8 years of age and a lower risk of depressive symptoms at ages 10.6 and 13.8.
- Vitamin D levels were measured in 7,358 people aged fifty and older with heart disease. Based on the results, they were placed in the optimal, normal, low, or very low vitamin D group. They were also evaluated for depression. When compared with those in the optimal

vitamin D group, those in the normal, low, and very low groups were more likely to be depressed.

- Italian researchers checked the vitamin D levels and mental health status of 954 senior citizens at the beginning of a six-year study. The level of depression, if any, was checked again after three and six years. Both men and women with lower levels of vitamin D were more likely to have worsened depression or to develop depression if they did not have it at the beginning than those with higher levels.
- Duke University Medical Center researchers looking at forty-two studies found that a vitamin D shortage was quite common among senior citizens living in the community (rather than in nursing or retirement homes) and that lower levels of the vitamin were linked to a greater likelihood of depression.
- A vitamin D shortage may even set the stage for depression while one is still in the womb. An interesting paper published by Danish researchers noted that patients with both schizophrenia and bipolar disorder are more often born in winter and spring, when mothers have the lowest amounts of vitamin D in their blood.
- A Swedish study showed low vitamin D levels in fifty-four depressed teens, a positive link between vitamin D and well-being, and an improvement in symptoms with vitamin D supplementation.
- A study of suicide attempters, nonsuicidal depressed patients, and healthy patients found that suicide attempters had much lower levels of vitamin D than the other subjects. In fact, 58 percent of those who had attempted suicide lacked vitamin D. Similarly, a study of active-duty service members showed that low vitamin D is common in this group and that lower levels of vitamin D are linked with a higher risk of suicide.
- In two different studies looking at whether low vitamin D levels are linked with depression after stroke, researchers found that depressed post-stroke patients had reduced levels of vitamin D.
- Researchers looking at whether vitamin D levels were linked to symptoms of depression in young women found that low vitamin D levels predicted significant depressive symptoms, regardless of season, body mass index, race/ethnicity, physical activity, time in nature, or diet.
- A 2015 study found that low vitamin D levels appear to be linked to psychiatric distress, but not violence, in adolescents. In fact, the

teens who had low vitamin D levels were 1.5 to 1.8 times more likely to report feelings of anger, depression, sadness, worry, anxiety, and poor sleep.

Research has also shown that vitamin D treatment can relieve symptoms of depression. For example, a 1999 study of patients with SAD found that those given a one-time oral dose of 100,000 international units (IU) of vitamin D experienced greater relief from depression than those given light therapy (a standard treatment for SAD). A 2009 pilot study arrived at similar results, finding that supplemental vitamin D given to women with low levels of the vitamin in their blood caused their levels to rise and their depression ratings to fall. The vitamin has even been used to improve the mood of healthy, nondepressed people during winter, when there is less sunshine to spur the body to make vitamin D.

> I was asked to see a seventeen-year-old depressed teen whose family did not want her to take any medications. Her depression was overwhelming, causing her to drop out of athletic activities and affecting her ability to complete her course work at school. When I checked her vitamin D levels, I found that she was severely lacking, with a level of 7 nanograms per milliliter (ng/mL). I quickly started her on 3,000 IU of vitamin D for two months. As her vitamin D level rose to 35 ng/mL, her mood improved and she was able to return to schoolwork and her activities. This case is striking, as vitamin D supplementation was the only biological intervention needed to treat her depression.

Determining if there is enough vitamin D

For a long time, vitamin D blood levels between 20 and 30 ng/mL were accepted as normal and healthy. We now know that this range is too low, and even people who were thought to be safely in the middle of range may need more of the vitamin. Even some people in the upper reaches may need more. Vitamin D is measured with a simple blood test assessing the 25-hydroxyvitamin D level. I prefer to see a 25-hydroxyvitamin D level of 40–60 ng/mL in my patients.

How much to take

Vitamin D is in foods such as mackerel, salmon, sardines, and vitamin D–fortified milk. The body also makes its own vitamin D when the skin is exposed to sunlight, so it would seem that a shortage in the vitamin would be rare. However, in truth, millions of people are deficient in vitamin D, especially those living in areas where there is not year-round sunshine or those who avoid sunlight.

Biochemical individuality plays a large role in vitamin D status. Although environmental factors such as nutrition and sun exposure influence how much vitamin D you make, genetics are responsible for a large portion of the variation in serum 25-hydroxyvitamin D. A Swedish study involving 204 same-sex twins aged thirty-nine to eighty-five living in a northern region found that genetic factors were responsible for one-fourth of the variation in serum 25-hydroxyvitamin D, no matter the season. During the summer alone, genetics were responsible for half of the variability in 25-hydroxyvitamin D.

I recommend vitamin D supplementation only after testing 25-hydroxyvitamin D levels. Supplementation is based on blood levels and may range from 2,000 to 10,000 IU. Vitamin D supplementation needs to be monitored by blood testing every few months until levels are no longer below 60.

As always when you take vitamin supplements, your doctor should monitor you carefully to ensure that you are getting ample amounts, but never too much, according to your biochemical individuality.

SAMe

The body uses the amino acid methionine to create a substance commonly called SAMe. In turn, SAMe helps make neurotransmitters, proteins, and hormones. Among the neurotransmitters it helps create is the mood enhancer serotonin.

SAMe and depression

Several studies have shown that supplemental SAMe can help relieve depression. A 2014 twelve-week study of 144 adults with major depression found that SAMe was better than placebo starting in week 1 and was better than the antidepressant escitalopram during weeks 2, 4, and 6. Response rates for SAMe were 45 percent; they were 31 percent for escitalopram and 26 percent for placebo.

In 2008, the National Center for Complementary and Alternative Medicine published a meta-analysis on SAMe and depression. Combining the results of twenty-eight different studies, researchers found that SAMe produced a very large improvement in depression compared with placebo.

A 2010 study found SAMe to be an effective add-on to traditional medication for patients with major depression whose depression did not respond to antidepressant treatment. In the study, seventy-three people with major depression who did not respond to SSRI antidepressants were given either an oral dose of SAMe (800 mg twice daily) or a placebo, in addition to their current medication. At the end of six weeks, they were evaluated based on the HDRS. Patients treated with add-on SAMe showed more improvement in their Hamilton scores and had higher rates of recovery than those receiving add-on placebo.

Reading studies is reassuring, but there's nothing like seeing the positive effects in a patient. I remember a fifty-seven-year-old artist who didn't want to take antidepressants because of a side effect he'd had several years previously. "I'd rather be sad than go through those side effects again," he said. He agreed to try SAMe, and within a few months, he reported that his depression was "almost entirely gone," without any side effects.

How much to take

SAMe is available as a supplement; no prescription is required. A standard dose of SAMe has not been set; SAMe studies have used doses ranging from 400 to 1,600 mg per day. I recommend 800–1,600 mg of SAMe per day for depression.

Side effects of SAMe include insomnia, anxiety, and stomach upset. The combination of SAMe and certain antidepressants may trigger serotonin syndrome, which can produce symptoms such as rapid heartbeat, agitation, and shaking. Although SAMe is available without a prescription, it should always be taken under the supervision of a doctor.

Remember, with SAMe—as with any other supplements—you should work with a doctor or other health care professional.

Inositol

Inositol (also known as vitamin B_8) helps form healthy cell membranes and maintains proper electrical energy and nutrient transfer between cells. Inositol is changed into a substance that regulates the action of serotonin, the lack of which is linked to depression, panic disorder, and OCD. Restoring normal levels of this vitamin may help improve psychiatric symptoms, including depression, feelings of panic, and obsessive thoughts.

Inositol and depression

Low levels of inositol in the CSF have been found in depressed people. Several studies have shown that the vitamin can help improve symptoms of depression at dosages of 12 g per day. In some studies, patients took inositol in addition to antidepressant medications; in others, they took only inositol or a placebo. The results were the same: depression improved when inositol was taken. One study went one step further, showing that, when inositol treatment was stopped, depression symptoms returned. Then, when inositol treatment was begun again, symptoms of depression disappeared again. A 2014 study also showed that inositol was marginally more effective than placebo in depressed patients and that it seemed to work best in patients with premenstrual dysphoric disorder.

Two studies support the use of inositol in reducing the frequency and severity of panic attacks, a problem that sometimes occurs with depression. One reported that a group of patients taking inositol had far fewer panic attacks than a group taking a placebo. The other compared inositol with the psychiatric medication fluvoxamine (Luvox). Subjects with active panic disorder were treated with up to 18 grams of inositol per day or up to 150 mg of fluvoxamine per day. The researchers found that inositol and fluvoxamine were equally effective in treating panic disorder, but inositol was better at reducing the number of panic attacks.

Inositol can also help reduce obsessive thinking, another feature often seen in depression. One study found that people with OCD who took 18 g of inositol per day reported fewer obsessions and compulsions.

How much to take

Ideally, everyone would get enough inositol from foods such as wheat germ, brewer's yeast, grapefruit, liver, raisins, and unrefined molasses. But there is always the chance that the body cannot absorb or use the vitamin well, which increases the amount you need. In many cases, eating too much sugar may impair absorption. Inositol is a carbohydrate that the body can make from glucose, but eating too much sugar can disrupt the inositol shuttle system and other messenger pathways, leading to a shortage.

There is no RDA for inositol, but it is estimated that most people eat about 1 g per day.

I recommend that patients start with 1/2 teaspoon (1.4 g) of inositol powder twice a day. Over the course of four weeks, I suggest increasing the dose by 1/2 teaspoon every five days until you reach 12 g of inositol per day. Inositol can be taken alone or with medications.

Supplemental inositol appears to be safe, even in high doses. Common side effects include nausea, bloating, insomnia, and fatigue. Because it may stimulate contractions of the uterus, caution is strongly advised when giving it to pregnant women.

Vitamins B_1 (Thiamine), B_3 (Niacin), and B_6 (Pyridoxine) and Depression

Thiamine

The brain rapidly loses energy when thiamine is in short supply, leading to depression, fatigue, anxiety, irritability, insomnia, and memory problems. Decades ago, studies showed that thiamine is important for normal brain function and that those who lack it often become depressed and irritable and have difficulty concentrating and sleeping. In a study in 1942, eleven women consumed a diet that contained only half the recommended amount of thiamine for eight to twelve weeks. They developed troubling symptoms, including a decreased appetite and lower food intake, which grew worse the longer they remained on the diet. Most notably, most of the women became depressed. When the women began taking thiamine supplements at the end of the study, the symptoms gradually subsided.

Niacin

The "feel-good" neurotransmitter serotonin is made from an amino acid called tryptophan, which is usually plentiful in the food supply. However, when niacin is in short supply, tryptophan is used to make niacin instead of serotonin. Since making just 1 mg of niacin takes 60 mg of tryptophan, the body can easily run short of the raw material it needs to make serotonin when it is forced to make niacin. No wonder, then, that a niacin shortage can result in depression, agitation, and anxiety, all of which are linked to low amounts of serotonin.

Pyridoxine

Psychological and psychiatric conditions such as depression, confusion, and irritability can result from a vitamin B_6 shortage. This is most likely because B_6 is needed to make the neurotransmitters serotonin, dopamine, norepinephrine, and GABA—all of which have potent effects on the brain. Depressed patients often have low B_6 levels. One study found low blood levels of B_6 in 21 percent of 101 depressed outpatients. Another found much lower levels (48 percent lower) of active vitamin B_6 in depressed patients compared with controls. Moreover, B_6 is needed to support brain function, synthesis of RNA and DNA, and formation of the myelin sheath around the nerve cells, which helps to transmit signals through the brain.

Interfering with these three Bs

The body's supply of B vitamins can be depleted by eating too many refined carbohydrates—the simple sugars in white flour, cakes, candy, pies, syrups, sweetened breakfast cereals, and many processed foods. People with alcoholism or kidney failure may also lack sufficient B vitamins.

How much to take

In a perfect world, everyone would get enough of these vitamins from foods such as bananas, beans, lentils, broccoli, brown rice, eggs, fish, lean meat, oatmeal, soybeans, spinach, sunflower seeds, nuts, pork, whole-grain cereals, yeast, and poultry. But because some people have poor diets or problems absorbing the vitamins, taking vitamins is often wise.

I recommend a B-complex vitamin containing L-methylfolate—not folic acid—as L-methylfolate is readily available to cross the blood-brain barrier. B-Complex Plus from Pure Encapsulations includes the important B vitamins, as well as L-methylfolate that play a role in the conversion of carbohydrates into energy.

Check and Replenish Based on Your Unique Biochemical Needs

Throughout the early part of the twentieth century, numerous articles in the medical literature documented successful treatment of depression with B vitamins and other nutrients. Building on new understandings of the body and nutrition, pioneering doctors began developing a new approach to treating depression that showed great promise. However, as public health officials used this scientific knowledge to fortify our food supply, vitamin-shortage diseases started slowly disappearing. In the 1950s, drug companies introduced prescription medications for depression, and in the decades following, interest in nutritional treatment of mental disease waned.

Although the lion's share of research funds has been given to drug studies over the past fifty or sixty years, research into vitamins and other nutrients has continued, and impressive evidence has grown that folic acid, B_{12}, vitamin D, and other nutrients can be effective treatments for many people. Today, we can offer nondrug treatments that we know are successful. This is not to say that supplements are better than medications, or vice versa. For certain people, vitamins or other supplements, or even a simple change in diet, are exactly what's needed. For others, medications or a combination of medications and nutrients is the right prescription.

My experience has shown that better nutrition and nutritional supplementation are critical for almost everyone, because modern agricultural, processing, shipping, and selling practices have resulted in foods that lack nutrients. And not only are we not getting the nutrition we should, but refined foods filled with sugars can also force the body to "use up" the B vitamins. In the standard American diet, we do not get enough of the nutrients we need. As a result, many people have serious nutritional shortages. Often, depression can be helped by simply restoring nutritional health.

Because this chapter covers a lot of information, I want to emphasize the most important idea: Every depressed person should take a B-complex vitamin with L-methylfolate. Vitamin B_{12} and vitamin D levels need to be checked and supplemented accordingly. Everybody is biochemically and genetically unique, so it is vital that you have a health professional test your nutrient levels. If any shortages are discovered, they should be treated aggressively. The treatment of nutritional problems may be the way out of depression.

Chapter 15

R—Restore

"All disease begins in the gut," wrote Hippocrates, the father of medicine, more than two thousand years ago. The field of psychiatry is only now fully recognizing the profound wisdom behind this ancient observation.

New understanding of the close connection between the brain and the intestinal tract, or gut, opens a door to exciting possibilities for treating depression. The composition of the gut, which varies by individual, is affected by factors including diet, stress, exercise, and antibiotics. The potential to influence the bacterial makeup of the gut and thereby influence the brain has far-reaching implications for treatment that is safe and cost effective.

Scientists have long known that a balance of bacteria in the intestinal tract is important for digestive health. They have also known for a long time that the brain affects the gut. For example, people commonly develop "butterflies," or gastrointestinal symptoms, before going on stage or making an important presentation. But the revolution in the way we now understand brain-related disorders is based on a relatively new insight: the relationship between brain and gut works in both directions. Not only does the brain influence the gut; the gut also influences the brain.

The Microbiome

The human intestinal tract is a densely populated place. It is home to 100 trillion cells from more than one thousand species—a collection of nerves, microorganisms, and immune cells. The cells of the microbiome, the changing population of bacteria within the gut, outnumber the cells that are actually part of the human body by ninety to one. In fact, microbial genes outnumber human genes 150 to 1, with twenty-two thousand human genes and more than 3.3 million bacterial genes identified.

Many people think of bacteria as the culprits in a disease process that must be eradicated by antibiotics. Actually, the vast majority of organisms that comprise the microbiome are health-enhancing bacteria that protect the digestive system from illness and infection, break down food, and synthesize nutrients. Also living within the microbiome, however, are harmful bacteria, or pathogens, that cause disease, allergies, and inflammation. As long as the health-promoting bacteria dominate the unfriendly kind, the digestive system remains relatively healthy. But when harmful bacteria proliferate, they produce chemicals that damage the gut, disrupt the immune system, and cause inflammation.

The gut houses more than 70 percent of the immune system, and the microbiome plays a key role in regulating the body's immune response. The composition of the microbiome can make a difference between whether people get sick or stay well. Disruption of the balance of bacteria in the gut through stress, medication, a diet high in sugar, deficiencies in minerals and vitamins, or infection can set the stage for inflammation. Fructose lowers the activity of brain-derived neurotrophic factor (BDNF), a chemical that protects the immune system and sustains the plasticity of the nervous system. Sucrose alters the bacterial balance in the intestines, often overwhelming the health-promoting bacteria with *Candida* yeast. In addition to killing the pathogens they target, antibiotics also wipe out healthy bacteria in the gut. The resulting imbalance in bacteria, called *dysbiosis,* can produce inflammation, toxic metabolites, and a vast array of psychological symptoms.

The body reacts to all stress as if it were an infection. Changes in intestinal flora encourage the growth of pathogenic bacteria, raising an alarm in the immune system. Stress decreases the number of beneficial bacteria, such as *Lactobacilli* and *Bifidobacteria,* which leads to inflammation and the development of cytokines. Cytokines are proteins manufactured by immune cells that govern responses to foreign antigens and germs. Proinflammatory cytokines trigger an inflammatory response, while anti-inflammatory cytokines limit inflammation. A spike in proinflammatory cytokines can wreak havoc in the microbiome, and current research has demonstrated a direct correlation between inflammation and depression.

Factors That Decrease "Good" Bacteria

- Lack of zinc, B vitamins, and essential fatty acids
- Lack of sunlight
- Reduced social support
- Poor nutrition
- Lack of connection with nature
- Stress
- Diet high in sugars and processed fructose
- Use of antibiotics, alcohol, and birth control pills
- Use of corticosteroids and anti-inflammatory drugs
- Infections
- Use of laxatives
- Excessive use of antibacterial soap
- Consuming meat from animals treated with growth hormones or antibiotics
- Gluten-containing grains

The Gut–Brain Connection

The gut, where an inflammatory storm can begin, is connected to the brain through multiple overlapping pathways. It is controlled by the enteric nervous system, sometimes called the "second brain." The vagus nerve, which links the colon and the brain stem, is the primary conduit by which inflammatory markers travel from gut to brain. A chemical in the gut known as lipopolysaccharide (LPS) can permeate the gut wall, stimulate white blood cells to create cytokines, and transport them to the brain.

Not only does inflammation in the gut lead to an inflammatory reaction in the brain, intestinal microorganisms affect the neurotransmitter balance in the brain. Like the brain, the gut produces neuropeptides and neurotransmitters. In fact, the gut makes up to 95 percent of the body's serotonin by producing tryptophan, serotonin's precursor. Serotonin and other neurotransmitters that influence emotions and mood are sent from the brain to the gut and from the gut to the brain. Proinflammatory cytokines that reach the brain inhibit the metabolism of the neurotransmitter serotonin.

Because of mounting scientific evidence of intricate connections between the gut and the brain, the microbiome is now a central focus of psychiatric research.

The Gut Microbiome and Depression

The field of psychiatry long overlooked or underestimated the immune system's influence on mental and emotional disorders. Only in the past two decades have scientists begun to understand the molecular mechanisms connecting the immune system and the brain. The discovery of a type of brain inflammation, anti-NMDA receptor encephalitis, provided concrete evidence of an association between the immune system and psychiatric symptoms. This discovery opened a new line of inquiry into whether a similar mechanism could explain other psychiatric illnesses.

Recent research identifies inflammation as the common denominator of many diseases. Inflammation appears to underlie Alzheimer's disease, Parkinson's disease, autism, coronary heart disease, diabetes, and even cancer. Clinical observations show that about 70 percent of people who suffer from autoimmune disorders develop neurological and psychiatric symptoms. It is not always clear which precedes which—the unhealthy gut or the disorder. But whichever comes first, the immune system goes awry. Inflammation is now specifically implicated in neuropsychiatric disorders, including depression. Researchers have shown that elevated levels of the proinflammatory cytokine interleukin-6 (IL-6) are often present in patients with major depressive disorder.

The connection between inflammation in the gut and depression is perhaps most apparent in the case of the bacteria *Clostridium difficile.* This microorganism causes a potentially deadly disease, common in hospitals and nursing homes, that sometimes occurs after long-term treatment with antibiotics. It can multiply and wipe out good bacteria in the colon.

There are many different strains of Clostridia in our guts. An overgrowth of certain strains of *Clostridia* generates 3-hydroxyphenyl 3-hydroxpropionic acid (HPHPA). HPHPA molecules pass through the gut into the bloodstream and into the brain, where they inactivate the enzyme dopamine-beta-hydroxylase (DBH). DBH is necessary for transforming the neurotransmitter dopamine into the neurotransmitter norepinephrine and sustaining a balance between the two. Through the action of HPHPA, dopamine levels shoot up. Dopamine levels gone awry in combination with insufficient norepinephrine can culminate in a vortex of mental, emotional, and behavioral havoc.

Many of my patients struggling with depression have elevated levels of HPHPA, which can be detected through a simple urine test measuring organic acids. Small-scale studies have looked at levels of HPHPA in patients with autism and schizophrenia, and high HPHPA is usually associated with behavioral, gastrointestinal, and neuropsychiatric symptoms. In one study, the urine of a patient experiencing a psychotic episode had HPHPA levels up to three hundred times higher than the normal value. Elevations in HPHPA can typically be resolved by high-dose probiotics, or antibiotic medications for more severe cases. I have seen patients struggling with chronic depression improve dramatically after three months of high-dose probiotic supplementation.

The hypothesis that the immune system is implicated in psychiatric problems represents a paradigm shift. It not only provides a biological basis for many formerly inexplicable conditions; it also makes possible avenues for diagnosing, treating, and preventing these conditions by managing inflammation. The longer the patient's immune system is out of balance, the more severe the psychiatric symptoms can become.

Probiotics

A simple test can detect the presence of harmful bacteria, and a straightforward integrative treatment plan can restore balance. Probiotics can be used to repopulate the gut with health-enhancing bacteria. Probiotics are live microorganisms that may benefit health when administered in adequate amounts.

Benefits of probiotics have been known for centuries, and scientists have long documented the benefits of probiotic supplementation. The vast majority of this research has concentrated on gastrointestinal dysfunction and indigestion.

Cultures all over the world use specific foods to enhance digestion. Examples of food containing live, health-promoting bacteria include yogurt, kefir, and other fermented milk products and fermented foods such as sauerkraut, kimchi, tempeh, miso, and kombucha. In contrast, the typical Western diet, which underuses plant foods and overuses sugar, increases vulnerability to an unhealthy microbiome. A highly refined diet in combination with the high level of antibiotic use in the West increases the risk of inflammatory diseases.

The effectiveness of probiotic supplementation has been studied extensively in animals. One research team found that rats raised in an environment free of bacteria demonstrated increased response to stressors. Giving these rats probiotics helped normalize their stress responses. In another study, broth containing probiotics helped mice remain calmer in a maze test than mice fed plain broth. Mice that consumed probiotic broth explored open spaces, while those on a plain broth diet quivered next to the high walls. Probiotic-fed mice also had lower levels of the stress-induced hormone cortisol.

The first reports of using probiotic supplements specifically to treat depression occurred more than a century ago. In 1920, Dr. George Porter Phillips reported that live bacteria supplements improved symptoms of depression in adults with melancholia. Scientists now know that probiotics influence mood by inhibiting cytokine production. Specifically, they contribute to systemic downregulation of inflammatory processes by balancing pro- and anti-inflammatory cytokines.

Probiotics also contribute to neurotransmitter availability. A research study on probiotics and depression found that supplementation with a probiotic strain called *Bifidobacterium infantis* led to a lower inflammatory response and to an increase in the production of tryptophan, a precursor of serotonin, which is involved in mood regulation. This particular bacterial strain exerted antidepressant activity in animals under stress.

More research conducted in the last few years continues to demonstrate the importance of beneficial bacteria in the mental well-being of humans. When researchers from Norway examined the microbes in fecal samples of thirty-seven depressed and eighteen nondepressed patients, they found that the bacteria strain *Bacteroides* was significantly overrepresented in patients with depression compared with healthy controls. Previous studies have correlated *Bacteroides* bacteria with obesity and inflammation, which have also been linked to an increased risk of depression.

Another study found that probiotics were able to alter activity in the brain regions responsible for regulating emotions and sensations. The study split thirty-six healthy women into three groups: one treatment group that ate probiotic-rich yogurt; one group given a product that looked and tasted like yogurt, with no probiotics; and a control group that ate no product at all. All of the women underwent functional magnetic resonance imaging (FMRI) before and after four weeks of treatment to measure how the brain responded during emotional attention tasks. They were shown pictures of people with angry or frightened faces and instructed to match them to other faces showing the same emotions. Researchers observed increased blood flow to and activity in brain regions involved in emotion processing in the group receiving the probiotic.

A clinical trial, published in 2014, reinforced the beneficial effects of probiotics and their ability to alleviate symptoms of anxiety in humans. The study, from England, included forty-five healthy volunteers aged eighteen to twenty-five, who were given a probiotic or a placebo every day for three weeks. At the end of the study, they completed several computer tests to evaluate how they processed emotional information such as negative and positive words. People given the probiotic focused more on positive information and paid less attention to negative information, suggesting that they experienced less anxiety when presented with negative stimuli. Researchers also found that the probiotic-supplemented group had lower levels of the stress hormone cortisol compared with the nonsupplemented group. High levels of cortisol are often associated with symptoms of depression and anxiety.

Similarly, in a study published in a 2015 issue of the journal *Brain, Behavior, and Immunity*, researchers found that multispecies probiotics can help decrease rumination, or recurrent thoughts about the possible causes and consequences of distress that often precede depressive episodes. Participants who received probiotics expressed significantly fewer ruminative thoughts at the end of the study through a questionnaire assessing cognitive reactivity. Although the research looking at probiotic supplementation in humans is limited, it shows promise as a useful intervention in preventing the progression of depressive symptoms and as an adjuvant therapy.

Using probiotics

Probiotics are nutritional supplements based on strains of bacteria cultured, grown, and then introduced into the body. I have used probiotic supplements successfully to treat depression for more than a decade. They can lessen the need for drug treatment and instead change a patient's physiology by manipulating the microbiome.

While incorporating foods containing live bacteria into the diet is beneficial, supplementation with probiotics is often more effective. I have found that supplementation with bacteria numbering in the billions is necessary for restoring healthy gastrointestinal function.

Probiotics are generally sold as capsules, powder, tablets, or liquid. In whatever form, probiotic supplements can help restore health-promoting bacteria to the digestive tract, which in turn decreases inflammation. A good probiotic supplement has a special enteric coating to protect the capsule as it travels through the stomach. This enteric coating is composed of gelatin and pectin, which eventually dissolves in the intestinal tract. The coating ensures that the bacteria survive their journey through the stomach acid to the intestines, where they are needed.

Once a probiotic regimen is started, the good bacteria optimize the digestive terrain and improve immune function as they move through the digestive tract and form colonies along the intestinal walls. As these beneficial microbes multiply, they compete with the harmful microbes living there. The probiotic microbes eventually crowd out harmful organisms while establishing themselves throughout the digestive tract.

In fact, everyone with depression or digestive issues is likely to benefit from probiotics, as diversity in the microflora is associated with good health. Probiotic supplements can be obtained at health-food stores, although I highly recommend purchasing high-quality supplements from a trusted source, as quality may vary depending on the manufacturer. (For more information on where to purchase quality supplements, refer to the Resources section). For patients who are depressed or anxious and also have gastrointestinal symptoms, I recommend 100 to 200 billion colony-forming units (CFUs) per day for at least three months.

For testing bacterial levels to determine whether high doses are needed, I routinely use the Great Plains Laboratory's Organic Acid Test. The laboratory is directed by Dr. William Shaw, who discovered the link between HPHPA and psychiatric symptoms more than twenty years ago.

Restoring Brain Health

Integrative medicine is based on the perspective that the brain is not distinct from the body. Perhaps nowhere is the intricate interdependence of brain and body more clear than in the brain–gut connection. If depression is a combination of symptoms driven by inflammation, the source of the problem is a disruption in gut ecology.

Emerging research is focusing on the human microbiome and its influence on brain health. New molecular technologies have contributed insight about the role of the gut in many disorders, including depression. Recognizing that the gut microbiome interacts with other environmental risk factors such as stress and diet should help us develop better interventions for preventing and treating depression.

We can predict which individuals may have a microbial imbalance, but we can't yet say with certainty which probiotic is the most promising intervention for a particular disorder in a particular person. More research into microbial interventions is needed. We can look forward to better understanding how to use probiotics to improve both individual quality of life and the global burden of depression. The gastrointestinal tract and brain are in constant communication. Your individual microbiome yields clues to the factors in your brain that may bring on or sustain depression. By treating your gut, we can help restore your brain health.

Chapter 16

A—Amino Acids and Proteins

Finally, we've reached "A," the last of the components I advocate as part of THE ZEEBRA approach to treating depression. "A" stands for amino acids, which are important for their effect on neurotransmitters.

We don't completely understand the way antidepressants and similar medications work, but we do know that they influence neurotransmitters, important brain chemicals that help regulate mood and behavior. Prozac, for example, increases the amount of serotonin in the brain. But antidepressants don't work for everyone, which is why it's important to know that there are other ways to affect neurotransmitters.

One approach is to use amino acid precursors, foods or supplements that supply the body with extra amounts of the amino acids that influence neurotransmitter levels or activity. Over many years of practice, I've found these to be an invaluable aid in the treatment of depression.

I'm going to begin this chapter by making a statement that will sound heretical to most psychiatrists: *Sometimes the most important intervention for the treatment of depression is supplying the patient with amino acids.* These building blocks of protein can be some of the most powerful antidepressants. I've often seen that many depressed patients have low levels of amino acids and that often their moods improve dramatically when given amino acids. The basis of all psychiatric medications involves enhancing neurotransmitters. Amino acids can do the same thing, as they are the building blocks of the vast majority of neurotransmitters.

The Pieces That Make a Protein

Amino acids are the building blocks of protein. These molecules, which contain carbon, hydrogen, oxygen, and nitrogen atoms in specific shapes, can be strung together in unique sequences to form a huge variety of proteins. In addition to building proteins, amino acids build and repair muscle tissue, form enzymes and hormones (which are also proteins) crucial to the regulation of body processes, and provide the raw material to make neurotransmitters.

The liver makes eleven of the twenty amino acids needed for human health, while the remaining nine must be obtained through the diet. These nine are called the essential amino acids, because consumption of them is essential to good health. The nine essential amino acids are:

- Histidine
- Isoleucine
- Leucine
- Lysine
- Methionine
- Phenylalanine
- Threonine
- Tryptophan
- Valine

The other amino acids are considered nonessential. Because the body makes them, consuming them is not necessarily crucial to health.

Amino Acids and Mood

Certain amino acids, including GABA, glutamine, phenylalanine, taurine, tryptophan, and tyrosine, have been shown to influence mood. Some are changed into neurotransmitters that are critical to brain function, others affect the way the brain works, and one is actually a neurotransmitter itself. Some of the most useful amino acids for depression include phenylalanine, taurine, tyrosine, tryptophan, and 5-HTP.

Phenylalanine

Endorphins, natural substances that help moderate mood and block chronic pain, occur naturally in the body and are always being built and destroyed. Phenylalanine appears to protect endorphins from routine destruction, increasing their levels and improving depressed moods. While the amino acid tryptophan is responsible for the synthesis of serotonin, phenylalanine is responsible for the creation of the neurotransmitters dopamine and norepinephrine.

A phenylalanine deficiency can result in lower dopamine and norepinephrine production, triggering symptoms of poor energy, depression, lack of alertness, and memory problems. Norepinephrine also plays an important role in regulating our stress response system. If you experience chronic stress, a sufficient supply of phenylalanine is necessary.

Results from several small-scale studies looking at the effects of phenylalanine supplementation have demonstrated its ability to alleviate symptoms in patients with depression. In one study, twelve healthy male participants who were given a mixture of phenylalanine and tyrosine reported feeling more alert and less anxious five hours after consumption compared with placebo. Another study with female volunteers mimicked the same results: Women who were subjected to phenylalanine/tyrosine depletion also experienced lower moods after a series of physiological challenges compared with those who received proper supplementation.

Another study assessed phenylalanine levels in both healthy and depressed individuals through blood and urine tests and found that the depressed participants had significantly lower levels of phenylalanine in both samples. In further support of phenylalanine's role in depressive symptoms, the researchers supplemented the forty depressed patients with 500 mg of L-phenylalanine in the morning and at noon, eventually increasing up to 14 g per day, depending on the individual's response to therapeutic effect. At the end of the study, thirty-one out of the forty (77.5 percent) participants reported significant mood improvement.

Phenylalanine comes in two forms, D and L, which are mirror images in structure. The D form is made in a laboratory; the L form is natural. I recommend that any patient with depression complete serum amino acid testing (not a routine test for most physicians) to assess for deficiencies. All of the neurotransmitters and hormones involved in mood regulation are produced from amino acids obtained from one's diet. If phenylalanine deficiency is detected, I would recommend 500–1,000 mg of daily supplementation with DL-phenylalanine.

Tyrosine

Tyrosine is derived from phenylalanine and easily passes into the brain through the blood-brain barrier. In the brain, it is converted to dopamine and the hormones responsible for stress regulation, norepinephrine and epinephrine. Tyrosine is also the precursor for thyroxine, the thyroid hormone that helps control the metabolic rate and growth rate. Tyrosine also helps ward off stress-related depression.

Because of tyrosine's wide-ranging effects on the body in general and on neurotransmitters in particular, low levels of this amino acid can lead to several problems. A lack of dopamine increases the risk of addictive behaviors such as bingeing, drug use, alcoholism, and risk-taking behavior. As the body's stress hormones become more depleted, the risk of depression increases.

Results of a study involving mice suggest that supplemental tyrosine may help ease cognitive and mood problems. Researchers induced stress in the mice by separating them, which depleted their dopamine and norepinephrine levels, well-known causes of mood problems. However, when the mice were given supplemental tyrosine, their levels normalized and their stress response improved.

The *Journal of Psychiatry and Neuroscience* reported that L-tyrosine has been a topic of major interest for many military research studies for its ability to reduce stress. Many animal studies show that the level of L-tyrosine in the brain influences the available amount of dopamine and norepinephrine, which affect mood and alertness. During physical stress, brain neurons are firing rapidly, and this depletion can be normalized by L-tyrosine supplementation. Dr. Simon Young reports that military test subjects have continued to respond positively to L-tyrosine supplementation under physical duress. One study investigated whether tyrosine would be able to counteract adverse environmental conditions that military personnel commonly face. Military personnel were given 1,000 mg of L-tyrosine or a placebo and were subsequently exposed to cold and hypoxic (low oxygen) conditions. The military personnel who received 1,000 mg of L-tyrosine reported fewer adverse side effects and improved cognitive function and mood. L-tyrosine can be of important benefit for individuals struggling with environmental stress factors or low mood.

Tryptophan and 5-HTP

Supplying the brain with sufficient tryptophan (in the form of 5-HTP) can help increase serotonin levels and regulate appetite. Some studies have shown that 5-HTP, a form of tryptophan, boosts brain levels of serotonin and can be an important add-on in treating depression.

The body's synthesis of serotonin depends directly on the amount of tryptophan available in the brain. When the body does not get enough serotonin, low mood, irritability, and anxiety can result.

Tryptophan is found in large amounts in high-protein foods, most notably eggs, cheese, fish, poultry, beef, and soybeans. Like other amino acids, once tryptophan enters the bloodstream, it is sent wherever the body needs it most at the time. It may become part of a hormone, an enzyme, or another protein molecule. Then, when the body's needs have been satisfied, most of the leftover tryptophan is converted in the brain to 5-hydroxytryptophan (5-HTP), which in turn, with the help of vitamin B_6, is converted to serotonin.

Conversion of amino acids into active neurotransmitters requires the availability of nutrient cofactors that are commonly depleted in individuals as a result of medications, dietary deficiencies, and environmental stress. By ensuring that vitamin and mineral cofactors are adequate, we are able to optimize neurotransmitter synthesis in the brain to help address symptoms of depression.

The B vitamins (B_3, B_6, B_{12}) and L-methylfolate are important cofactors required to convert tryptophan into serotonin. Low levels of B_3 affect serotonin levels in two ways. First, the conversion of tryptophan to 5-HTP is limited, since vitamin B_3 facilitates this step. Second, the liver takes up even more tryptophan to compensate for the lack of the vitamin just to convert it to 5-HTP.

When vitamin B_6 levels are low, the conversion of 5-HTP to serotonin is disrupted, and less than 1 percent of the amino acid actually reaches the brain. Low levels of vitamin B_6 are usually observed in women who are pregnant, lactating, or taking oral contraceptives and in individuals struggling with alcohol or substance abuse. When vitamin B_6 supplements were given to research animals, the amount of 5-HTP in the brain was considerably more than in those without vitamin B_6 supplementation.

L-methylfolate is a form of folate that readily crosses the blood-brain barrier for use in neurotransmitter production. L-methylfolate is able to increase folate concentrations in the central nervous system and plays an active role in the crucial steps of serotonin and dopamine synthesis. Individuals deficient in L-methylfolate cannot use tryptophan appropriately to make serotonin.

Deficiencies in amino acids and vitamin and mineral cofactors may result in decreased production of critical chemicals that affect mood. Without sufficient cofactors to ensure optimal use of amino acids for neurotransmitter synthesis, individuals are at higher risk for depression.

For many years, physicians have found that 5-HTP is effective in treating anxiety and depression. All the current research supports that supplying the brain with sufficient 5-HTP can help increase serotonin levels and therefore improve depressive symptoms.

GABA

Gamma-aminobutyric acid (GABA) is itself a neurotransmitter, one of the main substances that help brain cells talk to each other. GABA helps brain cells calm down, aids in the control of muscle activity, and plays an important part in vision. Because it reduces brain cell excitability, GABA acts as a natural tranquilizer, reducing stress and anxiety while increasing alertness and helping keep other neurotransmitters in check. People with low levels of GABA often have anxiety, depression, irritability, headaches, and hypertension.

Glutamine

As the most abundant amino acid in the body, glutamine increases GABA levels in the brain. Glutamine also helps remove excess ammonia from the body, improves immune system function, protects the intestinal lining, and appears to be needed for normal brain function. Although the body usually makes enough glutamine on its own, extreme stress (for example, heavy exercise or an injury) can increase the need for this amino acid beyond the amount naturally made. Some experts believe that low levels of glutamine may contribute to depression, fatigue, and alcohol cravings.

Taurine

Taurine is a nonessential amino acid that can be obtained through dietary intake of fish and meat. Taurine has anti-inflammatory properties and works with GABA to help prevent overactivity of the neurotransmitters, easing anxiety and hyperactivity. Taurine can also function as a neurotransmitter, helping prevent the reuptake of serotonin and other catecholamines such as dopamine, epinephrine, and norepinephrine, preserving their levels in the brain.

Taurine levels decline significantly as we age, and taurine deficiency can result in anxiety, depression, hypertension, gout, organ failure, and other conditions. Previous animal studies imply that taurine plays an important role in the treatment of Parkinson's disease. Parkinson's disease typically affects middle-aged to elderly people and is linked to the degeneration of cells in the brain. In studies looking at the effects of taurine supplementation in patients with Parkinson's, researchers found that it could alleviate symptoms by encouraging brain cell growth in the hippocampus, the area of the brain responsible for regulating our emotions and memory. Taurine supplementation is incredibly important in this patient population, as the standard treatment for patients with Parkinson's disease is the drug levodopa, which has been shown to deplete taurine levels.

Recent research further supports taurine's unique ability to stimulate new neuron growth. In a 2015 study published in *Stem Cell Research*, researchers found that taurine was able to regenerate new brain cells in the regions associated with learning and memory in middle-aged mice. They found that taurine supplementation was able to stimulate inactive stem cells that were otherwise unable to mature into the next stages of cell development. Taurine also maximizes brain cell communication by enhancing the electrical impulses that occur between cells that work together to support memory and cognition. Toxins, stress, and other conditions related to aging can damage these cell connections, resulting in slower cognition or poor mood.

Recent studies looking at taurine's ability to restore neuron growth are truly revolutionary. Studies demonstrate its promising ability to help treat age-related disorders and brain conditions. I typically recommend 1,000–2,000 mg of taurine supplementation daily for depressed individuals.

Amino Acids and Depression

While there's no doubt that low levels of amino acids are linked to depression, anxiety, and other negative moods, no one has yet figured out all the connections. We cannot say, for example, that an X percent drop in tryptophan absorption will lead to a Y percent increase in one's depression rating. Researchers have, however, put several pieces of the puzzle into place. For example, they have learned the following:

- Changes in amino acid levels affect mood. In particular, low levels of tryptophan have been linked to depressive symptoms and negative mood. In one study, researchers deliberately depleted the tryptophan levels of fifteen women who had had repeated episodes of major depression. Within a short time, ten of the fifteen study subjects had significant symptoms of depression. Another study found that adding tryptophan to fluoxetine (Prozac) treatment decreased depression scores more than fluoxetine plus placebo.

- Amino acid levels change when depression sets in, and the severity of depression may be linked to amino acid and protein levels. One study found very important differences in blood protein levels between people with major depression and healthy controls and between those with major depression and those with dysthymia. Another study examining depressed and healthy patients found that blood levels of the amino acids glutamate, glutamine, glycine, and taurine were changed in depressed people compared with healthy people.
- The relative levels of certain amino acids in the blood may make a person with major depression more or less likely to respond to treatment with antidepressants.
- Complex fatigue, which includes both mental and physical fatigue, causes changes in amino acid levels and metabolism in multiple organs. A study of animals with complex fatigue found decreases in total amino acid levels and low levels of glutamine in the plasma, skeletal muscle, and liver; in the animals' brains, researchers found low levels of phenylalanine, tyrosine, arginine, and threonine.

Many mysteries remain, but the following is clear: Low levels of certain amino acids can set the stage for depression. Because depression often occurs with changes in amino acid metabolism, the levels and ratios of certain amino acids may make psychiatric medications more or less effective.

What Makes Amino Acid Levels Decrease?

A lack of sufficient amino acids can result from several problems, but perhaps the most common cause is poor digestion of protein. The breakdown of protein occurs in the stomach, which releases the powerful gastric acid hydrochloric acid. Hydrochloric acid doesn't simply "burn through" proteins; it also changes a substance called pepsinogen into pepsin, an enzyme that cuts up protein into smaller pieces known as polypeptides. In a sense, hydrochloric acid takes "dull" pepsinogen and turns it into "razor-sharp" pepsin. Without pepsin, the human body cannot digest protein, so a decrease in the making of hydrochloric acid means that protein digestion will be less efficient. In addition, hydrochloric acid helps the body absorb vitamin B_{12} and many essential minerals, destroy bacteria that enter the body through the digestive tract, and trigger satiety signals, letting the brain know that the belly is full. Thus, too little hydrochloric acid can translate into a decrease in nutrient absorption, greater exposure to bacteria, impaired satiety signals, and hampered digestion in general.

Who's at risk for declining hydrochloric acid levels?

The amount of gastric acid produced by the stomach falls sharply with age, dropping by roughly 40 percent from the teens to the thirties and by almost half again by the time a person reaches the seventies. This means that the ability to digest protein also decreases markedly with age.

Stomach acid levels are also lower in those who regularly use antacids and other prescription or over-the-counter medications that interfere with acid production. That means that nutrient absorption and digestive capabilities can decrease in younger people as well.

Besides poor digestion of protein, low hydrochloric acid levels are linked to many long-term digestive complaints, including pain or discomfort after eating, gas, bloating, and food sensitivities and allergies. They can also contribute to iron-shortage anemia, osteoporosis, gallstones, skin conditions, rheumatoid arthritis, periodontal disease, asthma, and chronic stress.

Low acid levels

We generally think of acid indigestion, heartburn, or GERD as problems caused by too much acid in middle-aged and older adults. What many people (including quite a few health professionals) don't realize is that *low* acid levels can also trigger symptoms of GERD, which include burning pain in the middle of the chest, nausea, and regurgitation.

Rather than avoid the foods that seem to cause the problem, most people pop a pill to "cool the burn." Thanks to ongoing ad campaigns as well as "educational materials" from drug companies, some 60 million prescriptions for GERD medications are written every year, in addition to the sale of millions of over-the-counter remedies such as Prilosec,

Rolaids, Tums, Maalox, and Nexium. This means that untold millions of people may be trying to treat symptoms of low stomach acid by lowering it even further, worsening problems with protein digestion and nutrient absorption. Low levels of stomach acid can also impair absorption of zinc, magnesium, and other minerals, as well as vitamin C and certain B vitamins. Of these problems, poor absorption of zinc may be the most important.

As we have discussed, zinc is involved in more than two hundred different enzyme reactions, including several having to do with digestion. All the digestive enzymes, including hydrochloric acid, depend on zinc to function properly.

Low acid can equal low mood

Low levels of stomach acid and digestive enzymes can also cause psychological consequences. When protein molecules are not broken down efficiently, sufficient levels of key amino acids may not be released into the bloodstream. Among the amino acids "missing in action" can be tryptophan, tyrosine, taurine, and phenylalanine, all of which play an important role in mood regulation. For example, tryptophan serves as raw material for serotonin, while phenylalanine is necessary to make dopamine and norepinephrine. In addition, to create neurotransmitters, ample supplies of zinc, copper, magnesium, folic acid, vitamin B_6, vitamin B_{12}, and other nutrients are required.

Making sure the body has enough nutrients, plus ample amounts of stomach acid and digestive enzymes, is a first and crucial step in helping normalize neurotransmitter levels. If any of these nutrients is in short supply, the making of neurotransmitters can falter. This can occur even when a patient is taking a medication such as Prozac, which lowers the reabsorption of serotonin by brain cells to boost serotonin levels. If the body has so few raw materials that it can make only small amounts of serotonin, the Prozac boost won't do any good.

Melinda, a thirty-six-year-old mother of two, was very concerned about her weight and was constantly trying the latest diet. She had had depression since college but had stopped taking antidepressants due to sexual side effects. She also constantly had bloating, gas, and what she described as chronic indigestion. To handle these problems, she popped over-the-counter antacids like candy. Even though Melinda was careful about her diet and ate plenty of protein, including fish and chicken, her tests revealed low levels of all essential amino acids. Without changing her diet, Melinda started taking hydrochloric acid and digestive enzymes. She not only noticed an improvement in her mood and energy, but her chronic indigestion problem resolved.

Increasing Stomach Acid

If you have stomach problems, heartburn, gas, bloating, or other digestive complaints and depressed mood, your problems might be caused by low levels of stomach acid, resulting in deficiencies in amino acids, zinc, or other nutrients.

Despite the potential harm antacids can cause your body, it's important to taper off antacids gradually rather than stopping all at once. Begin by taking the proper digestive enzymes, with hydrochloric acid and pepsin, and getting rid of foods that upset your stomach, such as alcohol, coffee, and soft drinks.

Once your digestive symptoms are under control, you can speak to your doctor about taking over-the-counter antacids rather than prescription antacids. Over-the-counter antacids such as Tagamet are not as strong as prescription antacids. To slowly ease your body back to its normal production of acid, gradually decrease the dose of over-the-counter antacid until you no longer need any. As internal acid production normalizes, many of my patients find that they can stop using antacids completely.

Maintaining Proper Amino Acid and Protein Levels

Sometimes amino acid levels are low for dietary reasons, especially with diets that exclude animal products. Fad diets or crash weight-loss diets can also lack protein. Depression itself may play a role in low levels of amino acids, as some depressed people lose interest in food, eat fewer kinds of food, and eat less food overall.

Amino acid supplementation

Some people can get enough protein by simply making sure they eat enough meat, poultry, fish, or dairy products with enough hydrochloric acid and digestive enzymes.

Others, especially those with dietary restrictions, malnutrition, or diseases that interfere with absorption, may need amino acid supplements. They come in the form of whey protein powder or free-form amino acids.

Whey protein powder: This is one type of protein powder I recommend to my patients. Whey, a liquid byproduct of the cheese-making process, contains alpha-lactoglobulin, beta-lactalbumin, and other highly bioavailable proteins. These bioavailable proteins contain all the essential amino acids and are rapidly digested. Whey protein powder is an excellent protein supplement for anyone not allergic to dairy.

Free-form amino acids: These are amino acids that are not attached to other amino acids, so they can be readily absorbed and easily used by the body to strengthen mental and physical health. Amino Replete from Pure Encapsulations is a blend of free-form amino acids that provides the building blocks of protein, supporting the synthesis of neurotransmitters and neuropeptides involved with mood regulation and energy production.

Free-form amino acids are available in capsules or powders and can be added to any nutritional or medication program for improved energy, concentration, and mood. Targeted amino acid supplements can also be added to Amino Replete. I routinely recommend 4 g of Amino Replete mixed with water or juice to be taken before breakfast and before dinner.

It is always best to work with a doctor or registered dietitian who is well versed in the proper usage of amino acids, as well as in potential drug interactions and side effects.

Increasing neurotransmitters with amino acid precursors

An initial goal of depression treatment should be to discover any shortages in essential amino acids that can be corrected with dietary changes, digestive enzymes such as hydrochloric acid, protein shakes, or free-form amino acid supplements.

It's not enough for psychiatrists to ask patients about their diets and then stop investigating if patients say they get enough protein or even describe what are obviously amino acid–rich diets. I have often seen patients who eat diets containing plenty of essential amino acids continue to struggle with depression.

For these people, targeted amino acids are excellent ways to enhance the making of neurotransmitters and produce an antidepressant effect. Studies involving depleting levels of phenylalanine and tyrosine demonstrate that mood is affected, as deficiencies in these amino acids are able to decrease the availability of dopamine and neurotransmission. As we can easily induce states of depression by limiting the availability of amino acids, doesn't it make sense to supply sufficient amino acid precursors in the treatment of depression?

As I mentioned earlier, the amino acid L-tryptophan is a precursor to serotonin, while phenylalanine and tyrosine are precursors to dopamine and norepinephrine. We know that getting more L-tryptophan in the diet increases serotonin levels in the brain, while increasing tyrosine and phenylalanine in the body can increase the making of dopamine.

For years, scientists have studied depression in both animals and humans by putting them on tryptophan-limited diets. The goal, routinely achieved, is to deplete their bodies of the amino acid, lower serotonin levels, and create a state of depression. Given that tryptophan depletion is so commonly used to trigger depression, I have never quite understood why the idea of giving additional tryptophan has never been considered a potential treatment. If lowering tryptophan is so effective at triggering depression, why aren't we giving it to depressed people, especially those with already-low levels? Why aren't we at least checking those levels in every patient? Why isn't the medical community encouraging the research to answer these questions?

In my practice, I use a combination of 5-HTP and phenylalanine. Normally, the body uses tryptophan to make 5-HTP, which easily crosses the blood-brain barrier to enhance the making of serotonin. Giving 5-HTP saves a step, and because 5-HTP is not incorporated into various proteins, more is available to increase brain serotonin levels. We usually see a response to this treatment in less than two weeks. It's true that only limited research supports the use of 5-HTP in combination with phenylalanine, but psychiatrists and healthcare professionals around the country have successfully used this combination for many years.

I have been using 5-HTP and phenylalanine together for many years, and my patients have experienced significant improvements from this combination. However, some people may need more of one amino acid or the other. Individual dosing is critical for successful treatment. I have found that patients with low energy tend to do better with higher doses of tyrosine, and patients with obsessive ruminations need higher doses of 5-HTP.

Although 5-HTP can trigger some side effects, including stomach distress, gas, and cramping, they can be eliminated by starting slowly with just 50 mg per day and gradually increasing to 300 mg in divided doses—for example, 100 mg at breakfast, 100 mg at lunch, and 100 mg at dinner. Some people become slightly tired after taking 5-HTP, so they may want to take smaller doses during the day and a larger dose before bed.

It's Worth Repeating

Sometimes the most important intervention in the treatment of depression is to get enough amino acids. I can't stress this enough. The diet and nutritional status of every depressed patient should be checked and corrected, if necessary. For many, this first step is the only one they'll ever have to take.

Chapter 17

Laboratory Tests Your Doctor May Order

Traditionally, reviewing nutrition has not been part of a psychiatric evaluation. Although you might be tempted to skip a comprehensive metabolic evaluation, it is a critical part of understanding potential treatable causes of depression. Results from this evaluation are used as a basis for developing a personalized nutritional program that optimizes function and helps ensure your recovery and long-term health.

Rather than treating symptoms, it makes more sense to treat the nutritional and metabolic imbalances that are getting in the way of positive mood and healthy functioning. With restored balance, the symptoms should lessen or even vanish. But first we must discover where those imbalances lie. One of the best ways is through lab tests.

In the nutritional assessment of a person with depression, a number of tests are critical. Some are commonly performed in a doctor's office, while others are not as well-known. It's also possible that they won't be covered by health insurance. However, all are important. Discovering nutrient shortages and correcting them with the proper amounts of supplements can do much to help you feel better mentally and physically and to make it easier for you to participate in your recovery.

Getting Started

For all patients, I recommend the following tests, which can be ordered by any physician:

- Amino acids
- Celiac disease (anti-tissue transglutaminase antibody and anti-gliadin antibody tests)
- Complete blood count (CBC) with differential
- Comprehensive chemistry panel

- Copper
- C-reactive protein
- DHEA-S and pregnenolone
- Essential fatty acids
- Folate and vitamin B_{12}
- Food allergies
- Genetic testing
- Homocysteine
- Iron and ferritin
- Lipids
- Lithium
- Magnesium
- Methylmalonic acid
- Red blood cell trace minerals
- Testosterone
- Thyroid panel and thyroid antibodies
- Urinary organic acids
- Urinary peptides (including casomorphin and gliadorphin)
- Vitamin D
- Zinc

Following is a brief summary of each of the laboratory tests listed above.

Amino acids

Building blocks of the proteins found in every tissue and organ of the body, amino acids help regulate neurotransmitters, form antibodies, and produce energy inside the cells. Shortages, especially in the nine essential amino acids, can cause serious health problems, including some related to mood and cognitive function. For example, too little tryptophan can lead to depression, while a lack of tyrosine or phenylalanine can contribute to fatigue and difficulty concentrating. Both blood and urine tests can be used to detect amino acid levels. Blood tests may mean a blood draw or just a finger stick. If amino acid levels prove to be abnormally low or high, they can usually be adjusted through supplementation or diet.

Celiac disease

Celiac disease is a sensitivity to the gluten found in wheat and other grains, meaning that the body mistakenly identifies gluten as a foreign invader and launches an immune attack. A good amount of evidence suggests that people with celiac disease have higher rates of anxiety and depression than others. It appears that an activation of the inflammatory response system occurs with major depression and that certain proinflammatory substances like cytokines can trigger symptoms of depression.

Screening for celiac disease involves examining a blood sample to determine the presence of two antibodies that the body makes in response to gluten: anti-tissue transglutaminase and anti-gliadin. To confirm a positive result, a biopsy of the small intestine can be obtained. An endoscope is inserted down the throat, through the stomach, and into the small intestine. Tissue samples taken from its lining are examined under a microscope to identify characteristic changes of celiac disease, including shrunken, flattened villi, the hairlike projections lining the intestine.

Complete blood count with differential

The CBC measures white blood cell count and types (called differential), red blood cell count and characteristics, hemoglobin, hematocrit, and platelets. Anemia, which can present symptoms of depression, is shown by low red blood cell count, low hemoglobin, and low hematocrit. Certain characteristics of the red blood cell, designated MCH, MCV, or MCHC, can pinpoint the nutrient shortage causing the anemia, whether it's copper, folate, iron, or vitamin B_{12}.

White blood cell levels can be abnormally high due to an infection, an allergic reaction, or leukemia, or abnormally low due to medication reactions or low levels of zinc, which is needed for white blood cell production. Platelets play a role in blood clotting, and both high and low levels are abnormal. Low levels can cause excessive bleeding and bruising.

Comprehensive chemistry panel

This group of blood tests is used to evaluate organ function and is a preliminary check for diabetes, liver disease, and kidney problems. The test results give important information about electrolyte status, acid-base balance, kidney function, liver function, and blood sugar and protein levels. This panel can also test a person's zinc status by measuring alkaline phosphatase, an enzyme produced in the presence of zinc. A low alkaline phosphatase level often indicates a zinc shortage.

Copper

Low copper levels can lead to symptoms of depression, which is not surprising considering that copper is required to make the neurotransmitters norepinephrine and dopamine. A shortage of a form of copper called ceruloplasmin can cause anemia, which itself can bring on symptoms of depression. On the other hand, abnormally high levels of copper can be linked to psychological symptoms such as aggression, paranoia, and anxiety. Copper levels are determined by blood tests or, in some cases, a urinary test. Levels that are abnormal may be treated with supplementation or dietary changes.

C-reactive protein

C-reactive protein (CRP) is produced by the liver and commonly used as a marker to ascertain inflammation in the body. Elevated CRP levels may be due to a lack of sleep, stress, excessive exercise, infections, overeating, or obesity. Chronic inflammation can lead to a higher risk of heart disease, diabetes, and depression. One large-scale study completed in Copenhagen examined 73,131 men and women aged twenty to one hundred and found that higher levels of CRP were associated with an increased risk of distress and depression. Several studies suggest that lifestyle changes such as regular exercise can help normalize levels, often resulting in improvement in treatment outcomes and symptoms. Levels of CRP can be detected through a simple blood test.

DHEA and pregnenolone

Dehydroepiandrosterone (DHEA), the most common steroid hormone in the body, is the raw material used to produce the sex hormones testosterone and estrogen and as many as 150 other steroid hormones. Production of DHEA is at its peak in the mid-twenties, after which it drops precipitously, falling about 90 percent between ages twenty and ninety. Age-related weight gain and abdominal obesity are believed to be at least partially due to this drop in DHEA. Low levels of DHEA have been linked to depression. Levels are checked by measuring a form of the hormone called DHEA-sulfate in the blood.

Pregnenolone is synthesized from cholesterol and is the precursor to several steroids and hormones. Similar to DHEA, pregnenolone levels decline as we age. A lack of pregnenolone is associated with impaired brain function, impaired memory, and depression. Researchers have found significantly lower levels of pregnenolone in the cerebrospinal fluid of depressed patients compared with healthy counterparts.

Essential fatty acids

Two kinds of fatty acids—the omega-3s and the omega-6s—are considered essential because the body cannot make them itself. The omega-3s,

EPA and DHA, help fuel the brain and control inflammation in degenerative brain diseases such as Alzheimer's disease. EPA helps maintain nerve cell membranes, while DHA improves communication between the brain cells. Studies support the use of omega-3 fatty acids in depressed pregnant women; omega-3s have no effect on the fetus. The omega-6s are also crucial to brain function. People who have essential fatty acid deficiencies are at risk for many symptoms, including depression. In addition, depression can result from omega-6 levels that are too high relative to omega-3s.

Tests of blood serum and red blood cells can reveal levels of omega-3s and omega-6s, as well as the ratio of the two. Abnormally high or low levels of various fatty acids can be treated with supplementation or dietary changes.

Folate and vitamin B_{12}

Folate and vitamin B_{12} are essential for normal psychological function. Shortages are often found in depressed people. Folate is needed to make brain neurotransmitters, while B_{12} is needed to make red blood cells. Folate shortages have been linked to depression and anemia, while vitamin B_{12} shortages can contribute to many psychiatric and neurological symptoms, including depression, anxiety, hallucinations, memory loss, and confusion.

Food allergies

Food allergies may contribute to many psychiatric illnesses, including depression, ADHD, and anxiety. It is clear that people with food allergies tend to have depression more often than their healthy counterparts.

Food allergies, as discussed in chapter 10, lead to the production of too many IgG antibodies. There are now several ways to test for IgG antibodies. For many years, the standard test for allergies to various kinds of foods was a skin-prick test. This consisted of scratching the patient's skin and then dropping an extract of a particular food into the wound. If a reddened bump that resembled a mosquito bite appeared, the person was considered allergic to that food. Now, a blood test, taken from either a blood draw or a finger prick, is often used. For this test, blood is drawn and sent to a lab, where extracts of individual foods are mixed with the blood to see if specific elements of the immune system in the blood, the IgG antibodies, react to them. The test measures whether IgG antibodies are produced. If so, the person is considered allergic to that food.

Genetic testing

Genetic research is a useful tool, and almost any physician can order a genetic test for a patient. Simple genetic tests, often done by saliva collection, can inform physicians of the most appropriate and effective treatment for the patient by analyzing their genetic and biological markers. The results reveal how a patient may metabolize or respond to different medications. One biological marker that is analyzed in genetic testing is the methylenetetrahydrofolate reductase (MTHFR) gene.

People with genetic mutations called MTHFR polymorphisms have impaired folate metabolism. As mentioned earlier in the book, several studies show that people with variants of the MTHFR gene have a higher incidence of depression and require higher levels of folate supplementation. Genetic testing to check whether you have MTHFR polymorphisms can be invaluable in changing the way your depression is treated.

Homocysteine

Homocysteine, an amino acid produced by the body, is normally changed quickly to another amino acid called cysteine. But if this change is somehow impaired, homocysteine levels rise. High homocysteine levels harm the body, as they are linked to an increase in free radical activity, the formation of blood clots, and heart disease. A link also exists between high homocysteine levels and major depression. Although not all depressed people have high homocysteine levels, and not all of those with elevated homocysteine are depressed, data from the Health in Men Study, which involved 3,752 men aged seventy and older, found that higher levels of homocysteine increased the risk of depression. On the other hand, lowering homocysteine by 0.19 mg/L reduced the odds of depression by about 20 percent.

Because folate, vitamins B_{12} and $B_{6,}$ and zinc convert homocysteine to the nonharmful cysteine, those lacking in these nutrients can develop a buildup of homocysteine. In fact, high homocysteine levels can indicate an early-stage shortage of folate or vitamins B_6 or B_{12} before blood levels of these nutrients reflect these problems. Oral doses of folic acid, $B_{6,}$ and B_{12} may help improve treatment outcomes in depression.

Iron and ferritin

Depression and anxiety are often symptoms of a chronic iron shortage. An iron shortage can cause depression, fatigue, and weakness because iron is needed to make hemoglobin, which helps the red blood cells move oxygen to the cells. Without enough iron intake, the cells can become starved of oxygen, leading to weakness, fatigue, and general malaise. Lack of iron can also impair memory and motor skills and worsen emotional and psychological problems.

Iron influences levels of two enzymes, tyrosine hydroxylase and tryptophan hydroxylase, which regulate the making of dopamine and serotonin, respectively.

Many tests are used to check a person's iron status. Two common tests screen levels of serum iron and ferritin, a protein that stores iron. They are often ordered together. Sometimes blood levels of iron appear normal, but the stored supplies are low. If ferritin levels are below normal, or even in the low-normal range (less than 100 ng/mL), I recommend additional iron supplements. Taking iron with vitamin C can help with absorption.

Lipids

A lipid panel measures levels of total cholesterol, triglycerides, HDL, and LDL through a blood test. As we discussed earlier in the book, recent studies suggest that low total cholesterol levels are linked to depression and suicidal thoughts. One study published in the *Journal of Psychiatric Research* in 2009 found that death from suicide, accidents, and other unnatural causes was seven times more likely to occur in men with low total cholesterol (below 165 mg/dL) than in men with healthy levels. Some experts think that having low levels of cholesterol results in lowered production of serotonin and fewer serotonin receptors. And, of course, low serotonin levels are linked to depression as well as decreased levels of progesterone and testosterone (both of which are also linked to depression).

Lithium

Lithium is present in our environment, food, and water and is an essential nutrient for the human body. The most potent source of lithium in the modern diet is tap water. In the mid-nineteenth century, mineral water containing high lithium levels from springs in Europe and the United States was bottled and sold to grocers, pharmacists, and other merchants. The popular drink now known as 7UP originally contained trace amounts of lithium and was marketed to cure hangovers and lift mood.

Research has associated low levels of environmental lithium with increased rates of depression, volatile mood, aggressive behavior, and suicide. One study found that violent criminals had little to no stores of lithium in their hair. Lithium levels can be measured through a blood test or a hair tissue mineral analysis (HTMA). HTMA is a noninvasive and relatively inexpensive procedure that analyzes levels of minerals and toxic metals in a sample of hair. Hair samples are able to provide accurate information about mineral stores over the previous three months. Supplementation with low-dose nutritional lithium, 1–5 mg, has been particularly helpful in patients with a family history of depression, substance abuse, or bipolar disorder.

Magnesium

The mineral magnesium is needed for several hundred bodily functions, such as breaking down pcarbohydrates, fats, and proteins into energy, the maintenance of normal heartbeat, blood coagulation, insulin production, and muscle and nerve function.

A magnesium shortage can result in depression, anxiety, weakness, cardiac complications, insomnia, and difficulty concentrating, among other problems.

Testing for a magnesium shortage is not as simple as taking a blood sample. Most of the body's magnesium is stored in our cells; only about 1 percent of the body's total magnesium is in the blood. In other words, a blood test may not be the most accurate indicator of the body's magnesium levels. A person may have a normal blood level but still not have enough magnesium to smoothly run other biological functions.

While the most common test for magnesium is a blood test, an alternative method is a twenty-four-hour urine test to determine the amount of magnesium excreted from the body. The doctor then injects the patient with magnesium and collects urine for another twenty-four hours to determine a change, if any, in the amount of magnesium the patient's body has retained. If the patient retains more magnesium than normal, he lacks magnesium, because the body retained the injected magnesium to make up for the shortage.

Red blood cell trace minerals

When assessing any disorder linked to a zinc shortage, including depression, a red blood cell analysis is recommended. This test evaluates levels of a number of nutrients, including calcium, phosphorous, zinc, selenium, boron, chromium, and vanadium. The toxic elements also analyzed in this trace mineral analysis include arsenic, cadmium, lead, and mercury, all of which have important effects on blood cells or blood cell membranes.

Selenium, which is found in groundwater and is also available as a supplement, is thought to strongly protect against depression. One study showed that low levels of selenium increased the likelihood of major depressive disorder. Selenium levels should be in the range of 82–85 µg/L in adults; too-high levels of selenium have been shown to worsen depression. In one study, high doses of selenium were shown to elevate depressive symptoms, with a doubling of the selenium level linked to 56 percent higher odds of being depressed at an office visit.

Testosterone

All depressed men should have their testosterone levels checked. There is a strong link between depression and low levels of testosterone, and in some men, depression cannot be relieved until low testosterone levels are normalized. Testosterone levels are checked via a simple blood test. The "normal" values vary from laboratory to laboratory, with about 270 –1,000 ng/dL considered normal for men aged twenty to forty. The top of the range declines as men age, falling to the 700s for most men aged sixty and older. But remember, what may be normal for one man can be low for another, so the test results must be interpreted in light of all other findings.

Thyroid panel and thyroid antibodies

Thyroid hormones play a role in circadian rhythms and are responsible for regulating the rate at which the body uses energy. The thyroid gland takes up iodine and converts it into the thyroid hormones thyroxine (T_4) and triiodothyronine (T_3). When concentrations of these hormones drop too low, the pituitary gland releases thyroid-stimulating hormone (TSH), which prompts the thyroid gland to produce more hormones. When levels normalize, the thyroid stops producing these hormones.

A thyroid panel measures the amount of TSH, T_4, and T_3 in your blood. Too little T_4 and T_3 causes *hypothyroidism*, a condition that lowers the metabolic rate and increases the tendency toward weight gain, loss of appetite, fatigue, constipation, cold intolerance, and menstrual irregularities. On the other hand, too much T_4 and T_3 causes *hyperthyroidism,* which steps up the metabolic rate and causes weight loss, an increased heart rate, anxiety, insomnia, weakness, and again, a loss of appetite.

Low thyroid hormones contribute to depression, anxiety, and other psychological problems. Screening for thyroid problems is an important step in diagnosing and treating depression. Levels of thyroid hormones can be assessed through a simple blood test.

Urinary organic acids

Abnormally high levels of organic acids result from the blockage of one or more of the body's metabolic pathways, which prompts excretion of these acids through the urine. Organic acids in the urine indicate problems with biological processes, including neurotransmitter function, detoxification, digestive imbalances, energy production, and nutrient shortage.

For example, high levels of a urinary organic acid called methylmalonic acid can indicate a vitamin B_{12} shortage in its early stages, before it's detected through other methods. B_{12} is necessary for various chemical reactions that keep methylmalonic acid levels in check, so when B_{12} levels drop, methylmalonic acid levels rise. Combined with the results of a homocysteine test, high methylmalonic acid levels can confirm a mild or early vitamin B_{12} shortage—even if blood levels of B_{12} appear normal.

Similarly, high levels of an organic acid called kynurenate may indicate a shortage of vitamin B_6, a vitamin required to make all major neurotransmitters. When amounts of B_6 are too low, kynurenate levels increase in the urine.

Urinary organic acids are the best way to measure 3-hydroxyphenyl 3-hydroxpropionic acid (HPHPA) levels. Elevated levels of HPHPA can cause a build-up of dopamine in the brain, often resulting in many behavioral, gastrointestinal, and neuropsychiatric symptoms we see in patients with depression and other mood disorders.

Testing for urinary organic acids requires a first morning urine sample. Dietary changes, nutrient supplementation, or antifungal/antibiotic medications may be used to correct the underlying conditions leading to abnormally high levels.

Urinary peptides

The opiate peptides casomorphin and gliadorphin appear in the urine when the naturally occurring proteins casein (found in milk) and gluten (found in wheat, rye, barley, and certain other grains) are broken down incompletely. These problems in breakdown occur because the protease enzyme DPP IV occurs in too-low quantities in the small intestine or is simply inactive. Abnormally high levels of the opiate peptides cause psychological symptoms, including depression.

The test requires a first morning urine sample. Normally, test results should be negative, meaning that casomorphin and gliadorphin are not in the urine. If they are, casein and/or gluten should be removed from the diet. Supplementation of the diet with the enzyme DPP IV helps completely digest these neuroactive peptides.

Vitamin D

A shortage of vitamin D may be linked to depression, an increased stress response, high blood pressure, high blood sugar levels, or a host of diseases, including heart disease, cancer, and multiple sclerosis.

Vitamin D is changed in the liver to 25-hydroxyvitamin D, the form found in the bloodstream and typically used to evaluate an individual's vitamin D status. Low levels of 25-hydroxyvitamin D indicate that a person is not getting enough dietary vitamin D or exposure to sunlight or has a problem absorbing the vitamin. Low levels should be treated with vitamin D_3 supplementation, and the 25-hydroxyvitamin D status should be monitored every three months until levels are within the target range.

Zinc

Low levels of zinc have been linked to depression, and the lower they are, the worse the depression. Research has shown that people with major depression have zinc levels that are 12 to 16 percent lower than those who are not depressed. A meta-analysis of seventeen studies, including 1,643 depressed people and 804 healthy controls, concluded that those with depression had lower serum zinc concentrations. Zinc deficiencies also set off a cascade of other biological actions that impair cognitive function and disrupt mood regulation.

Taking zinc supplements has been shown to relieve depression and make antidepressants work better. Because the body cannot store zinc, daily intake is necessary. Symptoms of zinc deficiency include hair loss, skin lesions, acne, diarrhea, and depression. White marks on the fingernails are an early sign of zinc deficiency.

However, measuring blood levels of zinc is not always a reliable way to detect a zinc shortage. A better way to assess zinc status is to take the zinc taste test (see chapter 11). This test can identify even a subtle shortage.

It's Worth the Effort

Very few psychiatrists routinely request these laboratory tests. That's an oversight, for they don't take much time and they cost relatively little compared with the costs of paying for the wrong medication and the emotional toll of remaining in the grips of depression. I have found that running a few blood tests can guide doctors toward the right treatment. I believe we need to investigate the causes of depressed mood with the same energy and passion that we use to detect causes of other illnesses. If we can find all the factors causing depression, we can come closer to finding the correct therapies to produce complete recovery and permanent remission.

As we have described in this chapter, testing not only helps determine nutrient shortages or metabolic imbalances, but it can also help better predict which medications may be better for you. This process helps minimize some of the frustrating and often costly guesswork involved when prescribing medications and prevents unwanted side effects.

Chapter 18

Psychotherapy for Depression

The previous sections of this book discussed biological underpinnings of depression and their effects on the brain. I focused on interventions that actually change the molecular magic of the brain and form the neurochemical basis for recovery from depression.

But recovery from the fog of depression often involves more than changing your neurochemistry. It also involves building on your inner strengths and exploring the potential of meaningful connections with the outside world. It is just as important to nurture the mind as it is to nourish the brain. Psychotherapy, a spiritual life, and forms of relaxation and meditation can help you forge a path back to well-being.

What causes and sustains depression and influences the prospect of recovery depends on the interaction of psychological, social, and cultural factors in combination with genetics and biochemistry. Biochemistry is not an entity separate from thinking style, personal values, and life experience.

Just as your personality, beliefs, and expectations can influence the development of depression, they can also heal. For too long, Western medicine viewed a patient as a passive entity to be made compliant. The reality is more complicated; we must take an active role in examining the assumptions, beliefs, and behaviors that define our lives. Depression is isolating and a source of stigma in part because it is invisible. Although one can make inferences based on behaviors, no outsider can see its signs and symptoms.

Psychotherapy is intended to foster communication and expression of feelings. Through dialogue with a mental health professional, you learn how to understand thoughts and behaviors that may contribute to depression. The psychotherapist helps you recognize the negative patterns of thinking that contribute to sadness and hopelessness and to consider the support or toxicity provided by social networks. Psychotherapy for depression encourages positive self-care and lifestyle changes. It equips you with strategies to cope with psychological, behavioral, and interpersonal factors that have reinforced your depression.

Many of you struggling with depression are hostage to negative thoughts and feelings. You regret the past, find the present empty, and lack hope for the future. You may think obsessively, pursuing long chains of pervasive, negative thoughts. The negative thoughts are automatic because you make assumptions about yourself without shining a skeptical light on them. These assumptions invariably limit your progress and prevent recovery.

Cognitive-Behavioral Therapy

Psychotherapy helps illuminate the negative thoughts that are the hallmark of your depression. Cognitive-behavioral therapy (CBT) is the most thoroughly studied and one of the most effective therapies for treating depression. It involves your active participation in understanding the behaviors and emotional components embedded in your depression. Rather than exploring the past or searching for causes of problem behaviors from early family dynamics, CBT addresses your current struggles and challenging behaviors.

CBT was developed by Dr. Aaron Beck at the University of Pennsylvania. Beck suggested that one's thoughts about oneself are frequently destructive, and by reprogramming the mind to think differently, you can actually change your reality. Beck viewed depression as the result of false logic. As a patient in CBT, you develop objectives to help reprogram this false logic.

By correcting negative reasoning, you can achieve better mental health. CBT helps you identify negative thoughts that sustain a depressed mood and replace them with more positive and realistic thoughts. It offers you a guided process for dealing with the self-defeating tendency to ruminate. CBT is based on the observation that depressed individuals tend to have a negative view of themselves and the future. Instead of being considered unpleasant but haphazard events, unhappy circumstances become confirmation of your "essential worthlessness."

CBT posits that thoughts (or cognitions), feelings, and behaviors operate in a feedback loop. If the perception that you are a bad person looms continuously in your mind, this leads to sadness and a sense of shame. Behavior then reflects low self-worth. CBT therapists will help you interrupt this feedback loop by deconstructing the thoughts and questioning the logic of this negative judgment. Once critical and corrosive self-assessments are replaced by more hopeful and self-forgiving—as well as realistic—ones, your mood lifts. As you become conscious of the thoughts that were once automatic, you learn to challenge these assumptions. CBT does not simply challenge your thoughts; it also helps you identify strategies and alternatives to behaviors that keep old patterns in play.

CBT is now used throughout the world. It has been studied extensively in both small clinical studies and in large randomized controlled trials. CBT has been shown to be as effective in treating depression as antidepressant medication, and it appears to be superior to antidepressants at warding off relapse. CBT provides strategies for changing unhealthy patterns of thinking and behavior, should they reemerge.

Researchers have studied the potential of CBT to alleviate depression in different subgroups. As measured by higher scores on the Beck Depression Inventory after treatment, CBT is proven to improve mood and quality of life in adolescents. Studies in patients at particular life stages or with co-occurring mental health or physical problems also find the treatment promising. CBT is effective for preventing and treating perinatal depression. At the other end of the adult age spectrum, CBT has been modified and used successfully with older adults. This therapeutic approach would seem compatible with the needs of the elderly because it focuses on enhancing skills, and it is present-oriented and straightforward.

The setting and form of delivery of CBT have also been extensively studied. In patients with neurological conditions or limited mobility, Internet-delivered CBT has shown effectiveness in reducing depression while overcoming a significant barrier to treatment. Internet-delivered CBT in youth has also demonstrated significant positive effects on both anxiety and depression. When the therapy targeted the young person's depression, the researchers discovered that it also reduced the patient's anxiety, and vice versa. This finding is especially important, as anxiety and depression are often intertwined in adolescents. Positive effects of Internet-based CBT were shown to be long-lasting, whether or not parents were involved in the treatment.

A large study of CBT delivered by Internet was conducted in Australia. The researchers found that this psychotherapy was successful for both lessening depression and reducing thoughts of suicide. The older the patients, the greater the reduction in depression. Although both men and women experienced improvements in their mood, the results were most impressive in women.

The positive effects of Internet-delivered CBT are evident from scores on rating scales for depression after therapy has ended. Researchers explored long-term outcomes in patients with depression who participated in CBT Internet-delivered CBT. The improved moods experienced by most patients were sustained at a follow-up assessment 3.5 years afterward. Although half of the participants had sought and received help from a therapist after receiving the Internet-based CBT, the results show that Internet-delivered CBT can have long-standing effects either as a complement or as an alternative to more therapist-intensive psychotherapy.

Researchers have also explored the potential usefulness of Internet-delivered CBT with additional direct therapist involvement. One study addressing Internet-based CBT with therapist assistance found that treatment for depression was effective. Even though patients had less contact with the therapist than in regular face-to-face therapy, the therapeutic alliance they developed was determined to be both as effective and as satisfying as the therapeutic relationship in face-to-face therapy. When delivered within the context of routine psychiatric care, Internet-based CBT proved highly effective in both treating depression and in diminishing sleep difficulties and suicidal thinking.

So many patients with depression are untreated, and a methodology as easy to implement as Internet-delivered CBT could help close the gap between those with depression and those who are treated. These results show CBT as an alternative to face-to-face therapy when that is not possible or desirable. Internet-delivered CBT is promising because it can address the needs of patients on a large scale without dramatic changes in the structure of the healthcare system. What was surprising to many is that, when researchers compared Internet-based versus face-to-face CBT, they found the modes equally effective, though the effects actually seemed to last longer in the patients who received Internet-based therapy.

Cognitive-behavioral therapy in groups

CBT in a group setting has also been the subject of research. Group CBT was compared with individual CBT in older adults with both anxiety and depression. The researchers found improvement in both symptoms of depression and in social function and a similarly significant improvement in patients in group and individual therapy.

In one study, group CBT was found to be an effective treatment for major depressive disorder in patients with breast cancer. Patients not only reported less intense depression after the intervention; they also demonstrated higher scores in quality of life and self-esteem. Results of this study suggest the importance of integrating CBT into cancer treatment.

Group CBT is more cost-effective than individual CBT. Moreover, the group setting offers social support to participants and provides an avenue for them to normalize their experience by sharing it with peers. When compared with other types of group therapy, CBT group therapy has shown the most impressive results.

Narrative Therapy

Another type of psychotherapy that has proven helpful in treating depression is narrative therapy. In a sense, all therapy is narrative therapy, as it encourages you to reshape the stories by which you have explained your life experiences and helps you view them as sources of insight rather than confirmation of a destiny of doom. Recent research reveals that the way you describe an event shapes the choices you see. The opportunity to rework your personal narrative in collaboration with a therapist can allow you to see the past in a new way and to envision a more hopeful future.

In the 1980s, family therapists Michael White and David Epston formulated a specific approach to treating psychological problems that they labeled as narrative therapy. They emphasized the power differential between doctor and patient; those who classify the behavior and give the patient a diagnosis hold a great deal more power than the patient. By embodying the diagnostic label they have been assigned, patients often forfeit the opportunity to create the narratives they have of themselves. By assimilating what is expected of them, as "a depressive," for instance, they become complicit in someone else's narrative, a story that they have not even authorized.

Narrative therapy is based on the understanding that you organize your life experiences in a narrative form in a sequence over time. Understanding your narrative helps the therapist determine your pattern of interpretation. The therapist may notice that you fall back on a single or dominant narrative that highlights perceived or actual deficits. Using your stories coalesced around problems as a theme, the therapist serves as a consultant and helps you discover exceptions and generate alternative preferred stories as you rewrite your life's narrative.

The effectiveness of narrative therapy has been studied in various patient groups. In young people who self-harm, reconstructing a more positive and hopeful life narrative in conjunction with a therapist has been shown to help diminish depressive symptoms and foster emotional well-being and resilience.

Narrative therapy has also been used effectively with cancer patients. One intervention added a mindfulness component to narrative therapy and helped cancer patients destabilize their depressive outlook through mindfulness and acceptance rather than concentrating on changing the life script. The success of narrative therapy with cancer patients shows that narrative therapy can be effectively adapted to patients with serious and chronic conditions.

Older adults who have engaged in a life review based on the principles of narrative therapy have experienced less depression at the end of therapy. A randomized controlled trial explored the effect of life story review on depression in older Chinese people in Singapore. The researchers found that participation in a storybook creation process led to diminished symptoms of depression and a more passionate and proactive view of the self and self-agency. Other studies support the findings that life review in the company of a narrative therapist helps lift depressed mood in older adults.

Narrative therapy has also been shown to be successful when administered by trained nurses. Patients in a study in which nurses served as the narrative therapists completed their treatment with greater hope and a greater sense of agency over their lives. Their symptoms of depression were markedly reduced.

CBT and narrative therapy are similar in that they both focus on your existing negative concepts and encourage you to develop new, more hopeful interpretations.

Other Forms of Therapy

Psychodynamic therapy explores the potential roots of your emotional state, often focusing on unconscious motives and defenses. This type of therapy delves into the past, offering you opportunities to come to terms with early psychological trauma that was too overwhelming to master at the time it occurred. According to the theory behind psychodynamic therapy, these overwhelming experiences were left unassimilated, and chaotic memory traces were split off. Psychodynamic therapy focuses on the psychological defenses that preserve these old memory traces. With the support of the therapist, you will acknowledge the past as well as understand how the past may perpetuate the dysfunctional dynamics learned early in childhood. According to Harvard Medical School faculty member and psychiatrist Dr. Martha Stark, through therapy, your resistance is transformed into awareness. The relentless hopelessness and struggle to grieve the past evolves into acceptance. Childhood dramas are reenacted and then understood, allowing you to replace old patterns with more functional adaptations.

Do patients find relief from depression because of a particular therapy or because of the therapeutic relationship itself? Research studies have shown positive outcomes and diminished symptoms of depression after treatment with psychodynamic therapy, CBT, and narrative therapy. Currently, there is no overwhelming evidence that supports the superiority of one therapeutic school over another in treatment for depression. Large studies that compare the results from many clinical trials of different forms of therapy have found no appreciable differences in outcomes. In a 2010 article in *American Psychologist,* J. Shedler calls this situation the "dodo bird verdict," from the dodo bird's exclamation in the book *Alice in Wonderland.* At the end of a contest, the dodo bird proclaims, "Everybody has won, and all must have prizes!"

The lack of a clear winner among styles of therapy may be because a patient's ongoing, trusting relationship with a therapist is more important than the content of the therapist's theories. Indeed, many researchers believe that this relationship is key to overcoming depression. While depression leads to passivity and social withdrawal, the act of participating in a therapeutic process can restore confidence and a sense of control. If interpersonal difficulties have been a factor in the depression, the opportunity to work some of these out with a person who does not react in the predictable and sometimes dysfunctional ways of family members can help the patient achieve a more positive resolution. Psychotherapy helps you understand the meanings and dimensions of your depression and makes you a partner in regaining health and recovery.

There are endless names, forms, and variations of psychotherapy, including but not limited to:

- Acceptance and commitment therapy
- Motivational interviewing
- Interpersonal psychotherapy
- Internal family systems model
- Rational emotive behavioral therapy
- Humanistic psychology
- Jungian psychotherapy

Any of these forms of therapy can help patients move past a negative understanding of themselves and their pasts and develop hope for their futures. Family and friends can also help an individual emerge from the isolation of depression. In my clinical practice, I have observed that some patients—often busy, successful professionals—come to my office alone and are fairly secretive about their struggles with depression. Others come with a spouse or other family member. Almost invariably, those who are accompanied by supportive family members are more likely to continue with their treatment and eventually achieve relief from the symptoms of depression.

During your search for a therapist, choose someone who is supportive of your needs and respects you not only as a patient but as an individual. A good therapist does not believe that only one therapy is the answer for everyone. A good therapist recognizes and understands that everyone is unique and responds to different types of therapies.

Chapter 19

Spirituality and Faith

Recent research has yielded fascinating findings about the connections between depression and a religious or spiritual life. These findings are overturning the old psychiatric perspective on religion from the time of Sigmund Freud. For a very long time, psychiatry took a dim view of patients' beliefs about God and religion, analyzing these beliefs as proof of obsessional tendencies and as obstacles to mental health. For instance, psychiatrists believed that the image of an angry, punitive God hurt rather than helped a patient recover from depression. Even today, a recent national survey of U.S. psychiatrists revealed that the vast majority never ask about patients' attitudes toward religion or spirituality. When they do, their questions focus on the contribution of religion to pathology, not health or wellness.

Recent research shows that spirituality and religion enhance, rather than inhibit mental health. Being part of an established religious tradition can help you connect with and feel part of a larger whole. A personal sense of spirituality often gives you a comforting perspective about your place in the world and the meaning of life.

In this chapter, "spirituality" is defined as an experience of connectedness to the sacred. What is considered sacred depends on you—it may be the idea of a transcendent being, ultimate values, or a sense of meaning and purpose in life. "Religion" is defined as the formalized expression of spirituality through the application of beliefs and practices within a faith community. Because most research uses the terms "spirituality" and "religion" interchangeably, they are considered together in this chapter.

A very high percentage of the U.S. population considers themselves spiritual or religious. According to Gallup polls, four-fifths of Americans say their spiritual life is "fairly important," and more than half say it is "very important." About 62 percent of Americans claim to be affiliated with some religious group. Even more turn to their religion when they face difficult times. About 80 to 90 percent of people with mental health conditions draw on spirituality to cope, yet very few discuss this with their mental health providers. One-fourth of people who seek help for a mental disorder do so from a clergy member.

As many as three thousand studies have focused on the relationship between religion or spirituality and mental health. By far, most of these report positive findings. These studies have occurred in different settings, with people of different ethnic backgrounds, religions, and age groups. Most demonstrate an inverse relationship between religion/spirituality and depression: the more religious a person perceives himself or herself to be, the lower the risk of depression. People who have faith in religion seem to cope better with stress than those who do not define themselves as religious or spiritual.

People across many religions draw on their religious beliefs and spiritual teachings to cope with life's difficulties. Those with religious backgrounds are more likely to use positive coping techniques to manage bad feelings. They are also more likely to sustain a sense of hope and purpose and a belief that an individual's life has meaning and makes a difference.

Research has clearly demonstrated that individuals who identify religion or spirituality as important to them are at lower risk for depression. Many research studies suggest that neither the particular religious group nor regular attendance at religious services has a significant influence on outcome. Whether you are religiously liberal or conservative also appears to make no difference. A high value on spirituality makes a greater difference in preventing recurrence of depression than in preventing a single depressive episode.

Research also shows that symptoms of depression are of shorter duration in religious people. Belief in a caring God, a basic tenet of many religions, appears to help you recover more quickly from depression and even improves your response to medical treatment. Accordingly to scientists, praying to a God who is perceived as a source of unconditional support may lead you to find a way out of your depression.

Religious belief seems to be especially important in elderly people who are depressed. Although membership in a church or synagogue may provide social support (which in itself is a good thing), scientific research has demonstrated that religious belief alone helps older people recover from depression more quickly than social support alone. A recent study of nine thousand Europeans older than age fifty found that participation in a religious community led to greater benefits in diminishing depression than did volunteering or working with a charity, taking educational courses, or joining a political or other community organization.

The protective effect of spirituality and religion is also seen in adults with a history of parental depression. Generally, adult offspring of depressed parents are at high risk for depression during their lifetimes. A recent study that followed adult children ten and twenty years after a parent's depressive episode found that a personal sense of spirituality protects against depression. Adult children of depressed parents who say that religion is important to them are ten times less likely to suffer from depression than their counterparts without this priority.

Spirituality and religion, then, are associated with lower rates of depression, reduced severity and duration of depression, and faster remission. A systematic review of 850 studies of religion and mental health found that religion was linked to greater well-being in nearly 80 percent of patients, lower suicidality in 84 percent, lower rates of depression in 66 percent, and lower rates of anxiety in 51 percent. An intrinsic spiritual orientation—holding onto religious beliefs because they are important to oneself rather than socially acceptable to others—is associated with less hopelessness than an extrinsic spiritual orientation. Those who consider their beliefs integral to themselves experience less depression than those who say their beliefs are not strong or are based on social convention.

Spirituality and the Brain

Spirituality and religion can actually contribute to chemical, structural, and functional changes in the brain. They do this in several ways. One is through neurochemistry. Serotonin, norepinephrine, and dopamine have long been implicated in depression and are targeted by antidepressant medications. Spirituality and religious practices have been shown to boost the production and release of neurotransmitters. Some studies have shown up to a 65 percent increase in dopamine during meditation, which can be generalizable to any contemplative practice. The sense of calm and peace is associated with neurochemical changes.

In addition, these practices can have functional effects on the brain. Depression contributes to deactivating the prefrontal cortex, while spirituality and religion can stimulate parts of the brain that activate the prefrontal cortex, leading to better emotional regulation.

Also, spirituality and religious practices may even affect brain structure. While depressed patients and those at risk for depression based on family history exhibit cortical thickening of the prefrontal cortex and decreased gray matter, spirituality is associated with greater cortical thickness and increased gray matter.

Implications for Treatment

Religious beliefs can offer opportunities to see meaning in life beyond the narrow constructs of success and failure, satisfaction and disappointment. Like psychotherapy, religious beliefs often provide hope to move beyond depression. Both hope and forgiveness are pillars of many religions and channels to breaking free from depression. In his memoir *Darkness Visible*, writer William Styron describes his own experiences with depression as more about loss of hope and faith than about pain: "In depression . . . faith in deliverance, in ultimate restoration, is absent. The knowledge that no remedy will come—not in a day, an hour, a month, or a minute. . . . It is hopelessness even more than pain that crushes the soul." Strengthening or renewing contact with the spiritual dimensions of life can help you reawaken hope and engagement with life.

Religious traditions also encourage forgiveness, which is inversely related to depression. In order to forgive, you must let go of feelings of indignation and fantasies of revenge toward people who have wronged you. This doesn't mean behaving as if you were never hurt or letting people who have caused you pain back into your life. It merely means releasing the negative emotion that is preventing you from moving forward. Letting go for many is often accompanied by a lessening of depression and renewing a sense of hope and faith.

The ability to forgive confers many benefits. Forgiveness is positively correlated with higher satisfaction in life. According to scientific research, a forgiving disposition predicts relationship satisfaction and overall positive moods. Moreover, forgiveness is a factor promoting resilience, or the ability to recover from illness, modulate stress, and adapt to change. Forgiveness of others seems to be even more important to middle-aged and older adults than to young adults. Perhaps most important of all is the ability to foster forgiveness of yourself. It is you, after all, who supplies the critical voice, with every imperfection and transgression held up to an inner magnifying glass. Depression can feel dark and lonely, but forgiveness is one of the sources of light and hope.

Incorporating a spiritual or religious component into integrative treatment may make treatment more acceptable, encourage engagement with recovery, and improve response. Spiritual and religious practices do not carry the same stigma that mental health care sometimes does. Moreover, these practices tend to be ongoing, thereby diminishing a risk of relapse.

One of the most promising spiritual integrative therapies is based on CBT, which has been proven to treat depression effectively. Religiously integrated cognitive behavioral therapy (RCBT) has been shown to be even more effective than standard CBT in treating depressed people who are religious. A religious component fits logically within CBT. A core CBT intervention is cognitive restructuring—identifying, challenging, and replacing distorted thoughts. Distortions often involve spiritual and religious content—for instance, a view of the self as entirely sinful or life events as punishment from God. More hopeful and forgiving spiritual and religious beliefs can be drawn upon through RCBT to challenge distorted thinking. Patients treated with RCBT in various settings—Christians, Jews, and Muslims—have shown significantly lower scores on measures of depression after RCBT therapy.

Given the worldwide prevalence of both spirituality and depression, researchers need to better understand ways to which they are intertwined. If you consider yourself spiritual or religious, integrating this dimension into your treatment may offer you the best chance for full recovery from depression.

Chapter 20

Mindfulness and Yoga

Both psychotherapy and spirituality can nurture the mind. Unlike medications, they have no side effects, and their benefits can last longer than the treatment itself. They promote habits of thinking that not only help relieve depression but also protect against its recurrence. Another promising way to nurture the mind involves cultivating mindfulness. Mindfulness involves bringing one's full attention to the present moment with acceptance and compassion and without striving and judgment.

Mindfulness and our awareness of its effectiveness in treating depression come from research focused on Eastern philosophy using Western scientific technology. Perhaps the merger of ancient wisdom and modern technology is most succinctly captured through the launch of the iPhone application Headspace. Tibetan Buddhist monk Andy Puddicombe designed Headspace to teach meditation and mindfulness techniques through widespread technology. After its launch in 2012, three million people had downloaded Headspace by the middle of 2015. There are many other applications that guide individuals on how to meditate and relax. Understanding and appreciating the power of mindfulness can be helpful in achieving and sustaining emotional health.

Many Westerners first became aware of meditation in the 1960s, when the Beatles popularized transcendental meditation, a mantra-based technique developed by Maharishi Mahesh Yogi. It was based partly on yoga, a spiritual discipline that focuses on breath control and the adoption of certain body postures. Yoga is one of the most ancient of the mind-body techniques. According to the philosophy of yoga, the greatest stress in life comes from the mind's fluctuations, which allow it to become mired in thoughts about past frustrations and mistakes, also known as rumination. Deep mindful breathing, called *pranayama* in yoga, helps train the mind to stay in the present moment. Breathing is the only aspect of the autonomic nervous system that is both voluntary and involuntary, allowing us to practice deep breathing to elicit a relaxed state. Focusing on breathing can interrupt the negative cycle of thinking, lower stress levels, slow down both body and mind, and encourage patience. Dr. Richard Brown, an associate professor of clinical psychiatry at Columbia University College of Physicians, teaches breathing techniques to people around the world to alleviate symptoms of anxiety, depression, and post-traumatic stress disorder.

Mindfulness derives from Buddhist and yoga practices. Instead of concentrating on a mantra, the practitioner attempts to pay attention to bodily sensations, particularly breathing. Regular practice enables one to develop an attentive, nonjudgmental mind-set. The aim is a state of moment-to-moment awareness. This allows the development of insight into thoughts and feelings, which are then experienced as transient mental activity instead of absolute reality confirming a negative outlook. The goal is direct experience rather than experience filtered through reactivity and judgment.

While cultivating mindfulness through meditation and yoga was associated with the counterculture during the 1960s, today it is very much mainstream. Interest in Eastern breathing practices is growing, and breathing techniques are being adapted to diverse cultures and medical settings to improve the health of both body and mind. Research has consistently demonstrated benefits from mindfulness practices to combat the rise of stress-related illnesses. Business leaders now turn to practices like mindfulness that alleviate stress and lessen depression. A recent article in the *Harvard Business Review* even suggested that mindfulness is taking on cult status in the business world.

Becoming aware of habitual negative thinking is a critical component of mindfulness-based psychotherapy, a practice defined by Harvard psychologist Ellen Langer and numerous psychiatrists and therapists. It involves increasing one's self-awareness and living deliberately. This means turning off the "automatic pilot" that steers you mindlessly through your life and paying attention to your thoughts, feelings, and bodily sensations. Once you are no longer "zoned out," you can start to notice variability, question knee-jerk decisions that actually rob you of your choices, and reclaim your vitality. Langer calls this the power of possibility and encourages you to become more aware of what could be, rather than assuming that what is or what has always been is the way things have to be. Langer writes that one of the most painful aspects of depression is the belief that it has lasted since the beginning of time and will continue forever. If you pay closer attention, even when you are depressed, you realize that you are not depressed every minute of every day. Seeing that depression is not relentless helps you regain some ability to manage it.

The popularity of today's mindfulness movement is often attributed to Jon Kabat-Zinn, who was a Massachusetts Institute of Technology graduate student in molecular biology when he heard a lecture by a Zen teacher. Later, while working at the University of Massachusetts, he developed a program called mindfulness-based stress reduction (MBSR) to help patients at the university hospital who were coping with serious medical conditions.

The eight-week MBSR courses involve formal and informal meditation and mindfulness practices, including sitting meditation, mindful hatha yoga, and mindful eating. MBSR is a form of mindfulness frequently studied by scientists. It is used extensively in the field of medicine to treat complaints from psoriasis to intractable medical conditions to depression. Because it is a standardized intervention and secular, it lends itself well to scientific studies.

Study of MBSR shows that it is effective in decreasing depression in a variety of types of patients. It was proven effective in helping college students learn how to manage stress and depression. Meditative practice helped them achieve distance and perspective on their negative thoughts as well as greater psychological flexibility.

MBSR has been shown to play a significant role in improved depression, anxiety, and mental health scores among veterans. The content of the training and thc experience of a supportive environment, positive expectation of change, and development of new coping strategies contribute to the positive effect. Especially given the frequent preference of veterans to participate in treatment that does not involve medication, MBSR is a promising intervention in this population.

MBSR is one of the explicitly recognized therapies that use mindfulness methods. Others are mindfulness-based cognitive therapy (MBCT) and dialectical behavioral therapy (DBT).

MBCT, an eight-week skills-training intervention, appears to be as effective as medications. In fact, many patients exposed to MBCT as described in several studies were able to discontinue antidepressant medications. Several studies have shown the superiority of MBCT over psychoeducation for subjects who had major depression and did not achieve remission with antidepressant treatment. MBCT has specifically been shown to decrease cognitive reactivity to sad mood states and to heighten compassion for the self.

MBCT has been shown helpful as initial treatment for depression but is especially useful for depression that has been difficult to treat. In fact, this therapy may offer the most benefit to patients at greatest risk for relapse. Review studies have indicated that adding mindfulness meditation to conventional CBT is both effective and cost-efficient in preventing relapse in patients whose depression has subsided.

This finding is important, because depression is tenacious. Up to 80 percent of depressed people relapse. Antidepressant medications can lose their effectiveness. MBCT has shown the largest effect on patients who have the most risk due to a history of child abuse. Perhaps it confers resilience in groups at highest risk because patients learn skills that address underlying mechanisms of relapse or recurrence.

Long known to practitioners of yoga, the importance of breathing as a sign of well-being is increasingly accepted by medical science. Western medical researchers are now studying the specific role of yogic breathing in treating depression. In small studies, after just four days of yogic breathing practice, depressed patients showed an improvement in symptoms according to the Beck Depression Inventory. Moreover, the benefits were sustained as the study subjects were periodically rechecked.

Yoga has been added to both MBSR and MBCT with effective results. A number of studies have shown improvement in depression after MBSR and yoga in diverse groups. The impact on depression and stress was studied in medical students and in healthy young adult professional musicians. Both groups experienced decreases in depression that appear to have resulted directly from the yoga and meditation techniques themselves.

Dialectical behavior therapy (DBT), was developed by Dr. Marsha Linehan in the 1990s to treat suicidal patients and those with borderline personality disorder. More recently, DBT has also been shown to be helpful in treating a range of psychiatric disorders; some studies suggest its usefulness in treating major depressive disorders. DBT blends CBT with elements of Zen Buddhist mindfulness practice to foster mindful awareness and tolerance of distress. Central to its philosophy, DBT teaches dialectical thinking, an approach to tolerating conflict with awareness and flexibility instead of rigid and dichotomous thinking. DBT diverges from traditional CBT by providing more direct support to the patient and validating difficult thoughts rather than encouraging the patient to struggle with them. Recent research studies of DBT show significant relief in treatment-resistant depression in adults who did not respond to medication.

As neuroscience technologies have improved, science can now examine the effects of meditation on the brain. Quantifiable results now include reduction of stress and anxiety and relief from depression. A recent review of research studies looking at mindfulness effects found that mindfulness meditation yields quantifiable results in reducing the effects of depression on the brain, with results as significant as those of antidepressants. Other research on changes in neural activity suggests that the activity of the insula, a brain area associated with internally generated emotions, is linked with sad mood states in both healthy and depressed individuals. Insular activity is partly modulated by meditation, and the degree of activation has been shown to correlate with the amount of meditation practice.

Mindfulness through meditation and yoga is a promising way for you to nurture your mind. It has no side effects and can be practiced anywhere. It has been shown not only to help people overcome depression but it can also foster changes in attitudes toward life to prevent relapse of symptoms. Current scientific studies are demonstrating the effectiveness of mindfulness in treating depression. This represents a complementary perspective of ancient Eastern philosophy and modern neuroscience—a core fundamental of integrative medicine.

Chapter 21

Beyond Mindfulness

Both patients' individual stories and recent research demonstrate that mindfulness practices, including meditation and yoga, help alleviate depression. There are other ways to nurture the mind as well. Although we may intuitively sense their potential for restoring a sense of well-being, scientists now have evidence of the ways they directly influence the brain and help heal depression. The first of these is a sense of connection with nature—with green space and with blue space, or water.

Nature

From the wisdom of ancient peoples to writers of nineteenth-century America, we have long known that the natural world is a tonic for emotional health. Henry David Thoreau observed, "There can be no very black melancholy to him who lives in the midst of nature."

The latest scientific research confirms the wisdom of Thoreau's observation. Researchers at Stanford University studied the potential mental health benefits of nature by comparing the thought patterns of volunteers who took a walk through a lush green wooded area with the patterns of others who walked through an urban area congested with heavy traffic. After the walks, they studied blood flow configurations in the brains of these volunteers.

Unsurprisingly, the group who walked in the woods reported more peace of mind and life satisfaction. They also had lower levels of stress hormones than those who took the city walk. In particular, the volunteers who walked in nature exhibited less blood flow to the subgenual prefrontal cortex, a narrow band in the lower part of the brain related to depression.

When you can't stop thinking about your weaknesses, mistakes, and imperfections, and you keep entertaining the thought of failing, you are ruminating. This type of thinking shows up as heightened activity in the subgenual cortex, and it is both a precursor of and a hallmark trait of depression. While common sense would tell us that a walk in the woods is more calming than a walk through a crowded city, the research study shows what actually happens in our brains. The brains of those who walked in nature revealed decreased activity in the subgenual cortex, illustrative of less rumination. As rumination declines, so do feelings of depression.

Research links our indoor and increasingly urban lifestyle with increased aggression, violence, loss of emotional control, and depression. Renewing a connection with nature, then, would offer opportunities to improve mental health.

One study attempted to assess the optimal exposure to green exercise, or activity in the presence of nature. The researchers found large benefits from short exposures and, afterward, diminishing but still positive returns. Every green environment studied improved participants' moods; the presence of water led to the greatest improvements in mood. Those with mental health issues, including depression, achieved the most significant mood benefits.

A meta-analysis found the presence of water—or blue space—had even greater positive effects on mental health than green space in the absence of water. This finding should be important to architects and landscape designers, in addition to mental health professionals.

A growing body of research connects spending time in nature with high levels of well-being. Exposure to nature has been shown to reduce stress, improve the capacity for attention and cognitive functioning, increase concentration and impulse control, and speed healing. Because of the clear connection between nature and mental health, considerable research has focused on incorporating nature into mental health counseling. One group pioneered a course in ecotherapy for mental health practitioners, who would offer counseling in the context of the natural world. Participants felt that the course gave them a deeper understanding of themselves and a greater appreciation for different cultures. In addition, courses delivered in a natural setting allowed psychology students at a Canadian university to experience higher levels of well-being. A subfield offering horticultural therapy, or counseling in the setting of planting and gardening, has reported that participating patients experience sustained relief from depressive symptoms.

Researchers who have explored nature-based therapies advocate including these approaches in professional practice. Future research about the underlying mechanisms of the effects of nature on mental health and depression is ongoing. Activities outdoors or near water can be easily incorporated into an integrative treatment program; previous studies have demonstrated notable improvements in mood, energy, and brain chemistry with such programs.

Laughter

Smiling and laughter have been studied as ways to lift depression immediately. The simple act of smiling releases endorphins in the brain. In turn, the release of dopamine causes a smile. Some studies suggest that facial movement modulates emotion—that is, if people can be induced to express an emotion, they may then feel that emotion. If they smile, they feel better. Studies to date are equivocal about this facial feedback hypothesis, but it is still being explored. Although it may seem strange to expect mental health benefits from a "pretend smile," this is not a new idea. "Even the simulation of an event tends to arouse it in our mind," wrote Charles Darwin in 1872.

We know intuitively that a sense of humor encourages a pleasant feeling and is a wonderful asset in life, contributing to resilience and helping us weather life's inevitable indignities. Humor involves the whole person on cognitive, emotional, behavioral, and social levels and is linked to favorable adjustments to life losses and depression. Evidence shows that humor can also play a positive role in physical healing.

Laughter causes the body to release into the bloodstream high concentrations of different hormones and peptides related to happiness, bonding, tolerance, and generosity. This release also precludes the production of other hormones and neuropeptides related to hatred, violence, fear, jealousy, and aggression.

The importance of humor to mental health has led to the study and cultivation of laughter. In patients with cancer, four sessions of a therapeutic laughter program led to a significant reduction in both anxiety and depression.

A recently popularized form of yoga centers on laughter. Laughter yoga was popularized as an exercise routine by Indian physician Madan

Kataria. In 1995, Kataria launched his first Laughter Yoga Club. Now more than six thousand laughter clubs exist in sixty countries. Practitioners begin by simulating laughter that develops into real, contagious laughter. In the form of yoga, the laughter is physical and does not involve humor or comedy. Just the act of laughing leads to increased oxygen consumption and can stimulate the immune system.

Depression is common and often difficult to treat in elderly persons. A study comparing those who received humor therapy with those who received standard therapy found that those who received the humor therapy showed the greatest improvement in depression

Humor can also help relieve depression in other patient groups. Humorous movies shown on a near daily basis to hospitalized patients with chronic schizophrenia contributed to a decrease in the patients' depression and other symptoms of pathology after a month of this regimen. The patients also showed improved social competence and a decline in anger.

A therapeutic laughter program comprising four sessions was piloted in breast cancer patients. The patients experienced a significant reduction in anxiety, depression, and stress.

The outcomes of these programs show that cultivating laughter can be a therapeutic tool in helping people overcome depression and other negative emotions.

Hope

Research has shown that hope, the antithesis of depression, can also be cultivated. The theory on which hope therapy is based does not consider hope a passive emotion experienced only in a life crisis but a cognitive process through which people actively pursue goals. It is designed to increase hopeful thinking and encourage goal setting. This therapeutic perspective comes from positive psychology, which encourages therapists not to focus on pathology but instead to identify patients' strengths.

In a program of hope therapy over eight sessions, participants expressed more self-esteem and a greater sense of agency, or control over their own lives, and decreased depression and anxiety. Hope therapy was also shown to be effective for depressed women who were mothers of children with cancer. After the study concluded, participants showed significant decreases in depression and significant increases in hope.

Nature, laughter, and hope are strategies that attempt to dislodge everyday thinking, to help you get outside the corrosive confines of your depression. Spending time in nature is perhaps the easiest way to become open to the world outside the self. A sense of humor is a strong indicator of recovery. Hope is the foundation of healing, and if you can keep or find a sense of humor, you can also overcome depression.

Chapter 22

The Future Treatment of Depression

As I conclude this book, I'd like to repeat a plea for better care for the most vulnerable of patients. These are the individuals at each end of the age spectrum, children and seniors. Depressed children and seniors are often poorly served by psychiatry, although they make up a large percentage of the patients seeking help for depressed moods. I would also like to discuss some of the new developments on promising treatment modalities for depression, including transcranial magnetic stimulation (TMS), neurofeedback, and ketamine infusion therapy.

Adolescents

At any given time, as many as 15 percent of adolescents are depressed, making depression a more common problem than asthma and most other chronic problems in this age group.

Beth's story illustrates the cost of psychiatry's hit-or-miss prescription patterns. At seventeen, Beth was brought to my office by her worried mother, who explained that Beth had been an active, engaged child who did well in school and played on the school lacrosse team until her sophomore year. When Beth did not make the cut for the varsity team, she stopped playing lacrosse altogether and no longer spent time with her friends, most of whom she had met through the sport. Instead she began to isolate herself in her room, spending her time online. While she had always been an honor student, she began to get Cs and Ds on her report card, just when grades were becoming increasingly important to her future.

Beth's parents were painfully aware of her downward spiral, and they had taken her to see a psychiatrist a year before. The psychiatrist had diagnosed Beth with major depressive disorder and prescribed Lexapro after she didn't respond to the Zoloft prescribed by her primary care physician. This drug made Beth restless and unable to concentrate. So the psychiatrist prescribed Paxil instead. Beth's restlessness decreased, but she began to experience dramatic shifts in mood. The drug Abilify was added to stabilize Beth's mood. This drug combination made Beth sleepy all the time, and a stimulant drug was prescribed in addition to the two medications Beth was already taking. Beth continued to be depressed, and her parents were concerned that their teen daughter was taking three drugs, none of which were approved by the FDA for her illness. They brought her to me for a second opinion.

I tested Beth for nutritional deficiencies and looked at her genetic profile for metabolizing medications. Testing revealed that Beth was lacking in zinc, magnesium, and vitamin B_{12}. After reviewing her genetic test, I determined that the drug Wellbutrin was most likely to be effective, as Beth had a variant of the serotonin transporter gene. This gene has been helpful in predicting poor response to SSRI medications, which may explain why she did not get better on any of three previous SSRI medications she tried.

Beth got steadily better on this new regimen. In time, she was able to turn her record around before applying to college, reconnect with old friends, and get some pleasure from her remaining time in high school.

So many depressed teens do not get effective treatment even when they are under psychiatric care, and the stakes are high. Three-fourths of lifetime psychiatric disorders first emerge in adolescence or early adulthood. Depressed young people are also more likely to have behavioral problems, to underachieve, and to engage in substance abuse than other teens. More depressed college students have used alcohol than their peers who do not have depression. Moreover, once teens have participated in high-risk behaviors, they are more likely to continue to engage in them as they become adults. For all these reasons, depression in teens is of special concern.

Elderly Persons

Depression is also of special concern for elderly persons. Diagnosis in this group is more challenging because these patients often do not show the typical signs of depression. Depressed seniors may express no feelings of sadness; they may simply appear apathetic or uninterested in activities that used to bring them pleasure. They may not be as forthcoming about their feelings in general as those who have grown up in an era of relatively free personal expression. Instead, they may report more physical symptoms than painful feelings, so that symptoms of depression are hidden in other medical complaints. A shuffling gait may suggest arthritis, while difficulty breathing could mean pulmonary disease. The erosion of cognitive processes can look like Alzheimer's disease. But all these symptoms can be signs of depression.

How often do you hear that an elderly relative has little interest in food? Or that food doesn't taste good? If you remember, poor taste is a symptom of zinc shortage. Zinc shortage, a treatable contributing factor in depression, is common in the elderly.

Depression in elderly persons is also likely to respond poorly to antidepressant therapy, requiring the use of alternative approaches. A 2015 study in eighteen elderly patients with major depression showed that taking the omega-3 fatty acids DHA and EPA three times a day for twelve weeks significantly improved their depressive symptoms.

Medications

Elderly and young patients are particularly vulnerable to psychiatric medications. The use of these drugs is studied in young and middle-aged adults, not in teens and seniors. For seniors, these drugs may interact with other medications they take to treat other chronic conditions.

For adolescents, even greater dangers may be involved. Because antidepressant drugs can increase agitation and suicidal thinking in teens during the early phase of treatment, the FDA has required since 2004 that these drugs contain a "black-box warning," the most serious warning placed on medication labels. In addition, the effects of these powerful drugs on the developing brain are not fully understood. Most clinical studies of their effectiveness have been of short duration and have been conducted on small numbers of participants.

Some psychiatrists concerned about the growing use of antidepressants argue that this treatment model could actually be fueling an epidemic of mental illness among adolescents. The prescription rate of antidepressant medication for young people has increased sevenfold since 1990, and the rate of mental illness in young people itself continues to accelerate. If antidepressants continue to be prescribed at the current rate, within a generation, half of American children will be taking psychiatric medication. Some studies show that, even if young patients get relief when they begin to take these drugs, the depression comes back. Instead of a problem that comes and goes, depression becomes a chronic one.

Medical professionals can no longer continue treating vulnerable patients like teens and seniors as if there is but one answer to depression: medication.

Given that many members of these groups are malnourished, do not exercise enough, lack support, and have other diseases, it's vital that treatment addresses all of these areas. Indeed, for these groups and for all patients, we need to use every tool available to treat depression.

Although THE ZEEBRA is the most complete, personalized, and integrative approach for dealing with depression, medical science is continuing to advance, offering new hope for successful diagnosis and treatment. New research involves novel approaches for treating depression, including transcranial magnetic stimulation (TMS), neurofeedback, and ketamine infusion therapy.

Transcranial Magnetic Stimulation

One of the new treatment techniques recently approved by the FDA for major depressive disorder is transcranial magnetic stimulation (TMS). TMS sends carefully targeted magnetic field impulses into the prefrontal cortex, an area of the brain that plays a major role in regulating mood and that has been specifically linked to depression. Researchers believe that depression changes the prefrontal cortex. The mild electrical current from the magnetic impulses appears to improve the function and behavior of the prefrontal cortex.

Studies involving more than ten thousand TMS treatments show that it is safe and effective. In one study, about 50 percent of patients enjoyed a significant improvement in depressive symptoms, with the symptoms being completely resolved in 33 percent of the participants. The benefits lasted through the six months that the patients were monitored. Side effects included mild to moderate scalp discomfort and headache, with the problems occurring less often after the first week of treatment.

The first study looking at the long-term effects of TMS therapy in treatment-resistant depressed patients was presented at the American Psychiatric Association's 2013 Annual Meeting. All patients involved in this study initially received the standard TMS treatment protocol (or one adjusted to meet the patient's needs) daily for four to six weeks. From the total study population, 257 patients entered a long-term follow-up phase in which they tapered off this treatment regimen and were observed for fifty-two weeks. At the one-year follow up, 68 percent reported significant improvement, while 45 percent experienced complete remission.

The treatment sessions are easy and uneventful for the patient, who sits in a large chair with a small "arm" that generates the magnetic impulses positioned off to the left side of the head. Typically, twenty to thirty treatment sessions are given over the course of four to six weeks, with each session lasting less than forty minutes. Anesthesia and sedation are not necessary, and patients can return to work or personal activities right away.

TMS is prescribed by psychiatrists for adults with major depressive disorder who have not been helped by the proper application of at least one standard antidepressant. TMS therapy can be incorporated into an integrative psychiatry program. I've been encouraged by the results, but it is not yet possible to predict who will benefit from TMS therapy. It is worth talking to your psychiatrist about TMS treatment.

Although TMS is a large step forward, the best results are part of an integrated program following identification and treatment of underlying nutritional shortages.

Neurofeedback

Neurofeedback, also known as neurotherapy or biofeedback, is a simple, painless, and noninvasive procedure in which we are able to improve an individual's brain activity with gradual training exercises. It is typically done by a mental health professional, and electrodes are applied to different parts of the scalp to monitor brainwave activity. Signals are then processed and analyzed, and this information is shared with the patient. The brain is rewarded when it changes its own activity to more appropriate patterns, where it will eventually achieve self-regulation. Self-regulation is important for the brain's ability to function effectively and allows some people struggling with depression to better improve their mood.

The left frontal area of the brain has been associated with positive emotions and motivation, while the right frontal area of the brain is associated with depression and fear. When there is less brainwave activity in the left area, the right area becomes dominant, leaving the individual vulnerable to becoming depressed and withdrawn. Studies have shown that mood was improved in college students when the left side of the brain was trained to be more active than its right counterpart using neurofeedback technology.

Ketamine Infusion Therapy

Traditional medications for depression typically take weeks or months for any noted improvement in symptoms. However, in 2000, ketamine, an anesthetic medication, was reported to minimize depressive symptoms in patients with major depressive disorder within a few hours with a single, intravenous, subanesthetic dose. One 2011 study published in *Nature* showed that ketamine is able to quickly boost levels of the brain compound BDNF, which is generally low in patients with depression.

At higher doses, ketamine can render a person unconscious, but at lower doses, it can induce feelings of euphoria and possibly hallucinations, making it a popular drug of abuse. However, most studies use doses that are too low to induce any psychotic effects. Although the drug has been demonstrated to work quickly and effectively, ketamine infusion therapy is often reserved for patients with severe depression that is considered treatment resistant. Ketamine is typically given in a small dose over a forty-minute session.

Several small studies have explored the effectiveness of ketamine infusion therapy, yielding mostly positive results. Most patients in these studies report rapid and considerable improvement in their mood, typically lasting twenty-four to seventy-two hours. In a 2013 study published in *Biological Psychiatry*, twenty-four patients with treatment-resistant depression and off antidepressant medications were given a series of as many as six ketamine intravenous infusions over a twelve-day period. Participants were monitored for as many as eighty-three days after the last infusion was given. About 71 percent of study participants experienced improvement in symptoms, and the average time to relapse after the last infusion therapy was eighteen days.

There is also research that examines ketamine's ability to minimize the stress response. One of the greatest risk factors for depression is stress exposure. The ability to experience stress without developing affective disorders, also known as stress resilience, varies from one person to another. Increasing stress resilience would therefore decrease the risk of developing depressive symptoms caused by stress. In a 2015 study, researchers tested if a single dose of ketamine would be able to protect mice from developing depressive behavior after their exposure to a series of stressful test models for three weeks. Researchers found that ketamine was able to enhance stress resilience, as they performed better during the stress tests compared with placebo.

The Future

The psychiatric treatment of depression currently is not good enough. New treatments are being researched, but too many patients are still suffering. Psychiatry continues to blame patients for its failures. You can see this in the terms doctors use, saying that a patient has "failed treatment" and is "treatment resistant." But if a patient is taking medication prescribed by her doctor and doesn't recover, who has failed?

We *can* do better, much better, if we take advantage of decades' worth of largely ignored research that shows that depression is not "all in your head." The mind and body are one; what happens in the body affects the mind. Nutritional shortages, hormones, allergies, and other physical diseases are important in the development and course of depression.

It's time for an approach to depression that combines traditional medical science with nutritional and metabolic therapies. To be truly successful, this approach must also be scientific, basing each and every prescription or recommendation on objectively measured problems in the body instead of subjectively compiled lists of symptoms matched to equally subjective lists in a manual.

Such an approach to depression based on our different biochemical makeups does not ignore medications but integrates metabolic abnormalities that may be contributing to the symptoms. This approach, integrative medicine, successfully treats many individuals suffering from depression.

Chapter 23

Integrative Psychiatry

I am passionate about THE ZEEBRA approach. It helps both doctors and patients view depression in a new way and opens the door to solutions that millions have been waiting for.

So many patients arrive at my office for the first time already discouraged. They are tired of promised treatment and tired of being depressed. That they are still depressed is not for lack of trying. Most have tried at least one medication (and sometimes as many as seven) and every new therapy or self-help guide promising relief and recovery. Although their individual stories differ, the common theme is a feeling of helplessness and the sense of being let down by psychiatry.

It is for these patients that I have written this book.

I've covered a lot in this book, looking at everything from amino acids to zinc. I've discussed current psychiatric practices and focused on biochemical individuality. I'd like to review and summarize some of the central features of THE ZEEBRA approach.

- Each individual has a unique biochemistry. Levels that are normal in one person may be high or low in the next. Indeed, a measure that may be normal or healthy for thousands or even millions of patients may not be optimal for you.
- Depression is a complex state influenced by body chemistry and metabolism, genetics and epigenetics, nutrient intake and absorption, hormones, food sensitivities, life events, social support, and many other factors that define our lives.
- Treatment for depression must begin with testing to identify all contributing factors. No stone should be left unturned, because even a slight mineral shortage or hormone imbalance can result in symptoms of depression or prevent full recovery.
- Antidepressant medications are not magic bullets to treat depression. Although they are tools in the doctor's toolbox, they must share space with other available treatments.

- Integrative psychiatry offers the best approach for treating depression. It focuses on each person's unique personality, metabolism, and environment.

Recognizing that nutrition is key to brain health is a fundamental premise of integrative psychiatry. Instead of focusing on just one type of treatment, integrative medicine tries to address all factors that may contribute to your depression—bringing together nutritional supplements, medications, psychotherapy, and lifestyle changes.

With an integrated approach to psychiatry, assessment of nutritional factors is standard practice. Identifying and correcting nutritional shortages often restores brain health, allowing you to live free of symptoms. Because of what we now know about the impact of nutrition on the brain and therefore on the mind, nutritional assessment needs to be part of mainstream psychiatry.

Nutritional factors are not the only determinants of depression, of course. Integrative medicine brings together research findings from genetics as well as from neurobiology. Your genetic blueprints are the gift or curse you inherit from your ancestors, and they have an impact on your biological potential for health and illness. Rather than being random, these differences are often the result of predictable differences in genetics and an interaction between your genes and the environment. In fact, one-third of genetic variations are linked to your body's ability to use and absorb nutrients. These variations mean that each individual has unique metabolic needs and that the metabolism of essential nutrients varies in different individuals. Although genetic predispositions may be a metabolic liability in some cases, understanding them can make a difference in which of your genes are expressed. Genetics is not destiny.

The researchers Leroy Hood and David J. Galas describe integrative medicine as based on the "four Ps": *personalized, predictive, preventive, and participatory*. Unlike traditional medicine, its approach is based on prevention rather than reaction to illness or disease. Prevention is possible—even before the development of symptoms—because of the availability of new techniques for measurement and visualization and new information about biochemistry. There is no longer a need to wait until the patient shows signs of illness to treat underlying biochemical processes.

In the practice of integrative medicine, treatments are targeted precisely toward your particular genetic factors and nutritional imbalances. Treatment is no longer hit or miss but predicted to be effective.

All of these principles are incorporated into THE ZEEBRA approach, a program for treating you, not a diagnosis, through personalized medicine.

If you do not ask the questions, how can you find the answers? If you do not look for causes, how do you find the cures? If you understand that you are a unique biochemical, psychological, and spiritual person, you will understand that a new approach is desperately needed for the treatment of depression.

As I finish this book, I ask the same question that prompted me to write the book in the first place. *Why?*

- Why are vitamin B_{12} and folate levels not routinely checked in every patient who is depressed?
- Why are depressed patients not routinely screened for celiac disease?
- Why are so many psychiatrists so reluctant to explore more deeply the relationship between depression and trace metals such as zinc, chromium, and iodine?
- Why do health insurance companies cover memberships in health clubs but not nutritional supplements, even when lab tests reveal a clear nutritional shortage?
- Why do health insurance companies pay thousands of dollars each month for psychotropic medications yet not offer assistance for $50 worth of nutritional supplements?

I am impatient. We do not have more time. As Chief Medical Officer of a psychiatric hospital, I regularly see patients in crisis. Too often my desk holds the charts of depressed patients who have either attempted or committed suicide after shuttling for years between therapies and hospitals, trying one medication after another. The decision to end their life is their incomprehensible, tragic ending.

The science is available to change the current model of trial-and-error prescribing. The science is available to correct nutritional and metabolic influences on mood. Right now we have the tools we need to identify and improve the treatment of depression.

It's time.

You are in charge of your own health. I hope this book has given you the knowledge and tools you need to begin to heal. I encourage you to engage your health professional in a broad search for things that may contribute to your depression. Through this search, you can find the help you need and the peace of mind you deserve.

Depression is treatable. You will get well.

References

Introduction

Part I: UNDERSTANDING THE PROBLEM

Chapter 1: Personalized Medicine

Berwick DM. Disseminating innovations in health care. JAMA. 2003;289(15):1969–1975.

Goodwin JS, et al. The tomato effect: Rejection of highly efficacious therapies. JAMA. 1984;251(18):2387–2390.

Levin A. Time to apply cutting edge to the brain, Nobelists say. Psychiatric News. 2010;45(10):4.

Chapter 2: What Is Depression?

Altshuler LL, et al. Course of mood and anxiety disorders during pregnancy and the postpartum period. J Clin Psychiatry. 1998;59(Suppl 2):29–33.

Bostwick JM, et al. Affective disorders and suicide risk: A reexamination. Am J Psychiatry. 2000;157(12):1925–1932.

Conwell Y, et al. Suicide and aging. I: Patterns of psychiatric diagnosis. Int Psychogeriatr. 1995;7(2):149–164.

Goldman LS, et al. Awareness diagnosis and treatment of depression. J Gen Intern Med. 1999;14(9):569–580.

González HM, et al. Depression care in the United States: Too little for too few. Arch Gen Psychiatry. 2010;67(1):37–46.

Green RC, et al. Depression as a risk factor for Alzheimer's disease: The MIRAGE Study. Arch Neurol. 2003;60(5):753–759.

Hellerstein DJ, et al. Impairment in psychosocial functioning linked to dysthymic disorder in the NESARC study. J Affect Disord. 2010;127(1):84–88.

Huang TL, et al. T-helper 1/T-helper 2 cytokine imbalance and clinical phenotypes of acute-phase major depression. Psychiatry Clin Neurosci. 2007;61(4):415–420.

Kessler RC, et al. Lifetime prevalence and age-of-onset distributions of DSM-IV disorders in the National Comorbidity Survey Replication. Arch Gen Psychiatry. 2005;62(6):593–602.

Knol MJ, et al. Depression as a risk factor for the onset of type 2 diabetes mellitus. A meta-analysis. Diabetologia. 2006;49(5):837–845.

Mark TL, et al. Datapoints: Psychotropic drug prescriptions by medical specialty. Psychiatr Serv. 2009;60(9):1167.

Sansone RA, et al. Dysthymic disorder: The chronic depression. Am Fam Physician. 1996;53(8):2588–2596.

Chapter 3: How Do We Evaluate Depression?

Kennedy N, et al. Residual symptoms at remission from depression: Impact on long-term outcome. J Affect Disord. 2004;80(2–3):135–144.

Mojtabai R, et al. National trends in psychotrophic medication polypharmacy in office-based psychiatry. Arch Gen Psychiatry. 2010;67(1):26–36.

Trivedi MH, et al. Evaluation of outcomes with citalopram for depression using measurement-based care in STAR*D: Implications for clinical practice. Am J Psychiatry. 2006;163(1):28–40.

Turner EH, et al. Selective publication of antidepressant studies and its influence on

apparent efficacy. N Engl J Med. 2008;358(3):252–260.
Ustün TB, et al. Global burden of depressive disorders in the year 2000. Br J Psychiatry. 2004;184:386–392.

Chapter 4: Current Treatments Are Less Effective Than We Think

Bekelman JE, et al. Scope and impact of financial conflicts of interest in biomedical research: A systematic review. JAMA. 2003;289(4):454–465.
Food and Drug Administration. Antidepressant Use in Children, Adolescents and Adults. 2007. Available at: http://wwwfdagov/Drugs/DrugSafety/InformationbyDrugClass/ucm096273htm. Accessed July 29, 2015.
Fournier JC, et al. Antidepressant drug effects and depression severity: A patient-level meta-analysis. JAMA. 2010;303(1):47–53.
Gellad ZF, et al. Direct-to-consumer advertising of pharmaceuticals. Am J Med. 2007;120(6):475–480.
Gregorian RS, et al. Antidepressant-induced sexual dysfunction. Ann Pharmacother. 2002;36(10):1577–1589.
Kaplan A. Antidepressants: How well do they work? Psychiatric Times. 2010;27(3).
Moncrieff J. Are antidepressants overrated? A review of methodological problems in antidepressant studies. J Nerv Ment Dis. 2001;189(5):288–295.
Robinson AR, et al. Direct-to-consumer pharmaceutical advertising: Physician and public opinion and potential effects on the physician-patient relationship. Arch Intern Med. 2004;164(4):427–432.
Zimmerman M, et al. Symptom severity and exclusion from antidepressant efficacy studies. J Clin Psychopharmacol. 2002;22(6):610–614.

Chapter 5: Depression and Biochemical Individuality

Goldman E. Hippocampal neurogenesis: Key to antidepressants? Clinical Psychiatry News. 2007;35(6):16.
Mayberg HS, et al. Deep brain stimulation for treatment-resistant depression. Neuron. 2005;45(5):651–660.

Chapter 6: Genetics, Epigenetics, and Personalized Medicine

Dolinoy DC, et al. Maternal genistein alters coat color and protects Avy mouse offspring from obesity by modifying the fetal epigenome. Environ Health Perspect. 2006;114(4):567–572.
Dolinoy DC, et al. Maternal nutrient supplementation counteracts bisphenol A-induced DNA hypomethylation in early development. Proc Natl Acad Sci USA. 2007;104(32):13056–13061.
Fang MZ, et al. Tea polyphenol (-)-epigallocatechin-3-gallate inhibits DNA methyltransferase and reactivates methylation-silenced genes in cancer cell lines. Cancer Res. 2003;63(22):7563–7570.
Hughes LA, et al. Early life exposure to famine and colorectal cancer risk: A role for epigenetic mechanisms. PLoS One. 2009;4(11):e7951.
Liu Y, et al. Alcohol exposure alters DNA methylation profiles in mouse embryos at early neurulation. Epigenetics. 2009;4(7):500–511.
Maestripieri D. Early experience affects the intergenerational transmission of infant abuse in rhesus monkeys. Proc Natl Acad Sci USA. 2005;102(27):9726–9729. Epub 2005 Jun 27.
Murgatroyd C, et al. Genes learn from stress: How infantile trauma programs us for depression. Epigenetics. 2010;5(3):194–199.

Sullivan P, et al. Genetic epidemiology of major depression: Review and meta-analysis. Am J Psychiatry. 2000;157(10):1552–1562.

Chapter 7: Personalized Medicine with THE ZEEBRA Approach

Boscarino JA, et al. Low serum cholesterol and external-cause mortality: Potential implications for research and surveillance. J Psychiatr Res. 2009;43(9):848–854.

Eby GA, et al. Rapid recovery from major depression using magnesium treatment. Med Hypotheses. 2006;67(2):362–370.

Hintikka J, et al. High vitamin B_{12} level and good treatment outcome may be associated in major depressive disorder. BMC Psychiatry. 2003;3:17.

Levenson CW. Zinc: The new antidepressant? Nutr Rev. 2006;64(1):39–42.

Nemets H, et al. Omega-3 treatment of childhood depression: A controlled, double-blind pilot study. Am J Psychiatry. 2006;163(6):1098–1100.

Papakostas GI, et al. Serum folate, vitamin B_{12}, and homocysteine in major depressive disorder, Part I: Predictors of clinical response in fluoxetine-resistant depression. J Clin Psychiatry. 2004;65(8):1096–1098.

Pope HG Jr, et al. Testosterone gel supplementation for men with refractory depression: A randomized, placebo-controlled study. Am J Psychiatry. 2003;160(1):105–111.

Su KP, et al. Omega-3 fatty acids in major depressive disorder. A preliminary double-blind, placebo-controlled study. Eur Neuropsychopharmacol. 2003;13(4):267–271.

Sublette ME, et al. Omega-3 polyunsaturated essential fatty acid status as a predictor of future suicide risk. Am J Psychiatry. 2006;163(6):1100–1102.

Tai SS, et al. Promoting physical activity in general practice: Should prescribed exercise be free? J R Soc Med. 1999;92(2):65–67.

Young SN. Has the time come for clinical studies on the antidepressant effect of vitamin D? J Psychiatry Neurosci. 2009;34(1):3.

Part II: NOURISHING THE BRAIN: THE ZEEBRA APPROACH

Chapter 8: T: Take Care of Yourself

Akbaraly TN, et al. Adherence to healthy dietary guidelines and future depressive symptoms: Evidence for sex differentials in the Whitehall II study. Am J Clin Nutr. 2013;97(2):419–427.

Chang KJ, et al. Perceived sleep quality is associated with depression in a Korean elderly population. Arch Gerontol Geriatr. 2014;59468-59473.

Eby GA, et al. Rapid recovery from major depression using magnesium treatment. Med Hypotheses. 2006;67(2):362–370.

Fernandez-Mendoza J, et al. Insomnia and incident depression: Role of objective sleep duration and natural history. J Sleep Res. 2015;24(4):390–398.

Fried EI, et al. The differential influence of life stress on individual symptoms of depression. Act Psychiatrica Scandinavica. 2015;131(6):465–471.

Gangwisch GE, et al. High glycemic index diet as a risk factor for depression: Analyses from the Women's Health Initiative. Am J Clin Nutr. 2015;102(2):454–463.

Grossi G, et al. Self-reported sleep lengths ≥9 hours among Swedish patients with stress-related exhaustion: Associations with depression, quality of sleep and levels of fatigue. Nordic J Psychiatry. 2015;69(4):292-299.

Jacka FN, et al. Association of Western and traditional diets with depression and anxiety in women. Am J Psychiatry. 2010;167(3):305–311.

Jacka FN, et al. Does reverse causality explain the relationship between diet and depression? J Affective Dis. 2015;175:248-250.

Jacka FN, et al. Associations between diet quality and depressed mood in teens: Results from the Australian Healthy Neighbourhoods Study. Aust N Z J Psychiatry. 2010;44(5):435–442.

Koetter U, et al. A randomized, double blind, placebo-controlled, prospective clinical study to demonstrate clinical efficacy of a fixed valerian hops extract combination (Ze 91019) in patients suffering from non-organic sleep disorder. Phytother Res. 2007;21(9):847–851.

Livingston WS, et al. Improved sleep in military personnel is associated with changes in the expression of inflammatory genes and improvement in depression symptoms. Front Psychiatry 2015 Apr 30;6:59.

Lovato N, et al. A meta-analysis and model of the relationship between sleep and depression in adolescents: Recommendations for future research and clinical practice. Sleep Med Rev. 2014;18(6):521–529.

Lucas M, et al. Inflammatory dietary pattern and risk of depression among women. Brain Behav Immun. 2014;36:46–53.

O'Neil A, et al. Relationship between diet and mental health in children and adolescents: A systematic review. Am J Pub Health. 2014;104(1):331–342.

Paunio T, et al. Poor sleep predicts symptoms of depression and disability retirement due to depression. J Affect Disord. 2014;172C:381–389.

Pina-Camacho L, et al. Maternal depression symptoms, unhealthy diet and child emotional–behavioural dysregulation. Psychol Med. 2015;45(9):1851-1860.

Poyares DR, et al. Can valerian improve the sleep of insomniacs after benzodiazepine withdrawal? Prog Neuro-Psychopharmacol Biol Psychiatry. 2002;26(3):539–545.

Sánchez-Villegas A, et al. Fast-food and commercial baked goods consumption and the risk of depression. Pub Health Nutr. 2012;15(3):424–432.

Slykerman RF, et al. Maternal stress during pregnancy is associated with moderate to severe depression in 11-year-old children. Acta Paediatrica 2015;104:68–74.

Solnick SJ, et al. Soft drinks, aggression and suicidal behavior in US high school students. Int J Injury Control Safety Promot. 2014;21(3):266–273.

Urrila AS, et al. Sleep in adolescent depression: Physiological perspectives. Acta Physiol (Oxf). 2015;213(4):758–757.

Zhai L, et al. Sleep duration and depression among adults: A meta-analysis of prospective studies. Depress Anxiety. 2015 Sep;32(9):664-670.

Zahedi, H. et al. Association between junk food consumption and mental health in a national sample of Iranian children and adolescents: The CASPIAN-IV study. Nutrition 2014;11-12:1391.

Chapter 9: H—Hormones and Herbs

Akhondzadeh S, et al. Comparison of *Crocus sativus L.* and imipramine in the treatment of mild to moderate depression: A pilot double-blind randomized trial. BMC Complement Altern Med. 2004;4:12.

Almeida OP, et al. Low free testosterone concentration as a potentially treatable cause of depressive symptoms in older men. Arch Gen Psychiatry. 2008;65(3):283–289.

Amanatkar HR, et al. Impact of exogenous testosterone on mood: A systematic review and meta-analysis of randomized placebo-controlled trials. Ann Clin Psychiatry; 2014;26(1):19–32.

Aronson R, et al. Triiodothyronine augmentation I the treatment of refractory depression. A meta-analysis. Arch Gen Psychiatry. 1996;53(9):842–848.

Berent D, et al. Thyroid hormones association with depression severity and clinical outcome in patients with major depressive disorder. Molecular Biol Rep. 2014;4:2419.

Bergman J, et al. Curcumin as an add-on to antidepressive treatment: A randomized double-blind, placebo-controlled, pilot study. Clin Neuropharmacol. 2013;36(3):73–77.

Bloch M, et al. Dehydroepiandrosterone treatment of midlife dysthymia. Biol Psychiatry. 1999;45(12):1533–1541.

Bonjiorno P. *Holistic Solutions for Anxiety and Depression in Therapy: Combining Natural Remedies with Conventional Care.* 2015. New York: W. W. Norton & Co.

Borrow AP, et al. Estrogenic mediation of serotonergic and neurotrophic systems: Implications for female mood disorders. Prog Neuropsychopharmacol Biol Psychiatry. 2014;54:13–25.

Bukhari IA, et al. Behavioral profile of *Hypericum perforatum* (St. John's Wort) extract. A comparison with standard antidepressants in animal models of depression. Eur Rev Med Pharmacol Sci. 2013;17(8):1082–1089.

Chan S. *Panax ginseng, rhodiola rosea,* and *chisandra chinensis.* Int J Food Sci Nutr. 2012;63(S1):75–81.

Deligianndis KM, et al. Complementary and alternative therapies for perinatal depression. Best Pract Res Clini Obstet Gynaecol. 2014;28:85–95.

Dwyer AV, et al. Herbal medicines, other than St. John's wort, in the treatment of depression: A systematic review. Alt Med Rev. 2011;16(1):40–49.

Giltay EJ, et al. Salivary testosterone: Associations with depression, anxiety disorders and antidepressant use in a large cohort study. J Psychosomatic Res. 2012;72(3):205–213.

Hurley L, et al. Antidepressant-like effects of curcumin in WKY rat model of depression is associated with an increase in hippocampal BDNF. Behav Brain Res. 2013;239:27–30.

Jiang H, et al. Antidepressant-like effects of curcumin in chronic mild stress of rats: Involvement of its anti-inflammatory action. Progress Neuropsychopharmacol Biol Psychiatry. 2013;47:33–39.

Kalra S, et al. Euthyroid depression: The role of thyroid hormone. Recent Pat Endocr Metab Immune Drug Discov. 2014;8(1):38–41.

Kasper S, et al. Efficacy of St. John's wort extract WS® 5570 in acute treatment of mild depression. Eur Arch Psychiatry Clini Neurosci. 2008;258(1):59–63.

Khera M, et al. The effect of testosterone supplementation on depression symptoms in hypogonadal men from the Testim Registry in the US (TRiUS). Aging Male. 2012;15(1):14–21.

Kulkami S, et al. Potentials of curcumin as an antidepressant. Sci World J. 2009;12:33.

Lifschytz T, et al. Basic mechanisms of augmentation of antidepressant effects with thyroid hormone. Curr Drug Targets. 2006;7(2):203–210.

Lopresti A, et al. Curcumin for the treatment of major depression: A randomized, double-blind, placebo-controlled study. J Affect Disord. 2014;167:368–375.

Lopresti A, et al. Multiple antidepressant potential modes of action of curcumin: A review of its anti-inflammatory, monoaminergic, antioxidant, immune-modulating and neuroprotective effects. J Psychopharmacol. 2012;26(12):1512–1524.

Lopresti AL, et al. Saffron *(Crocus sativus)* for depression: A systematic review of clinical studies and examination of underlying antidepressant mechanisms of action. Hum Psychopharmacol. 2014;29(6):517–527.

Mannuci C, et al. Serotonin involvement in *Rhodiola rosea* attenuation of nicotine withdrawal signs in rats. Phytomed. 2012;19:1117–1124.

Matusuzaka H, et al. Gender differences in serum testosterone and cortisol in patients with major depressive disorder compared with controls. Int J Psychiatry Med. 2013;46:203–221.

Mehta D, et al. Early predictive biomarkers for postpartum depression point to a role for estrogen receptor signaling. Psychol Med. 2014;44(11):2309–2322.

Melnyk JP, et al. Chemical and biological properties of the world's most expensive spice: Saffron. Food Res Int. 2010;8:1981.

Michael A, et al. Altered salivary dehydroepiandrosterone levels in major depression in adults. Biol Psychiatry. 2000;48(10):989–995.

Morita T, et al. Plasma dehydroepiandrosterone sulfate levels in patients with major depressive disorder correlate with remission during treatment with antidepressants. Hum Psychopharmacol. 2014;29:280–286.

Oulis P, et al. Testosterone and dehydroepiandrosterone sulfate in female anxious and non-anxious major depression. Int J Psychiatry Clin Pract. 2014;18(1):21–24.

Panahi Y, et al. Investigation of the efficacy of adjunctive therapy with bioavailability-boosted curcuminoids in major depressive disorder. Phytother Res. 2015;29(1):17–21.

Panossian A, et al. Mechanism of action of rhodiola, salidroside, tyrosol, and triandrin in isolated neuroglial cells: An interactive pathway analysis of the downstream effects using RNA microarray data. Phytomed. 2014;21:1325–1348.

Paturel A. Surprising saffron: There's more to these delicate strands than you'd expect. New research shows saffron can boost your mood. Health. 2006;20(1):161–162.

Pope HG Jr, et al. Testosterone gel supplementation for men with refractory depression: A randomized, placebo-controlled study. Am J Psychiatry. 2003;160(1):105–111.

Prange AJ Jr, et al. Enhancement of imipramine antidepressant activity by thyroid hormone. Am J Psychiatry. 1969;126(4):457–469.

Quereshi N, et al. Mood disorders and complementary and alternative medicine: A literature review. Neuropsychiatric Dis Treatment. 2013;9:639–658.

Rapkin AJ, et al. Pathophysiology of premenstrual syndrome and premenstrual dysphoric disorder. Menopause Int. 2012;18(2):52–59.

Sanmukhani J, et al. Efficacy and safety of curcumin in major depressive disorder: A randomized controlled trial. Phytother Res. 2014;4:579.

Schmidt PJ, et al. Dehydroepiandrosterone monotherapy in midlife-onset major and minor depression. Arch Gen Psychiatry. 2005;62(2):154–162.

Shahmansouri N, et al. A randomized, double-blind, clinical trial comparing the efficacy and safety of *Crocus sativus L.* with fluoxetine for improving mild to moderate depression in post percutaneous coronary intervention patients. J Affect Disord. 2014;155216–155222.

Solomon D, et al. Economic evaluation of St. John's wort *(Hypericum perforatum)* for the treatment of mild to moderate depression. J Affect Disord. 2013:148(2–3):228–234.

Solomon D, et al. Potential of St. John's Wort for the treatment of depression: The economic perspective. Austr N Z J Psychiatry. 2011;45(2):123–130.

Tizabi Y, et al. Relevance of the anti-inflammatory properties of curcumin in neurodegenerative diseases and depression. Molecules. 2014;19(12):20864–20879.

Zhu G, et al. Serum DHEAS levels are associated with the development of depression. Psychiatry Res. 2015; 229 (1-2): 447-453.

Chapter 10: E—Exclude

Arigo D, et al. Psychiatric comorbidities in women with celiac disease. Dis Chronic Illness. 2012;8(1):45–55.

Ciacci C, et al. Depressive symptoms in adult coeliac disease. Scand J Gastroenterol. 1998;33(3):247–250.

Elgun S, et al. Dipeptidyl peptidase IV and adenosine deaminase activity decrease in depression. Psychoneuroendocrinology. 1999;24(8):823–832.

Hallert C, et al. Psychic disturbances in adult coeliac disease. II. Psychological findings. Scand J Gastroenterol. 1982;17(1):21–24.

Hole K, et al. Attention deficit disorders: A study of peptide-containing urinary complexes. J Dev Behav Pediatr. 1988;9(4):205–212.

Hole K, et al. A peptide-containing fraction in the urine of schizophrenic patients which stimulates opiate receptors and inhibits dopamine uptake. Neuroscience. 1979;4(12):1883–1893.

Lillestøl K, et al. Anxiety and depression in patients with self-reported food hypersensitivity. Gen Hosp Psychiatry. 2010;32(1):42–48.

Ludvigsson JF, et al. Coeliac disease and risk of mood disorders: A general population-based cohort study. J Affect Disord. 2009;99(1–3):117–126.

Maes M, et al. Lower serum dipeptidyl peptidase IV activity in treatment-resistant major depression: Relationships with immune-inflammatory markers. Psychoneuroendocrinology. 1997;22(2):65–78.

Pedersen OS, et al. Serotonin uptake stimulating peptide found in plasma of normal individuals and in some autistic urines. J Pept Res. 1999;53(6):641–646.

Peters SL, et al. Randomised clinical trial: Gluten may cause depression in subjects with non-coeliac gluten sensitivity—an exploratory clinical study. Aliment Pharmacol Thera. 2014;39(10):104.

Reichelt KL, et al, Biologically active peptide-containing fractions in schizophrenia and childhood autism. Adv Biochem Psychopharmacol. 1981;28:627–643.

Saelid G, et al. Peptide-containing fractions in depression. Biol Psychiatry. 1985;20(3):245–256.

Smith DF, et al. Meta-analysis on anxiety and depression in adult celiac disease. Acta Psychiatrica Scandinavica. 2012;125(3):189–193.

Chapter 11: Z—Zinc and Other Minerals

Amani R, et al. Correlation between dietary zinc intakes and its serum levels with depression scales in young female students. Biol Trace Elem Res. 2010;137(2):150–158.

Barragán-Rodríguez L, et al. Efficacy and safety of oral magnesium supplementation in the treatment of depression in the elderly with type 2 diabetes: A randomized, equivalent study. Magnes Res. 2008;21(4):218–223.

Bauer M, et al. Lithium's emerging role in the treatment of refractory major depressive episodes: Augmentation of antidepressants. Neuropsychobiology. 2010;62(1):36–42.

Beard JL, et al. Maternal iron shortage anemia affects postpartum emotions and cognition. J Nutr. 2005;135(2):267–272.

Cipriani A, et al. Lithium in the prevention of suicidal behavior and all-cause mortality in patients with mood disorders: a systematic review of randomized studies. Am J Psychiatry. 2005;162(10):1805–1819.

Colangelo LA, et al. Selenium exposure and depressive symptoms: The coronary artery risk development in young adults trace element study. Neurotoxicol. 2014;41:167–174.

Conner TS, et al. Optimal serum selenium concentrations are associated with lower depressive symptoms and negative mood among young adults. J Nutr. 2014;145(1):59–65.

Crayton JW, et al. Elevated serum copper levels in women with a history of post-partum depression. J Trace Elem Med Biol. 2007;21(1):17–21.

Davidson JR, et al. Effectiveness of chromium in atypical depression: A placebo-controlled study. Biol Psychiatry. 2003;53(3):261–264.

Dé Montigny C, et al. Lithium induces rapid relief of depression in tricyclic antidepressant drug non-responders. Br J Psychiatry. 1981;138:252–256.

Diniz BS, et al. Lithium and neuroprotection: Translational evidence and implications for the treatment of neuropsychiatric disorders. Neuropsychiatric Dis Treat. 2013;9:493–500.

Dubey VK, et al. Possible involvement of corticosterone and serotonin in antidepressant and anti-anxiety effects of chromium picolinate in chronic unpredictable mild stress-induced depression and anxiety in rats. J Trace Elem Med Biol. 2015;29:222–226.

Eby GA 3rd, et al. Magnesium for treatment-resistant depression: A review and hypothesis. Med Hypotheses. 2010;74(4):649–660.

Grønli O, et al. Zinc deficiency is common in several psychiatric disorders. PLoS One. 2013;8(12):e82793.

Jacka FN, et al. Association between magnesium intake and depression and anxiety in community-dwelling adults: The Hordaland health study. Austr N Z J Psychiatry. 2009;43(1):45–52.

Johnson LA, et al. The impact of GPX1 on the association of groundwater selenium and depression: A project FRONTIER study. BMC Psychiatry. 2013;13:7.

Kim J, et al. Iron and mechanisms of emotional behavior. J Nutritional Biochem. 2014;25:1101–1107.

Kukreja S, et al. Polypharmacy in psychiatry: A review. Mens Sana Monogr. 2013;11(1):82–99.

Lai J, et al. The efficacy of zinc supplementation in depression: Systematic review of randomized controlled studies. J Affect Disord. 2012;136(1–2):e31–39.

McLeod MN, et al. Chromium treatment of depression. Int J Neuropsychopharmacol. 2000;3(4):311–314.

Mehrpouya S, et al. Iron administration prevents BDNF decrease and depressive-like behavior following chronic stress. Brain Res. 2015;1596:79–87.

Nowak G, et al. Effect of zinc supplementation on antidepressant therapy in unipolar depression: A preliminary placebo-controlled study. Pol J Pharmacol. 2003;55(6):1143–1147.

Nowak G, et al. Zinc and depression: An update. Pharmacol Rep. 2005;57(6):713–718.

Nunes MA, et al. Microdose lithium treatment stabilized cognitive impairment in patients with Alzheimer's disease. Curr Alzheimer's Res. 2013;10:104–107.

Pasco JA, et al. Dietary selenium and major depression: A nested case-control study. Complement Ther Med. 2012;20(3):119–123.

Peuranpää P, et al. Effects of anemia and iron shortage on quality of life in women with heavy menstrual bleeding. Acta Obstet Gynecol Scand. 2014;93:654–660.

Prange AJ Jr, et al. Enhancement of imipramine antidepressant activity by thyroid hormone. Am J Psychiatry. 1969;126(4):457–469.

Ranjbar E, et al. Effects of zinc supplementation on efficacy of antidepressant therapy, inflammatory cytokines, and brain-derived neurotrophic factor in patients with major depression. Nutr Neurosci. 2014;17(2):65–71.

Sara M, et al. Iron administration prevents BDNF decrease and depressive-like behavior following chronic stress. Brain Res. 2015;1596:79–87.

Sawada T, et al. Effect of zinc supplementation on mood states in young women: A pilot study. Eur J Clin Nutr. 2010;64(3):331–333.

Siwek M, et al. Zinc supplementation augments efficacy of imipramine in treatment-resistant patients: A double-blind, placebo-controlled study. J Affect Disord. 2009;118(1–3):187–195.

Slavich GM, et al. From stress to inflammation and major depressive disorder: A social signal transduction theory of depression. Psychol Bull. 2014;140(3):774–815.

Stefanson AL, et al. Dietary regulation of Keap1/Nrf2/ARE pathway: Focus on plant-derived compounds and trace minerals. Nutrients. 2014;6:3777–3801.

Stewart R, et al. Relationship between depressive symptoms, anemia, and iron status in older residents from a national survey population. Psychosom Med. 2012;74(2):208–213.

Swardfager W, et al. Potential roles of zinc in the pathophysiology and treatment of major depressive disorder. Neurosci Biobehav Rev. 2013;37(5):911–929.

Swardfager W, et al. Zinc in depression: A meta-analysis. Biol Psychiatry. 2013;74(12):872–878.

Szewczyk B, et al. Antidepressant activity of zinc and magnesium in view of the current hypotheses of antidepressant action. Pharmacol Rep. 2008;60(5):588–599.

Tarleton EK, et al. Magnesium intake and depression in adults. J Am Board Fam Med. 2015;28(2):249–256.

Vahdat Shariatpanaahi M, et al. The relationship between depression and serum ferritin level. Eur J Clin Nutr. 2007;61(4):532–535.

Vashum KP, et al. Dietary zinc is associated with a lower incidence of depression: Findings from two Australian cohorts. J Affect Disord. 2014;166:249–257.

Chapter 12: E—Essential Fatty Acids and Cholesterol

Beydoun MA, et al. Omega-3 fatty acid intakes are inversely related to elevated depressive symptoms among United States Women. J Nutr. 2013;143(11):1743–1752.

Boettcher E, et al. Dietary proteins and functional gastrointestinal disorders. Am J Gastroenterol. 2013;108(5):728–736.

Borgherini G, et al. Serum cholesterol and psychological distress in hospitalized depressed patients. Acta Psychiatr Scand. 2002;105(2):149–152.

Brown D, et al. The effect of moderate glycemic energy bar consumption on blood glucose and mood in dancers. Med Probl Perform Art. 2014;29(1):27–31.

Chiu CC, et al. Associations between n-3 PUFA concentrations and cognitive function after recovery from late-life depression. Am J Clin Nutr. 2012;95(2):420–427.

Du J, et al. The role of nutrients in protecting mitochondrial function and neurotransmitter signaling: Implications for the treatment of depression, PTSD and suicidal behaviors. Crit Rev Food Sci Nutr. 2014 Nov. 3:0.

Gagnon C, et al. Low serum 25-hydroxyvitamin D is linked to increased risk of the development of the metabolic syndrome at five years: Results from a national, population-based prospective study (The Australian Diabetes, Obesity and Lifestyle Study; AusDiab). J Clin Endocrinol Metab. 2012;97(6):1953–1961.

Gibbons RD, et al. Synthesis of 6-week patient-level outcomes from double-blind placebo-controlled randomized studies of fluoxetine and venlafaxine. Arch Gen Psychiatry. 2012;69(6):572–579.

Giles GR, et al. Omega-3 fatty acids influence mood in healthy and depressed individuals. Nutr Rev. 2013;71(11):727–741.

Golomb BA, et al. Low cholesterol and violent crime. J Psychiatr Res. 2000;34(4–5):301–309.

Grønli O, et al. Zinc shortage is common in several psychiatric disorders. PLoS ONE. 2013;8(12):e92793.

Grosso G, et al. Role of omega-3 fatty acids in the treatment of depressive orders: A comprehensive meta-analysis of randomized clinical studies. PLoS ONE. 2014;9(5):e96905.

Gude MF, et al. Fatal outcome after overdosage with antidepressants. Ugeskr Laeger. 2014;176(7A).

Hamzat H, et al. Inappropriate prescribing of proton pump inhibitors in older patients. Drugs Aging. 2012;29(8):681–690.

Hibbeln JR, et al. The potential for military diets to reduce depression, suicide, and impulsive aggression: A review of current evidence for omega-3 and omega-6 fatty acids. Military Med. 2014;11:117.

Hibbeln JR. Fish consumption and major depression. Lancet. 1998;351(9110):1213.

Jazayeri S, et al. Comparison of therapeutic effects of omega-3 fatty acid eicosapentaenoic acid and fluoxetine, separately and in combination, in major depressive disorder. Austr N Z J Psychiatry. 2008;42(3):192–198.

Keenan K, et al. Association between fatty acid supplementation and prenatal stress in African Americans. Obstet Gynecol. 2014;124(6):1080–1087.

Lalovic A, et al. Cholesterol content in brains of suicide completers. Int J Neuropsychopharmacol. 2007;10(2):159–166.

Lehto SM, et al. Low serum HDL-cholesterol levels are linked to long symptoms duration in patients with major depressive disorder. Psychiatry Clin Neurosci. 2010;64(3):279–283.

Lespérance F, et al. The efficacy of omega-3 supplementation for major depression: A randomized controlled study. J Clin Psychiatry. 2011;72(8):1054–1062. Epub 2010 Jun 15.

Logan AC. Omega-3 fatty acids and major depression: A primer for the mental health professional. Lipids Health Dis. 2004;3:25.

Lotrich FE, et al. Elevated ratio of arachidonic acid to long-chain omega-3 fatty acids predicts depression development following interferon-alpha treatment: Relationship with interleukin-6. Brain Behav Immun. 2013;31:48–53.

Mamalakis G, et al. Depression in serum adiponectin and adipose omega-3 and omega-6 fatty acids in teens. Pharmacol Biochem Behav. 2006;85(2):474–479.

Markus MW, et al. Low omega-3 index in pregnancy is a possible biological risk factor for postpartum depression. J Am Coll Cardiol. 2013;8(7):e67617.

Martin SS, et al. 2013 ACC/AHA Cholesterol Treatment Guideline. J Am Coll Cardiol. 2014;63(24):2674–2678.

Michikawa T, et al. Higher serum dehydroepiandrosterone sulfate levels are protectively linked to depressive symptoms in men, but not in women: A community-based cohort study of older Japanese. Am J Geriatr Psychiatry. 2013;21:11.

Mischoulon D, et al. A double-blind, randomized controlled clinical study comparing eicosapentaenoic acid versus docosahexaenoic acid for depression. J Clin Psychiatry. 2015;76(1):54–61.

Moran LJ, et al. Vitamin D is independently linked to depression in overweight women with and without PCOS. Gynecol Endocrinol. 2015;31(3):179–182.

Mosienko V, et al. Life without brain serotonin: Reevaluation of serotonin function with mice deficient in brain serotonin synthesis. Behav Brain Res. 2015;277:78–88.

Muñoz-Aguirre P, et al. The effect of vitamin D supplementation on serum lipids in postmenopausal women with diabetes: A randomized controlled study. Clin. Nutri. 2015; 34(5):799–804.

Naqvi AZ, et al. Docosahexaenoic acid and periodontitis in adults: A randomized controlled study. J Dent Res. 2014;93(8):767–773.

Nemets H, et al. Omega-3 treatment of childhood depression: A controlled, double-blind pilot study. Am J Psychiatry. 2006;163(6):1098–1100.

Pålsson E, et al. Markers of glutamate signaling in cerebrospinal fluid and serum from patients with bipolar disorder and healthy controls. Eur Neuropsychopharmacol. 2015;25:133–140.

Papadopoulou A, et al. Plasma total cholesterol in psychiatric patients after a suicide attempt and in follow-up. J Affect Disord. 2013;148:440–443.

Park H. An overview of eosinophilic esophagitis. Gut Liver. 2014;8(6):590–597.

Perez-Rodriguez MM, et al. Low serum cholesterol may be linked to suicide history attempt. J Clin Psychiatry. 2008;69(12):1920–1927.

Sallis H, et al. Perinatal depression and omega-3 fatty acids: A Mendelian randomization study. J Affect Disord. 2014;166:124–131.

Sarris J, et al. S-adenosyl methionine (SAMe) versus escitalopram and placebo in major depression RCT: Efficacy and effects of histamine and carnitine as moderators of response. J Affect Disord. 2014;164:76–81.

Schlögelhofer M, et al. Polyunsaturated fatty acids in emerging psychosis: A safer alternative? Early Interv Psychiatry. 2014;8(3):199–208.

Shabbir F, et al. Effect of diet on serotonergic neurotransmission in depression. Neurochem Int. 2013;62:324–329.

Stan AD, et al. Glutamate and GABA contributions to medical prefrontal cortical activity to emotion: implications for mood disorders. Psychiatry Res. 2014;223:253–260.

Stoll AL, et al. Omega-3 fatty acids in bipolar disorder: A preliminary double-blind, placebo-controlled study. Arch Gen Psychiatry. 1999;56(5):407–412.

Su KP, et al. Omega-3 fatty acids in major depressive disorder: A preliminary double-blind, placebo-controlled study. Eur Neuropsychopharmacol. 2003;13(4):267–271.

Su KP, et al. Omega-3 fatty acids in the prevention of interferon alpha-induced depression: Results from a randomized, controlled study. Biol Psychiatry. 2014;76:559–566.

Sublette ME, et al. Omega-3 polyunsaturated essential fatty acid status as a predictor of future suicide risk. Am J Psychiatry. 2006;163(6):1100–1102.

Teofilo MMA, et al. HDL-cholesterol concentrations are inversely linked to Edinburgh Postnatal Depression Scale scores during pregnancy: Results from a Brazilian cohort study. J Psychiatric Res. 2014;58:181–188.

Tsai AC, et al. Suicide mortality in relation to dietary intake of n-3 and n-6 polyunsaturated fatty acids and fish: Equivocal findings from 3 large cohort studies. Am J Epidemiol. 2014;179(12):1458–1466.

Vaz JS, et al. Omega-6 fatty acids and greater likelihood of suicide risk and major depression in early pregnancy. J Affect Disord. 2014;152–154:76–82.

Vilibić M, et al. Association between total serum cholesterol and depression, agitation, and suicidal ideations in war veterans with posttraumatic stress disorder: A cross-sectional study. Croat Med J. 2014;55:520–529.

Wissmann P, et al. Immune activation in patients with Alzheimer's disease is linked to high serum phenylalanine concentrations. J Neurol Sci. 2013;329:29–33.

Chapter 13: E—Exercise and Energy

Babyak M, et al. Exercise treatment for major depression: Maintenance of therapeutic benefit at 10 months. Psychomatic Med. 2000;62(5):633–638.

Blake H. Physical activity and exercise in the treatment of depression. Front Psychiatry. 2012;3:106.

Blumenthal JA, et al. Effects of exercise training on depressive symptoms in patients with chronic heart failure. JAMA. 2012;308(5):465–474.

Blumenthal JA, et al. Is exercise a viable treatment for depression? ACSMs Health Fit J. 2012;16(4):14–21.

Brown RA, et al. A preliminary, randomized study of aerobic exercise for alcohol dependence. J Substance Abuse Treatment. 2014;47:1–9.

Brown H, et al. Physical activity interventions and depression in children and teens: A systematic review and meta-analysis. Sports Med. 2014;43(3):195–206.

Callister R, et al. Healthy body healthy mind: Trialling an exercise intervention for reducing depression in youth with major depressive disorder. Int J Exercise Science. 2013;10(1):6.

Chaddock L, et al. A functional MRI investigation of the association between childhood aerobic fitness and neurocognitive control. Biol Psychol. 2012;89:260–268.

Chaddock-Heyman L, et al. Aerobic fitness is linked to greater white matter integrity in children. Frontiers Human Neurosci. 2014;8(584):1–7.

Chadler M, et al. Facilitated physical activity as a treatment for depressed adults: Randomised controlled study. BMJ. 2012;344:e2758.

Cooney GM, et al. Exercise for depression. Cochrane Database Syst Rev. 2013;12;9:CD004366.

Cooney G, et al. Exercise for depression. JAMA. 2014:311(23):2432–2433.

Goodwin RD. Association between physical activity and mental disorders among adults in the United States. Prev Med. 2003;36(6):698–703.

Danielsson L, et al. Exercise or basic body awareness therapy as add-on treatment for major depression: A controlled study. J Affect Disord. 2014;168:98–106.

Dopp RR, et al. Exercise for adolescents with depressive disorders: A feasibility study. Depression Res Treatment. 2012, article ID 257472:109.

Dunn AL, et al. Exercise treatment for depression: Efficacy and dose response. Am J Prev Med. 2005;28(1):1–8.

Erlij D, et al. Dopamine D4 receptor stimulation in GABAergic projections of the globus pallidus to the reticular thalamic nucleus and the substantia nigra reticulate of the rat decreases locomotor activity. Neuropharmacology. 2012;62:1111–1118.

Galper DI, et al. Inverse association between physical inactivity and mental health in men and women. Med Sci Sports Exerc. 2006;38(1):173–178.

Gardner A, et al. Mitochondrial energy depletion in depression with somatization. Psychother Psychom. 2008;77(2):127–129.

Gow AJ, et al. Neuroprotective lifestyles and the aging brain. Neurology. 2012;79:1802–1808.

He SB, et al. Exercise intervention may prevent depression. Int J Sports Med 2012;33:525–530.

Heyman E, et al. Intense exercise increases circulating endocannabinoid and BDNF levels in humans: Possible implications for reward and depression. Psychoneuroendocrinology. 2012;37:844–851.

Hillman CH, et al. Effects of the FITKids randomized controlled study on executive control and brain function. Pediatrics;134(4):e1063–1073.

Jones D, et al. The effect of relaxation interventions on cortisol levels in HIV-seropositive women. J Int Assoc Providers AIDS Care. 2014;13(4):318–323.

Josefsson T, et al. Physical exercise intervention in depressive disorders: Meta-analysis and systematic review. Scand J Med Sci Sports. 2014;24:259–272.

Kamimura A, et al. The relationship between body esteem, exercise motivations, depression, and social support among female free clinic patients. Women's Health Issues. 2014;24(6):656–662.

King WC, et al. Associations between physical activity and mental health among bariatric surgical candidates. J Psychosom Res. 2013;74:161–169.

Kuratsune H, et al. Acylcarnitine shortage in chronic fatigue syndrome. Clin Infect Dis. 1994;18(Suppl 1):S62–S67.

Leckie RL, et al. BDNJ mediates improvements in executive function following a 1-year exercise intervention. Frontiers Human Neurosci. 2014;8, Article 985:1–12.

Lieberwirth C, et al. The social environment and neurogenesis in the adult mammalian brain. Frontiers Human Neurosci. 2012;6, Article 118:1–19.

Liu R, et al. Cardiorespiratory fitness as a predictor of dementia mortality in men and women. Med Sci Sports Exerc. 2012;44(2):253–259.

Malaguarnera M, et al. L-carnitine treatment reduces severity of physical and mental fatigue and increases cognitive functions in centenarians: a randomized and controlled clinical study. Am J Clin Nutr. 2007;86(6):1738–1744.

Martin A, et al. Does active commuting improve psychological wellbeing? Longitudinal evidence from eighteen waves of the British Household Panel Survey. Prev Med. 2014;69:296–303.

McHugh JE, et al. Exercise and social support are linked to psychological distress outcomes in a population of community-dwelling older adults. J Health Psychol. 2011;17(6):833–844.

Michalak J, et al. How we walk affects what we remember: Gait modifications through biofeedback change negative affective memory bias. J Behav Ther Exp Psychiatry. 2015;46:121–125.

Mizuno K, et al. Antifatigue effects of coenzyme Q10 during physical fatigue. Nutrition. 2008;24(4):293–299. Erratum in: Nutrition 2008;24(6):616.

Mura G, et al. Efficacy of exercise on depression: A systematic review. Int J Psychosoc Rehab. 2014;18(2):23–36.

Oertel-Knöchel V, et al. Effects of aerobic exercise on cognitive performance and individual psychopathology in depressive and schizophrenia patients. Eur Arch Psychiatry Clin Neurosci. 2014;264:589–604.

Perales M, et al. Exercise during pregnancy attenuates prenatal depression: A randomized controlled study. Eval Health Professions. 2015;38(1):59–72.

Pinto Pereira SM, et al. Depressive symptoms and physical activity during 3 decades in adult life: Bidirectional associations in a prospective cohort study. JAMA Psychiatry 2014;71(12):1373-1380.

Pontifex MB, et al. Exercise improves behavioral, neurocognitive, and scholastic performance in children with attention-deficit/hyperactivity disorder. J Pediatr. 2013;162:543–541.

Prakash RS, et al. Physical activity and cognitive vitality. Annu Rev Psychol. 2015;66:769–797.

Rethorst CD, et al. Evidence-based recommendations for the prescription of exercise for major depressive disorder. J Psychiatr Pract. 2013;19(3):204–212.

Rezin GT, et al. Mitochondrial dysfunction and psychiatric disorders. Neurochem Res. 2009;34(6):1021–1029.

Ruggero CJ, et al. Does cardiorespiratory fitness protect against depression during middle school? J Adolesc Health. 2015;57(1):60–65.

Schuch FB, et al. Exercise and severe major depression: Effect on symptom severity and quality of life at discharge in an inpatient cohort. J Psychiatr Res. 2015;61:25–32.

Schutte NM, et al. Genetic modification of the effects of exercise behavior on mental health. Frontiers Psychiatry. 2014;5, Article 64:1–2.

Sidhu KS, et al. Exercise prescription. Curr Psychiatry. 2009; 8(6):39–51.

Smith AL, et al. Pilot physical activity intervention reduces severity of ADHD symptoms in young children. J Attention Disord. 2013;17(1):70–82.

Stine-Morrow EAL, et al. Psychol Aging. 2014;29(4):891–906.

Teitelbaum JE, et al. The use of D-ribose in chronic fatigue syndrome and fibromyalgia: A pilot study. J Altern Complement Med. 2006; 12(9):857–862.

Terracciano A, et al. Personality, metabolic rate and aerobic capacity. PLoS ONE. 8(1):e54746.

Vaccarino AL, et al. Prevalence and association of somatic symptoms in patients with major depressive disorder. J Affect Disord. 2008;110(3):270–276.

Verdelho A, et al; LADIS Study. J Neurol Neurosurg Psychiatry. 2013;84(11):1250–1254.

Voss MW, et al. The influence of aerobic fitness on cerebral white matter integrity and cognitive function in older adults: Results of a one-year exercise intervention. Human Brain Mapping. 2013;34:2972–2985.

Wang C. Tai Chi improves pain and functional status in adults with rheumatoid arthritis: Results of a pilot single-blinded randomized controlled study. Med Sport Sci. 2008;52:218–229.

Woolery A, et al. A yoga intervention for young adults with elevated symptoms of depression. Altern Ther Health Med. 2004;10(2):60–63.

Yuki A, et al. Relationship between physical activity and brain atrophy progression. Med Sci Sports Exerc. 2012;44(12):2362–2368.

Chapter 14: B—B Vitamins and Other Vitamins

Ataie-Jafari A, et al. The association of vitamin D deficiency with psychiatric distress and violence behaviors in Iranian adolescents: The CASPIAN-III study. J Diabetes Metab Disord. 2015; 14:62.

Bell KM, et al. S-adenosylmethionine treatment of depression: A controlled clinical study. Am J Psychiatry. 1998;145(9):1110–1114.

Black LJ, et al. Low vitamin D levels are linked to symptoms of depression in young adult males. Austr New Zealand J Psychiatry. 2014;48(5):464–471.

Coppen A, et al. Enhancement of the antidepressant action of fluoxetine by folic acid: A randomised, placebo controlled study. J Affect Disord. 2000;60(2):121–130.

Fava M, et al. Folate in depression: Efficacy, safety differences in formulations, and clinical issues. J Clin Psychiatry. 2009;70(Suppl 5):12–17.

Fava M, et al. Folate, vitamin B12, and homocysteine in major depressive disorder. Am J Psychiatry. 1997;154(3):426–428.

Ford AH, et al. Homocysteine, depression and cognitive function in adults. J Affect Dis. 2013;151:646–651.

Grudet C, et al. Suicidal patients are deficient in vitamin D, linked to a pro-inflammatory status in the blood. Psychoneuroendocrinology. 2014;50:210–219.

Han B, et al. Low serum levels of vitamin D are linked to post-stroke depression. Eur J Neurol. 2015 Sep;22(9):1269-1274.

Harris HW, et al. Vitamin D shortage and psychiatric illness. Curr Psychiatry. 2015;12(4):19–27.

Hörberg G, et al. Depressed teens in a case-series were low in vitamin D and depression was ameliorated by vitamin D supplementation. Acta Paediatrica. 2012;101:779–783.

Issac TG, et al. Vitamin B12 shortage: An important reversible co-morbidity in neuropsychiatric manifestations. Indian J Psychol Med. 2015;37(1):26–29.

Kerr DCR, et al. Associations between vitamin D levels and depressive symptoms in healthy young adult women. Psychiatry Res. 2015;227(1):46–51.

Milaneschi Y, et al. Serum 25-hydroxyvitamin D and depressive symptoms in older women and men. J Clin Endrocrinol Metab. 2010;95(7):3225–3233.

Milaneschi Y, et al. The association between low vitamin D and depressive disorders. Molecular Psychiatry. 2014;19:444–451.

Miyake Y, et al. Dietary vitamin D intake and prevalence of depressive symptoms during pregnancy in Japan. Nutrition. 2015;31:160–165.

Morris MC, et al. Dietary folate and vitamin B_{12} intake and cognitive decline among community-dwelling older persons. Arch Neurol. 2005;62(4):641–645.

Mukai T, et al. A meta-analysis of inositol for depression and anxiety disorders. Hum Psychopharmacol Clin Exp. 2014;29:55–63.

Nabi H, et al. Association of serum homocysteine with major depressive disorder: Results from a large population-based study. Psychoneuroendocrinology. 2013;38:2309–2318.

Papakostas GI, et al. Effect of adjunctive L-methylfolate 15 mg among inadequate responders to SSRIs in depressed patients who were stratified by biomarker levels and genotype: Results from a randomized clinical trial. J Clin Psychiatry. 75(8):855–863.

Papakostas GI, et al. Methylfolate as adjunctive therapy for SSRI-resistant major depression: Results of two randomized, double-blind, parallel-sequential studies. Am J Psychiatry. 2012:169:1267–1274.

Papakostas GI, et al. S-adenosyl methionine (SAMe) augmentation of serotonin reuptake inhibitors for antidepressant nonresponders with major depressive disorder: A double-blind, randomized clinical study. Am J Psychiatry. 2010; 167(8):942–948.

Polak MA, et al. Serum 25-hydroxyvitamin D concentrations and depressive symptoms among young adult men and women. Nutrients 2014;6:4720–4730.

Sarris J, et al. S-adenosyl methionine (SAMe) versus escitalopram and placebo in major depression randomized controlled trial: Efficacy and effects of histamine and carnitine as moderators of response. J Affect Disord. 2014;164:76–81.

Shelton RC, et al. Assessing effects of L-methylfolate in depression management: Results of a real-world patient experience study. Prim Care Companion CNS Disord. 2013;15(4):PCC.13m01520.

Shipowick CD, et al. Vitamin D and depression symptoms in women during the winter: A pilot study. Appl Nurs Res. 2009;22(3):221–225.

Snellman G, et al. Seasonal genetic influence on serum 25-hydroxyvitamin D levels: A twin study. PLoS One. 2009;4(11):e7747.

Spedding S. Vitamin D and depression: A systematic review and meta-analysis comparing studies with and without biological flaws. Nutrients 2014;6:1501–1518.

Stewart JW, et al. Low B6 levels in depressed outpatients. Biol Psychiatry. 1984;19(4):613–616.

Stewart R, et al. Relationship between vitamin D levels and depressive symptoms in older residents from a national survey population. Psychosom Med. 2010;72(7):608–612.

Tiemeier H, et al. Vitamin B12 folate, and homocysteine in depression: The Rotterdam Study. Am J Psychiatry. 2002;159(12):2099–2101.

Tolppanen AM, et al. The association of serum 25-hydroxyvitamin D3 and D2 with depressive symptoms of childhood: A prospective cohort study. J Child Psychol Psychiatry. 2012;53(7):757–766.

Umhau JC, et al. Low vitamin D status and suicide: A case-control study of active duty military service members. PLoS ONE. 2013;8(1):e51543.

Yue W, et al. Association of serum 25-hydroxyvitamin D with symptoms of depression after 6 months in stroke patients. Neurochem. 2014;39:2218–2224.

Zhang G, et al. Thiamine nutritional status and depressive symptoms are inversely associated among older Chinese students. J Nutr. 2013;143(1):53–58.

Chapter 15: R—Restore

Ackerman J. The ultimate social network. 2012. Available at: http://www.nature.com/scientificamerican/journal/v306/n6/full/scientificamerican0612-36.html. Accessed July 14, 2015.

Arnold C. Gut feelings: The future of psychiatry may be inside your stomach. The Verge. Aug. 21, 2013. Available at: http://www.theverge.com/2013/8/21/4595712/gut-feelings-the-future-of-psychiatry-may-be-inside-your-stomach. Accessed July 14, 2015.

Brown K, et al. Diet-induced dysbiosis of the intestinal microbiota and the effects on immunity and disease. Nutrients. 2012;4:1095–1119.

Cryan JF, et al. Mind-altering microorganisms: The impact of the gut microbiota on brain and behavior. Nat Rev Neurosci. 2012;13(10):701–712.

Cryan JF, et al. The microbiome-gut-brain axis: From bowel to behavior. Neurogastroenterol Motil. 2011;23:187–192.

Dash S, et al. The gut microbiome and diet in psychiatry: Focus on depression. Curr Opin Psychiatr. 2015;28(1):1–6.

Desbonnet L, et al. The probiotic *Bifidobacteria infantis:* An assessment of potential antidepressant properties in the rat. J Psychiatr Res. 2008;43(2):164–174.

Donaldson-James S. Anxiety in your head could come from your gut. September 12, 2013. Available at: http://abcnews.go.com/health/anxiety-head-gut/story?id=20229136. Accessed July 14, 2015.

Foster JA, et al. Gut-brain axis: How the microbiome influences anxiety and depression. Trends Neurosci. 2013;36(5):305–312.

Gangwisch JE, et al. High glycemic index diet as a risk factor for depression: analyses from the Women's Health Initiative. Am J Clin Nutr 2015; 102(2):453-463.

Ginty AT, et al. Short-term supplementation of acute long-chain omega-3 polyunsaturated fatty acids may alter depression status and decrease symptomology among young adults with depression: A preliminary randomized and placebo controlled study. Psychiatry Res. 2015; 299(1-2):485-489.

Moloney RD, et al. The microbiome: stress, health and disease. Mamm Genome. 2014;25(1–2):49–74.

Naseribafrouei A, et al. Correlation between the human fecal microbiota and depression. Neurogastroenterol Motil. 2014;26(8):1155–1162.

Neufield K-AM, et al. Effects of intestinal microbiota on anxiety-like behavior. Commun Integr Biol. 4(4):492–494.

Quigley EMM. Gut microbiota and the role of probiotics in therapy. Curr Opin Pharmacol. 2011;11(6):593–603.

Selhub EM, et al. Fermented foods, microbiota, and mental health: Ancient practice meets nutritional psychiatry. J Physiol Anthropol. 2014;33:2.

Steenbergen L, et al. A randomized controlled study to test the effect of multispecies probiotics on cognitive reactivity to sad mood. Brain Behav Immun. 2015 Apr 7. [Epub ahead of print]

Tillisch K, et al. Consumption of fermented milk product with probiotic modulates brain activity. Gastroenterology. 2013;114(7):1394–1401.

Vitetta L, et al. The gastrointestinal tract microbiome, probiotics, and mood. Inflammopharmacology. 2014;22(6):333–339.

Wu GD, et al. Linking long-term dietary patterns with gut microbial enterotypes. Science. 2011;334(6052):105–108.

Yano JM, et al. Indigenous bacteria from the gut microbiota regulate host serotonin biosynthesis. Cell. 2015;161(2):264–276.

Yasgur BS. Psychiatry and the gut: The role of microbiota in mood disorders. Psychiatry Advisor. April 24, 2015. Available at: http://www.psychiatryadvisor.com/mood-disorders/psychiatry-and-the-gut-the-role-of-microbiota-in-mood-disorders/article/410957/. Accessed July 14, 2015.

Chapter 16: A—Amino Acids and Proteins

Czysz AH, et al. Lateral diffusion of G_s in the plasma membrane is decreased after chronic but not acute antidepressant treatment: Role of lipid raft and non-raft membrane microdomains. Neuropsychpharmacol. 2015;40:766–773.

Jin G, et al. Changes in plasma and tissue amino acid levels in an animal model of complex fatigue. Nutrition. 2009;25(5):597–607.

Layman DK. Dietary guidelines should reflect new understandings about adult protein needs. Nutr Metab (Lond.). 2009;6:12.

Levitan RD, et al. Preliminary randomized double-blind placebo-controlled study of tryptophan combined with fluoxetine to treat major depressive disorder: Antidepressant and hypnotic effect. J Psychiatry Neurosci. 2000; 25(4):337–346.

Liew S-C, et al. Methylenetetrahydrofolate reductase (MTHFR) C677T polymorphism: Epidemiology, metabolism and the associated diseases. Eur J Med Genet. 2015;58:1–10.

Maes M, et al. Total serum protein and serum protein fractions in depression: Relationships to depressive symptoms and glucocorticoid activity. J Affect Disord. 1995;34(1):61–69.

Mauri MC, et al. Plasma and platelet amino acid concentrations in patients affected by major depression and under fluvoxamine treatment. Neuropsychobiology. 1998;37(3):124–129.

Mitani H, et al. Correlation between plasma levels of glutamate, alanine and serine with severity of depression. Prog Neuro-Psychopharmacol Biol Psychiatry. 2006;30(6):1155–1158.

Qureshi NA, et al. Mood disorders and complementary and alternative medicine: A literature review. Neuropsychiatr Dis Treatment. 2013;639–658.

Shears SB, et al. Defining signal transduction by inositol phosphates. Subcell Biochem. 2012;59:389–412.
Smith KA, et al. Relapse of depression after rapid depletion of tryptophan. Lancet. 1997;349(9056):915–919.
van Enkhuizen J, et al. The catecholaminergic-cholinergic balance hypothesis of bipolar disorder revisited. Eur J Pharmacol. 2014;753:114–126.
van Ijzendoorn MH, et al. Genetic differential susceptibility on study: Meta-analytic support from randomized controlled experiments. Dev Psychopathol. 2015;27:151–162.
Young SN. Appropriate amino acid mixtures for tryptophan depletion and tyrosine/phenylalanine depletion and the safety of long-term amino acid depletion in humans. Psychopharmacol. 2013;229:377–378.

Chapter 17: Laboratory Tests Your Doctor May Order

Almeida OP, et al. Homocysteine and depression later in life. Arch Gen Psychiatry. 2005;65(11):1286–1294.
Colangelo LA, et al. Selenium exposure and depressive symptoms: The Coronary Artery Risk Development in Young Adults Trace Element Study. Neurotoxicology. 2014;41:167–174.
Conner TS, et al. Optimal serum selenium concentrations are linked to lower depressive symptoms and negative mood among young adults. J Nutr. 2015;145(1):59–65.
Demartini B, et al. Depressive symptoms and major depressive disorder in patients affected by subclinical hypothyroidism. J Nerv Ment Dis. 2014;202:603–607.
Lord RS, et al. (Eds.). *Laboratory Evaluations for Integrative and Functional Medicine.* 2008. Duluth, GA: Metametrix Institute.
Lukaczer D, et al. "Assessment and Therapeutic Strategy—A Place to Start." *Textbook of Functional Medicine.* Ed. D.S. Jones, pp. 706–708. 2005. Gig Harbor, WA: Institute for Functional Medicine.

Part III: NURTURING THE MIND

Chapter 18: Psychotherapy for Depression

Amen DG. ANT Therapy: How to develop your own internal anteater to eradicate automatic negative thoughts. Available at: http://ahha.org/articles.asp?Id=100. Accessed August 23, 2015.
Ananth S. Developing healing beliefs. Explore (NY). 2009;5(6):354–355.
Andersson G, et al. A 3.5-year follow-up of Internet-delivered cognitive behavioral therapy for major depression. J Ment Health. 2013;22:155–164.
Andrews PW, et al. The bright side of being blue: Depression as an adaptation for analyzing complex problems. Psychol Rev. 2009;116(3):620–654.
Chan MF, et al. A randomized controlled study to explore the effect of life story review on depression in older Chinese in Singapore. Health Soc Care Community. 2013;21(5):545–553.
Cuijpers P, et al. A meta-analysis of cognitive behavioural therapy for adult depression, alone, and in comparison with other treatments. Can J Psychiatry. 2013;58(7):376–385.
Cuijpers P, et al. Psychotherapy for depression in adults: A meta-analysis of comparative outcome studies. J Consult Clin Psychol. 2008;76(6):909–922.
Ebert DD, et al. Internet and computer-based cognitive behavior therapy for anxiety and depression in youth: A meta-analysis of randomized controlled outcome trials. PLOS One. 2015;10(3):e0119895.

Feldman G. Cognitive and behavioral therapies for depression: Overview, new directions, and practical recommendations for dissemination. Psychiatr Clin North Am. 2007;30(1):39–50.

Fels A. Should we all take a bit of lithium? New York Times, September 14, 2014, pp. SR6.

Fernie BA, et al. Cognitive-behavioural interventions for depression in chronic neurological conditions: A systematic review. J Psychosom Res. 2015;78:411–419.

Hannen E, et al. Narrative therapy with an adolescent who self-cuts. Ed Psychol Pract. 2012;28:187–214.

Hedman E, et al. Effectiveness of Internet-based cognitive behaviour therapy for depression in routine psychiatric care. J Affect Disord. 2014;155:41–58.

Kapusta ND, et al. Lithium in drinking water and suicide mortality. Br J Psychiatry 2011;198(5):346–350.

Keri, S, et al. Blood biomarkers of depression track clinical changes during cognitive-behavioral therapy. J Affect Disord. 2014;164:188–122.

Laidlaw K, et al. Age-appropriate augmented cognitive behavior therapy to enhance treatment outcome for late-life depression and anxiety disorders. Gero Psych. 2015;28:57–66.

Lake J. Integrative management of depressed mood. Integrat Med. 2004;3:48–57.

Lee-Duckworth A, et al. Positive psychology in clinical practice. Ann Rev Clin Psychol. 2015;I:629–650.

Lopes RT, et al. Narrative therapy versus cognitive behavior therapy for moderate depression: empirical evidence from a controlled clinical trial. Psychother Res. 2013;24:662–674.

Mauer L, et al. Standard and trace-dose lithium: A systematic review of dementia prevention and other behavioral benefits. ANZ J Psychiatry 2014;48(9):809–819.

Mewton L, et al. Cognitive behaviour therapy via the Internet for depression: A useful strategy to reduce suicidal ideation. J Affect Disord. 2015;17:78–84.

Pugh NE, et al. A case study illustrating therapist-assisted cognitive behavior therapy for depression. Cog Behav Pract. 2014;21:64–72.

Qiu J, et al. A randomized controlled trial of group cognitive behavior therapy for Chinese breast cancer patients with major depression. J Psychosom Obstet Gynecol. 2013;34:60–67.

Ray O. How the mind hurts and heals the body. Am Psychol. 2004;59(1):29–40.

Renaud J, et al. Predicting who benefits most from cognitive behavior therapy for anxiety and depression. J Clin Psychol. 2014;70:924–932.

Seo M, et al. Narrative therapy with an emotional approach for people with depression: improved symptom and cognitive-emotional outcomes. J Psychiatr Ment Health Nurs. 2015;22(6):379–389.

Shedler J. The efficacy of psychodynamic psychotherapy. Am Psychol. 2010;65:98–109.

Singer AR, et al. A pilot study of cognitive behavioral therapy for depression in early psychosis. Cog Behav Pract. 2014;21:323–334.

Sokol LE. A systematic review of the efficacy of cognitive behavioral therapy for treating and preventing perinatal depression. J Affect Disord. 2015;177:7–21.

Solomon A. *The Noonday Demon: An Atlas of Depression.* 2001. New York: Scribner.

Spence D. *Narrative Truth and Historical Truth: Meaning and Interpretation in Psychoanalysis.* 1982. New York: Norton.

Stark, Martha. "Integrative Psychotherapy: Healing the Mind-Body Matrix." *Integrative Therapies for Depression: Redefining Models for Assessment, Treatment, and Prevention.* Ed. James Greenblatt, Ed. Kelly Brogan, chapter 27. 2015. Boca Raton, FL: CRC Press.

Thimm JC, et al. Effectiveness of cognitive behavior group therapy for depression in routine practice. BMC Psychiatry. 2014;14:292.

Titov N, et al. Clinical and cost-effectiveness of therapist-guided Internet-delivered cognitive behavior therapy for older adults with symptoms of depression: A randomized controlled trial. Behav Ther. 2015;46:193–205.

Trinidad A. "Narrative Therapy." *Integrative Therapies for Depression: Redefining Models for Assessment, Treatment, and Prevention.* Ed. James Greenblatt, Ed. Kelly Brogan, chapter 26. 2015. Boca Raton, FL: CRC Press.

Vega BR, et al. Mindfulness-based narrative therapy for depression in cancer patients. Clin Psychol Psychother. 2014;21:411–419.

Vromas LP, et al. Narrative therapy for adolescents with major depressive disorder: Improved symptom and interpersonal outcomes. Psychother Res. 2015;21:4–15.

Wagner B, et al. Internet-based versus face-to-face cognitive-behavioral intervention for depression: Randomized controlled non-inferiority trial. J Affect Disord. 2014;152–154:113–121.

Wuthrich VM, et al. Randomised controlled trial of group-cognitive behavior therapy for comorbid anxiety and depression in older adults. Behavior Res Ther. 2013;51:779–785.

Zu S, et al. A comparison of cognitive behavior therapy, antidepressants, their combination, and standard treatment for Chinese patients with moderate to severe major depressive disorder. J Affect Disord. 2014;152–154:253–267.

Chapter 19: Spirituality and Faith

Bonelli R, et al. Religious and spiritual factors in depression: Review and integration of the research. Depression Res Treat. Article ID 962860. 2012. Available at http://dx.doi.org/10.1155/2012/962860. Accessed August 23, 2015.

Bosworth HB, et al. The impact of religious practice and religious coping on geriatric depression. Int J Geriatr Psychiatry. 2003;18(10):905–914.

Croezen S, et al. Social participation and depression in old age: A fixed-effects analysis in ten European countries. Am J Epidemiol. 2015;182(2):168–176.

Friedman PH, et al. The relationship between forgiveness, gratitude, distress, and well-being: An integrative review of the literature. Int J Healing Caring. 2006;6:1–10.

Hill, Natalie. "Role of Spirituality and Religion in Depression and Treatment." *Integrative Therapies for Depression: Redefining Models for Assessment, Treatment, and Prevention.* Ed. James Greenblatt, Ed. Kelly Brogan, chapter 23. 2015. Boca Raton, FL: CRC Press.

Hovey JD, et al. Religion-based emotional social support mediates the relationship between intrinsic religiosity and mental health. Arch Suicide Res. 2014;18(4):376–391.

Kasen S, et al. Religiosity and resilience in persons at high risk for major depression. Psychol Med. 2012;42:509–519.

Koenig HG, et al. Religiosity and remission of depression in medically ill older patients. Am J Psychiatry. 1998;155:536–542.

Krause N, et al. Forgiveness by God, forgiveness of others, and psychological well-being late in life. J Sci Study Relig. 2003;42(1):77–94.

Miller, L, et al. Religiosity and major depression in adults a high risk: A ten-year prospective study. Am J Psychiatry. 2012;169:89–94.

Shafranske EP, et al. Spiritually oriented psychodynamic psychotherapy. J Clin Psychiatry. 2009;65:142–157.

Styron W. *Darkness Visible: A Memoir of Madness.* 2007. New York: Modern Library.

Thompson LY, et al. Dispositional forgiveness of self, others, and situations: The Heartland Forgiveness Scale. J Pers. 2005;73(2):313–359.
Touissant LL, et al. Forgiveness and health: Age differences in a U.S. probability sample. J Adult Devel. 2001;8:249–257.

Chapter 20: Mindfulness and Yoga

Broderick PC. 2005. Mindfulness and coping with dysphoric mood: Contrasts with rumination and distraction. Cog Ther Res. 2005;29:501–510.
Brown RP, et al. Yoga breathing, meditation, and longevity. Ann N Y Acad Sci. 2009;1172:54–62.
Chen F, et al. The effect of body-mind relaxation meditation induction on major depressive disorder: A resting-state fMRI study. J Affect Disord. 2015;183:75–82.
Langer EJ. *Counter Clockwise: Mindful Health and the Power of Possibility.* New York: Ballantine Books, 2009. Print.
Chiesa A, et al. Mindfulness-based cognitive therapy versus psycho-education for patients with major depression who did not achieve remission following antidepressant treatment: a preliminary analysis. J Altern Complement Med. 2012;226(2–3):474–483.
Gallego J, et al. Effect of a mindfulness program on stress, anxiety, and depression in university students. Span J Psychol. 2015;17:E109.
Kuyken W, et al. Effectiveness and cost-effectiveness of mindfulness-based cognitive therapy compared with maintenance antidepressant treatment in the prevention of depressive relapse or recurrence (PREVENT): A randomised controlled trial. Lancet. 2015;386(9988):63–73.
Liebman JL. *Peace of Mind.* 1946. New York: Simon & Schuster.
Oman D, et al. Meditation lowers stress and supports forgiveness among college students: A randomized controlled trial. J Am Coll Health. 2008;56(5):569–578.
Pradhan B. "Depression Specific Yoga and Mindfulness-Based Cognitive Therapy Model: Description, Data on Efficacy, and Differences from Contemporary Models." *Integrative Therapies for Depression: Redefining Models for Assessment, Treatment, and Prevention.* Ed. James Greenblatt, Ed. Kelly Brogan, chapter 24. 2015. Boca Raton, FL: CRC Press.
Ray O. How the mind hurts and heals the body. Am Psychol. 2004;59(1):29–40.
Serpa JG, et al. Mindfulness-based stress reduction reduces anxiety, depression, and suicidal ideation in veterans. Med Care. 2014;52(12 Suppl):S19–S24.
Smith, H., et al. "Meditation and Mindfulness." *Integrative Therapies for Depression: Redefining Models for Assessment, Treatment, and Prevention.* Ed. James Greenblatt, Ed. Kelly Brogan, chapter 25. 2015. Boca Raton, FL: CRC Press.
Widdicome L. The higher life: How mindfulness became the road to success. New Yorker, July 6 and 13, 2015.

Chapter 21: Beyond Mindfulness

Barton J, et al. What is the best dose of nature and green exercise for improving mental health? A multi-site analysis. Environ Sci Technol. 2010;44(10):3948–3955.
Bennett MP, et al. Humor and laughter may influence health: III. Laughter and Health Outcomes. Evid Based Complement Alternat Med. 2008;5(1):37–40.
Bratman GN, et al. Nature experience reduces rumination and subgenual prefrontal cortex activation. Proc Natl Acad Sci. 2015;112(28):8567–8572.
Cheavens J, et al. Hope therapy in a community sample: A pilot investigation. Soc Indicat Res. 2006;77:61–78.

David K, et al. Creating and teaching a course in ecotherapy: We went to the woods. J Human Counseling Ed Develop. 2004;43:211–218.
Foley E, et al. Effect of forced laughter on mood. Psychological Rep. 2002;90:184.
Ganz F, et al. 2014. The effect of humor on elder mental and physical health. Geriatr Nurs. 2014;35:205–211.
Gelkopf M, et al. The effect of humorous movies on inpatients with chronic schizophrenia. J Nerv Mental Disord. 2006;194:880–883.
Greenleaf A, et al. Nature-based counseling: Integrating the healing benefits of nature into practice. Int J Advance Counseling. 2014;36:162–174.
Howell A, et al. Nature connectedness: Associations with well-being and mindfulness. Pers Individ Dif. 2011;51:166–171.
Kim SH, et al. Laughter and stress relief in cancer patients: A pilot study. Evid Based Complement Alternat Med. 2015;2015:864739.
Lund DA, et al. Humor, laughter, and happiness in the daily lives of recently bereaved spouses. Omega. 2008;58:87–105.
McIntosh D. Facial feedback hypotheses: evidence implications, and directions. Motivat Emot. 1996; doi: 10.1.1007/BF02253868.
Morgan AJ, et al. Self-help interventions for depressive disorders and depressive symptoms: A systematic review. Ann Gen Psychiatry. 2008;7:13.
Neuhoff CC, et al. Effects of laughing, smiling, and howling on mood. Psychol Rep. 2002;91:1079–1080.
Solomon A. *The Noonday Demon: An Atlas of Depression.* 2001. New York: Scribner.
Walter M, et al. Humour therapy in patients with late-life depression or Alzheimer's disease: A pilot study. Int J Geriatr Psychiatry. 2007;22:77–83.
White M, et al. Blue space: The importance of water for preference, affect, and restorativeness ratings of natural and built scenes. J Environ Psychol. 2010;30:482–493.

PART IV: HOPE AND HEALING

Chapter 22: The Future Treatment of Depression

Komori T. The effects of phosphatidylserine and omega-3 fatty acid-containing supplement on late life depression. Ment Illn. 2015;7(1):5647.

Chapter 23: Integrative Psychiatry

Fried EI, et al. The differential influence of life stress on individual symptoms of depression. Acta Psychiatrica Scandinavica. 2015;131(6):465-471.
Logan AC, et al. Nutritional psychiatry research: an emerging discipline and its intersection with global urbanization, environmental challenges and the evolutionary mismatch. J Physiol Anthropol. 2014;33(1):22.
Sarris, J. et al. Personal View: Nutritional medicine as mainstream in psychiatry. Lancet Psychiatry. 2015;2271-2274.

Appendix

NUTRITIONAL SUPPORT FOR DEPRESSION		
Recommended	**Breakfast**	**Dinner**
NeuroMood Pure Pack	✓ 1 packet	
Amino Replete*	✓ 1 scoop	✓ 1 scoop
Optional		
Lithium (orotate) 5 mg*	✓ 1 capsule	

Simple Guidelines for Enhancing Nutritional Support

Mental and emotional health depends on the availability of nutrient building blocks and cofactors, such as amino acids, essential fatty acids, vitamins, and minerals for the biosynthesis of neurotransmitters. In addition to these essential factors, nonessential dietary components such as antioxidants and phytochemicals support neurotransmitter dynamics in a generalized manner by modulating enzymes and maintaining healthy reuptake systems.

Based on decades of research and clinical experience, Dr. James Greenblatt, in collaboration with Pure Encapsulations, developed the PureSYNAPSE™ product line to provide individualized, integrative support for mood, sleep quality, stress, memory, and healthy eating behavior.

DISCLAIMER: You should never stop taking an antidepressant medication without the supervision of a physician. These supplements should be taken at least sixty days before stopping any medication, and you should continue to take them sixty days after discontinuing antidepressant medications.

NUTRITIONAL SUPPORT FOR ANTIDEPRESSANT WITHDRAWAL		
Recommended	Breakfast	Dinner
NAC (N-acetylcysteine)	✓ 1 capsule	✓ 1 capsule
EPA/DHA Essentials	✓ 1 capsule	✓ 1 capsule
B-Complex Plus	✓ 1 capsule	
Inositol (powder)	✓ ½ teaspoon	✓ ½ teaspoon
Magnesium (glycinate)	✓ 1 capsule	✓ 2 capsules
Lithium (orotate) 5 mg	✓ 1 capsule	
Optional		
Amino Replete**	✓ 1 scoop	✓ 1 scoop

NUTRITONAL SUPPORT FOR ENHANCING ANTIDEPRESSANT MEDICATIONS		
Recommended	**Breakfast**	**Dinner**
Folate 1000 (L-methylfolate)	✓ 2 capsules	✓ 1 capsule
EPA/DHA Essentials	✓ 1 capsule	✓ 1 capsule
Trace Minerals	✓ 1 capsule	✓ 1 capsule
NAC (N-acetylcysteine)	✓ 1 capsule	✓ 1 capsule
Creatine (powder)		✓ 2 scoops
Lithium (orotate) 5 mg	✓ 1 capsule	

*Lithium (orotate) is highly recommended for individuals with a family history of substance abuse, depression, or bipolar disorder.

** Amino Replete should be taken *before* breakfast and *before* dinner for optimal results.

Index of Recommended Nutritional Supplements

AMINO REPLETE

Dosage directions: 1 to 2 scoops daily before meals, mixed with 8 oz of water or juice

Amino Replete is a formulation of free-form amino acids of more than a dozen important amino acid precursors involved in neurotransmitter synthesis, including tryptophan, tyrosine, and phenylalanine. By providing the precursors to several neurotransmitters and neuropeptides, Amino Replete supports cognitive function, positive mood, and appetite regulation.

B-COMPLEX PLUS

Dosage directions: 1 capsule per day with meals

B-Complex Plus is an exceptional combination of B vitamins, including vitamins B_1, B_2, B_3, B_5, B_6, B_{12}, biotin, and folic acid (as metafolinL-5-MTHF), all of which are provided in their optimal bioavailable and functional forms. The B vitamins are essential for hemoglobin formation, nerve impulse transmissions, mood, hormone synthesis, and energy metabolism.

CREATINE (powder)

Dosage directions: 4 g daily (or 2 tsp) with a meal, mixed with juice or water

Creatine supports the body's natural ability to regenerate the primary energy molecule ATP by enhancing levels of phosphocreatine.

DOPAPLUS

Dosage directions: 3 to 6 capsules daily before meals

Dopamine is a neurotransmitter that plays indispensable and diverse roles in cognition, learning, mood, and behavior. In the brain, this critical neurotransmitter controls the flow of information to maintain mental sharpness, alertness, memory, and cognitive performance. DopaPlus provides amino acids, cofactors, and enzyme modulators that support the synthesis and actions of dopamine. The formula also prevents the development of substances that interfere with neuronal communication systems in the brain. This formulation supports positive mood, alertness, cognitive performance, and healthy eating behavior.

DIGESTIVE ENZYMES ULTRA WITH BETAINE HCL

Dosage directions: 1 or 2 capsules with each meal

Digestive Enzymes Ultra with Betaine HCL offers a combination of digestive enzymes designed to support optimal gastric pH, important for the digestion of protein and other nutrients. Digestive enzymes help facilitate the breakdown of food so that the body can readily absorb the nutrients.

EPA/DHA ESSENTIALS

Dosage directions: 2 to 4 capsules per day, in divided doses, with meals

Omega-3 fatty acids work to provide the building blocks for creating neurotransmitters that regulate mood in the brain while also being able to reduce inflammation. Fatty acids are also present in myelin, the outer layer of neurons, which work to insulate and protect the neurons from damage. Fatty acids also aid in transmitting electrical signals quickly and efficiently between neurons. Omega-3 fatty acid supplementation can alleviate withdrawal symptoms known as "brain zaps," which are perceived as the sensation of mini-electrical shocks in the brain. EPA and DHA from fish oil help the brain heal and adjust to the rapid change of neurotransmitter synthesis when you taper off medications.

FOLATE 100

Dosage directions: 1 to 3 capsules daily, with or without food

L-methylfolate is the active form of folate, one of the body's essential B vitamins. L-methylfolate enhances the body's ability to produce neurotransmitters and can naturally improve mood so that you can get the most out of your antidepressant therapy.

INOSITOL (powder)

Dosage directions: ½ tsp twice daily with a meal, mixed with juice or water

Inositol is derived from glucose and is involved with metabolic regulation and growth in humans. It works to maintain proper electrical signals between cells and nutrient transfers across your cell membranes. Inositol also supports healthy central nervous system function, including emotional wellness and mood.

LITHIUM (OROTATE) 5 mg

Dosage directions: 1 capsule per day with a meal

Lithium is a mineral that is essential to human health. Present in trace amounts of the food we eat and the water we drink, lithium has a long history of clinical use for supporting healthy mood and behavior. Lithium is essentially "brain food," as it helps stimulate neuron growth in the brain, even in small amounts. Low-dose lithium has been shown to have a wide range of therapeutic effects, including improvement of mood, prevention of cognitive decline, and improvement of brain function by protecting neurons and enhancing neurotransmitter activity. Lithium is recommended for any individual with a family history of substance abuse, bipolar disorder, or depression.

MAGNESIUM (GLYCINATE)

Dosage directions: 3 capsules daily with a meal

Magnesium is considered an antistress mineral, and studies have found that magnesium can combat mood swings associated with tapering off a medication. Magnesium is necessary for the metabolism of carbohydrates, amino acids, and fats; it is also critical for energy production and the use of calcium, phosphorus, sodium, and potassium. This vital mineral also helps you use B-complex vitamins, vitamin C, and vitamin E.

N-ACETYL CYSTEINE (NAC)

Dosage directions: 3 capsules per day in divided doses between meals

N-acetyl-l-cysteine (NAC) is a derivative of the dietary amino acid l-cysteine. NAC is a powerful free radical scavenger and supports the body's natural defense system. NAC supports tissue levels of glutathione, a key component of the antioxidant defense system.

NEUROMOOD PURE PACK

Dosage directions: 1 packet daily (5 capsules)

PureSYNAPSE Pure Pack is a comprehensive daily packet providing B vitamins, minerals, essential fatty acids, amino acids, and curcumin for healthy cognitive function and positive mood. It contains:

- O.N.E. Multivitamin
- Magnesium (glycinate)
- EPA/DHA Essentials
- NeuroPure
- Taurine

NEUROPURE

Dosage directions: 2 to 4 capsules daily in divided doses between meals

NeuroPure offers combined support for both dopamine and serotonin. Amino acid precursors and nutrient cofactors in this formula support the synthesis of serotonin and dopamine, while polyphenols from curcumin prevent their degradation, maximizing the effects of these neurotransmitters in the brain. NeuroPure aims to enhance emotional balance, mood stability, and food cravings and offers overall neurotransmitter support.

SEROPLUS

Dosage directions: 2 to 4 capsules daily in divided doses between meals

Serotonin supports critical behavioral and physiological functions, including the regulation of mood, emotions, and appetite. SeroPlus delivers amino acids and vitamin and mineral cofactors to support serotonin synthesis and activity. This formula supports positive mood, relaxation, and healthy eating behavior.

Resources

Nutritional Supplement Resources

Integrative Psych MD
www.JamesGreenblattMD.com

Integrative Psych MD is a resource Web site for professionals, physicians, patients, and families. This Web site provides more information on research supporting the therapies and nutritional supplements discussed in *Breakthrough Depression Solution*. This Web site also features:

- Dr. Greenblatt's conference and speaking schedule
- Information on how to order quality nutritional supplements
- Evidence-based research to support integrative medicine for mood disorders

Pure Encapsulations, Inc.

490 Boston Post Road
Sudbury, MA 01776
800-753-2277
www.PureEncapsulations.com

Pure Encapsulations was founded to formulate and manufacture the highest-quality line of hypoallergenic supplements available. Since its inception, the company has been the industry leader in manufacturing excellence and quality control, as well as a pioneer in the production of research-based and clinically relevant formulas. Sixteen clinical trials involving Pure Encapsulations products are currently in progress. These include studies at Stanford University, Michigan State University, and Mayo Clinic. Dr. Greenblatt is retained as a medical advisor for Pure Encapsulations.

Available through health professionals, finished products are pure and hypoallergenic to optimize the long-term health of the most sensitive patients. An extensive product testing program involves verification of label claims, potency, and purity by third-party laboratories. Pure Encapsulations is NSF-GMP registered in the United States, is GMP certified in Canada, and exceeds the standards of the United States Pharmacopeia (USP) for supplement manufacturing.

PureSYNAPSE™

www.puresynapse.com

The PureSYNAPSE™ product line was developed in collaboration with James Greenblatt, MD, to provide individualized, integrative support for mood, sleep quality, stress, memory, and healthy eating behavior. The four main products are Amino Replete, NeuroPure, DopaPlus, and SeroPlus. The PureSYNAPSE™ Pure Pack contains a daily packet providing B vitamins, minerals, fish oil, and curcumin for healthy cognitive function. This Web site provides information on how and where to order the high-quality supplements discussed in this book, as well as easy-to-follow guidelines on how to use supplements based on your individual needs. The Web site also offers educational resources and webinars that provide evidence-based research supporting several nutritional therapies in the treatment of mood disorders.

Low Dose Lithium

http://www.lowdoselithium.org/

Pharmaceutical lithium has been used for years as a psychiatric drug with powerful mood-stabilizing influences on depression and other mental health disorders. At high doses, lithium has been associated with adverse effects, which often limit its use as a long-term solution. Now, after in-depth research and much clinical success, the authors behind lowdoselithium.org have found another way.

What many have failed to realize is that lithium is not only a medication—it is a mineral essential to human health. This website provides educational articles and resources on the incredible healing potential of low-dose lithium or doses of lithium that mimic those found naturally in our soils, food, and water.

On this website, you will find information on a broad range of topics, including where lithium is found in the environment, its growing uses in technology, and its long history as a dietary supplement and medication. The database is frequently updated with the latest scientific evidence supporting the clinical applications of low-dose lithium and is a practical resource for providers and patients alike. Also recommended is the book *Preserving Memory and Optimal Brain Health,* which explores the many ways in which low-dose lithium can improve mental health and contribute to longevity.

Testing Laboratories

Great Plains Laboratory

11813 W. 77th St.
Lenexa, KS 66214
913-341-8949
www.greatplainslaboratory.com

Great Plains Laboratory offers a broad range of nutritional and metabolic testing, including opioid peptide testing for casomorphin and gliadorphin, IgG food allergies, and urinary organic acids. Dr. Greenblatt is retained as a medical advisor for Great Plains Laboratory.

Genova Diagnostics

63 Zillicoa St.
Asheville, NC 28801
800-522-4762
www.gdx.net

Genova Diagnostics offers clinical testing that supports health care providers in the personalized treatment and prevention of mental illness. The group's ION (Individual Optimal Nutrition) Profile with 40 Amino Acids, a combination of analyses, measures levels of organic acids, fatty acids, vitamins, minerals, and antioxidants, with a specific focus on amino acid absorption and imbalances.

Assurex Health

6030 S. Mason-Montgomery Road
Mason, Ohio 45040
866-757-9204
www.assurexhealth.com

Assurex Health is a personalized medicine company that specializes in pharmacogenomics. It is dedicated to helping health care providers determine genetically appropriate medications for patients suffering from neuropsychiatric and other medical conditions. Assurex Health's proprietary technology is based on pharmacogenomics—the study of the genetic factors that influence an individual's response to drug treatments—as well as evidence-based medicine and clinical pharmacology. The GeneSight test was developed in the Assurex Health clinical laboratory and is based on patented technology licensed from two world-renowned medical centers, Mayo Clinic and Cincinnati Children's Hospital Medical Center, which continue to be research collaborators.

Genomind

2200 Renaissance Blvd., Suite 100
King of Prussia, PA 19406
877-895-8658
www.genomind.com/

Genomind is a personalized medicine company composed of innovative researchers and expert leaders in psychiatry and neurology. Genomind is committed to bringing science to psychiatry and to creating new innovations that will help clinicians improve their patients' lives. The Genecept Assay contains a proprietary panel of ten genes that have been individually selected for actionable clinical applicability to treat neuropsychiatric conditions. The panel is unique for its dual approach: it looks at how the body metabolizes certain drugs and how certain drugs affect the body. When certain drugs or neurotransmitters interact with a specific brain receptor, they modify the chemistry of the brain and directly influence behavior.

Integrative Medicine Resources

Integrative Medicine for Mental Health: Referral Registry & Resources (IMMH)

11813 W. 77th St.
Lenexa, KS 66214
800-288-0383
www.integrativemedicineformentalhealth.com

IMMH provides referrals to and information on integrative medicine practitioners. The website also offers resources concerning integrative medicine and mental health treatment.

American Board of Integrative Holistic Medicine (ABIHM)

5313 Colorado St.
Duluth, MN 55804
218-525-5651
Fax: 218-525-5677
www.holisticboard.org/

ABIHM is an association that establishes and promotes standards for integrative holistic medicine. It is also a resource for physicians desiring certification in integrative holistic medicine, as well as for those seeking physicians certified in holistic medicine.

American Holistic Medical Association (AHMA)

23366 Commerce Park, Suite 101B
Beachwood, OH 44122
216-292-6644
Fax: 216-292-6688
www.holisticmedicine.org/

AHMA is dedicated to the advancement of holistic and integrative medicine in health care. It is committed to increasing awareness and understanding of integrative, complementary, and alternative medicine techniques.

American College for Advancement in Medicine (ACAM)

8001 Irvine Center Dr., Suite 825
Irvine, CA 92618
800-532-3688
Fax: 949-309-3535
www.acam.org

ACAM is a nonprofit association dedicated to educating physicians and other health care professionals on the latest findings and emerging procedures in complementary, alternative, and integrative medicine.

International College of Integrative Medicine (ICIM)

P.O. Box 271
Bluffton, OH 45817
866-464-5226
Fax: 610-680-3847
www.icimed.com

ICIM is a community of dedicated health care professionals advancing emergent innovative therapies in integrative and preventive health care. They conduct educational sessions, support research and publications, and cooperate with other professional and scientific organizations.

Institute of Functional Medicine (IFM)

4411 Point Fosdick Dr. N.W., Suite 305
P.O. Box 1697
Gig Harbor, WA 98335
800-228-0622
Fax: 253-853-6766
www.functionalmedicine.org

IFM is a resource for training physicians and patients about the principles of functional medicine. IFM also provides referrals to functional medicine practitioners.

Natural Medicine Comprehensive Database

3120 W. March Lane
Stockton, CA 95219
209-472-2244
www.naturaldatabase.com

This organization provides information on natural products for the treatment of a variety of medical disorders. It offers a database of potential interactions between prescription medications and supplements.

About the Authors

James M. Greenblatt, MD

A pioneer in the field of integrative medicine, James M. Greenblatt, MD, has treated patients with mood disorders and complex eating disorders since 1990. After receiving his medical degree and completing his psychiatry residency at George Washington University, Dr. Greenblatt went on to complete a fellowship in child and adolescent psychiatry at Johns Hopkins Medical School. An acknowledged integrative medicine expert and one of the founders of Integrative Medicine for Mental Health (IMMH), Dr. Greenblatt has lectured throughout the United States on the scientific evidence for nutritional interventions in psychiatry and mental illness. His expertise in integrative medicine has made him a highly sought-after speaker at various national and international conferences in Canada, England, and Asia.

His books, *Answers to Anorexia*, *The Breakthrough Depression Solution,* and *Answers to Appetite Control,* draw on his many years of clinical experience and expertise in integrative medicine while treating patients with eating and mood disorders. *The Breakthrough Depression Solution* has been translated into Chinese and Japanese and has allowed Dr. Greenblatt to train physicians in Asia on complementary therapies for the treatment of mood disorders. The concepts from *The Breakthrough Depression Solution* were also adapted into a textbook for medical professionals by CRC Press. *Integrative Therapies for Depression* is the first textbook for professionals that reviews the current treatment models for depression and presents evidence-based research to support integrative medicine for mood disorders with practical, clinical recommendations

Dr. Greenblatt continues to provide educational workshops and trainings for physicians throughout the United States. He is committed to educating professionals on the limitations of the current models of treatment for mental illness and offers practical integrative solutions based on personalized biochemical testing.

Dr. Greenblatt currently serves as Chief Medical Officer and Vice President of Medical Services at Walden Behavioral Care in Waltham, Massachusetts. Dr. Greenblatt is also Assistant Clinical Professor in the Department of Psychiatry at Tufts University School of Medicine in Boston. He is currently working on several book projects for the consumer audience, including books on the use of nutritional lithium for the prevention of cognitive decline and integrative therapies for the treatment of attention-deficit hyperactivity disorder.

For more information about this author, please visit www.JamesGreenblattMD.com.

Winnie To, BS

After graduating from the University of San Francisco in 2012 with a concentration in biology, Winnie began working as a research assistant in a busy integrative outpatient practice in Boston. She prepared presentations for national conferences and webinars, developed educational materials for local seminars, and wrote content for newsletters and *Psychology Today* blogs.

Winnie provided research support and editorial assistance in the successful publication of *Answers to Appetite Control* and served as a project coordinator for *Integrative Therapies for Depression*, which was published by CRC Press in 2015.

Winnie is currently enrolled in a graduate nursing program at Regis College. She is studying to become an integrative nurse practitioner specializing in the treatment of mood disorders.

Index

O

P

T

Also Available from Sunrise River Press

Award-winning publisher of ground-breaking health, self-help & medical resources

ANSWERS TO ANOREXIA
A Breakthrough Nutritional Treatment That Is Saving Lives

by James M. Greenblatt, MD Offers the first new medical treatment plan in 50 years for anorexia nervosa. This book is based on cutting-edge research on nutritional deficiencies in anorexia that have been long ignored, and the use of a simple but revolutionary brain test that can help psychiatrists select the best medication. Dr. Greenblatt, explains that anorexia is a complex disorder with genetic, biological, psychological, and cultural contributing factors. In other words, anorexia is not primarily a psychiatric illness; rather, it is a medical illness of starvation that causes malnutrition in the body and the brain. Successful treatment must focus on correcting this malnutrition. Softbound, 6 x 9 inches, 304 pages. ***Item # SR607P***

TAKING ANTIDEPRESSANTS
Your Comprehensive Guide to Starting, Staying On, and Safely Quitting

by Michael Banov, MD Antidepressants are the most commonly prescribed class of medications in this country. Yet, consumers have few available resources to educate them about starting and stopping antidepressants. Dr. Michael Banov walks the reader through a personalized process to help them make the right choice about starting antidepressants, staying on antidepressants, and stopping antidepressants. Readers will learn how antidepressant medications work, what they may experience while taking them, and how to manage side effects. Softbound, 6 x 9 inches, 304 pages. ***Item # SR606P***

LIVING YOUR BEST WITH EARLY-STAGE ALZHEIMER'S
An Essential Guide

Lisa Snyder, MSW, LCSW Recent medical advances have made it possible to diagnose Alzheimer's when symptoms are only mild. Today, when a person is diagnosed they may have many years ahead with only mild symptoms. This is a straightforward, practical guide on coping with the diagnosis, managing symptoms, finding meaningful activity, planning for the future, communicating, participating in research and clinical trials, and much more. This book helps the person with Alzheimer's feel empowered to move forward in life in light of this challenging diagnosis. 7 x 9 inches, 288 pages. Softbound. ***Item # SRP603***

AUTISM CAUSES, PREVENTION AND TREATMENT
Vitamin D Deficiency and the Explosive Rise of Autism Spectrum Disorder

by John J. Cannell, MD Autism affects 1 in every 68 American newborns. Cases of autism are increasing at a rate of 12% every year. What has caused this rapid rise in the incidence of autism spectrum disorder? Who's the most susceptible? And what can be done about it? Autism researcher John Cannell, MD, founder of the Vitamin D Council, provides the most comprehensive and compelling explanation to date regarding the causes, prevention strategies, and treatment protocols that, in many cases, reverse autistic symptoms. Hardcover, 6 x 9, 208 pages. ***Item # SRP646***

SUNRISE River Press

838 Lake Street South, Forest Lake, MN 55025
Phone: 651-277-1400 or 800-895-4585 Fax: 651-277-1203

Like us on Facebook
www.facebook.com/SunriseRiverPress

1-800-895-4585
www.sunriseriverpress.com